A Socio-Legal History of the Laws of War

Emerald Advances in Historical Criminology

Series Editors: David Churchill and Christopher Mullins

This series embraces a broad, pluralistic understanding of "the historical" and its potential applications to criminology. Providing an inclusive platform for a range of approaches which, in various ways, seek to orient criminological inquiry to history or to the dynamics of historical time, the series also offers a platform both for conventional studies in the history of crime and criminal justice, but also for innovative and experimental work which extends the conceptual, theoretical, methodological, and topical range of historical criminology. In this way, the series encourages historical scholarship on nontraditional topics in criminology (such as environmental harms, war, and state crime) and inventive modes of theorizing and practising historical research (including processual approaches and futures research). The series thus makes a valuable contribution to criminology irrespective of disciplinary affiliation, theoretical framing, or methodological practice.

Previous Titles

- History & Crime: A Transdisciplinary Approach by Thomas J. Kehoe and Jeffrey E. Pfeifer
- The First British Crime Survey: An Ethnology of Criminology within Government by Julian Molina

A Socio-Legal History of the Laws of War: Constraining Carnage

BY

CHRISTOPHER W. MULLINS

Southern Illinois University, USA

emerald
PUBLISHING

United Kingdom – North America – Japan – India – Malaysia – China

Emerald Publishing Limited
Howard House, Wagon Lane, Bingley BD16 1WA, UK

First edition 2023

British Library Cataloguing in Publication Data
A catalogue record for this book is available from the British Library

ISBN: 978-1-78769-858-1 (Print)
ISBN: 978-1-78769-857-4 (Online)
ISBN: 978-1-78769-859-8 (Epub)

Printed and bound by CPI Group (UK) Ltd, Croydon, CR0 4YY

INVESTOR IN PEOPLE

Table of Contents

About the Author

Christopher W. Mullins, PhD, is Associate Dean of Academic and Student Affairs for the College of Health and Human Services and Professor in the School of Justice and Public Safety at Southern Illinois University, Carbondale, USA. His research focuses on the structural, cultural, and legal aspects of violence, especially mass atrocity. He has published four books, one coedited volume, and over 60 peer-reviewed articles and book chapters in a variety of outlets.

Preface

This book examines how over the course of centuries different human societies and cultures have structured and enclosed their war making with norms that are designed to either maintain good military order or to reduce the impact of the violence inherent in warfare on soldiers and citizens. This book has attempted to survey and analyze values that address the root problem of warfare: that its effects go well beyond those actively engaged in hostilities. Most societies looked at in this volume have norms and practices which attempt to curtail the damage caused by warfare in various ways. Of course, what is important varies in time and place and earlier concerns do not always mirror later concerns. Yet all societies acknowledge the inherent danger in allowing war to be uncontrolled. What is perceived as needing control and what sort of controls are needed vary widely, especially early on. By the tenth century CE in Europe we see the emergence of attempted theological control of warfare for humanitarian reasons by the medieval Catholic church.

Through the thirteenth and fourteenth centuries we would see armies adopting formal articles of battle which dictated the behavior allowed and not allowed of troops in battle, camp, or on the march. While rarely followed to the letter, they were enforced. The fifteenth through nineteenth centuries saw an increase in the use of formal articles which proscribed certain behaviors and prescribed others. Later articles begin to contain procedural law aspects as well as substantive law. They become longer, come complex, and more legalistic. During the nineteenth century, we will see these codifications of norms become more extensively used by militaries and we will begin see a strong civilian push for humanitarian law, a social movement that lay dormant since the Church's ninth- and Tenth-century campaigns. This book stops at end of the eighteenth century. At this historical juncture we see fully codified articles of battle that are law in all but name (i.e., the Continental Congress' articles of 1775 and 1776). The nineteenth, twentieth, and twenty-first centuries see proliferation of military law, both domestic and international; it is a story that requires its own book.

The main assumptions behind my analyses here come from social science approaches to understanding law by placing it in its sociohistorical context. As a scholar, I come out of anthropological and sociological theoretical worldviews and traditions, and thus look at both macro and micro level forces shaping behavior. My thinking is driven from a cultural materialist standpoint (See Harris, 1968) that sees nonmaterial culture, such as norms and laws, as deriving from the material conditions of a society's existence. Economics, in the anthropological sense, drive social structure and some aspects of cultural norms. These norms will frame certain phenomena as "problems" to be solved, and other norms and cultural forces will influence how those "problems" are approached, if they are dealt with at all. Existing elements of material and nonmaterial culture will influence formation or transformation of norms and laws. As will broader contexts, including interactions with other societies or communities.

As examined early on in the book, war is an inversion of daily social norms of interaction. The central acts of war – injuring and killing people and the destruction of property – are typical prohibited by mores and ordinary law. The fundamental aspects of the social contract that focuses on peaceful coexistence and cooperation are abandoned and a new set of rules adopted: the laws of war, whatever they may be in the given context. Often symbolic and ritual observances mark the beginning and ending of a war, to mark the transitions between norm sets. It also makes war an isolated social space, a liminal space where warfare can occur without the total elimination of civilian and international rules. It is a social space that both belligerent parties agree to create and enter, though the closing of the space may depend more upon one belligerent party than the other. All social spaces and contexts have rules, be they formal or informal (see Goffman, 1959). Warfare is not an abandonment of rules. Armies couldn't function without them, as our early chapters here show. But entering the liminal space of war indicates that different rules apply. While this gives soldiers permission to violate central social mores around the harming of others, all conflicts appear to have norms designed to reduce the harm caused by war and by the armies. They create boundaries to reduce and constrain carnage. As with any law, they are not always going to be successful in every case. Yet historical evidence shows that strong rules can keep armies behaving appropriately toward citizens, property, and the like most of the time (i.e., Gustavus' Swedish Army of the Thirty Years' War) (Macmunn, 1920).

This book follows the evolution and codification of norms surrounding the behavior of soldiers on the battlefield in the western context. Its analysis is limited to the west and what is often seen as the cultural roots of the west (i.e., the Levant and Mesopotamia). This is done for a number of reasons. First, while there are cultural differences across the societies examined, there are strong similarities in the way they approach war, especially by the first century CE. There is a traceable tradition of military norms, values, tactics, and attitudes from the Ancient near-east through eighteenth-century Europe and her colonies. This does not mean there is not a rich tradition of military norms and laws in other cultural traditions. The Laws of Manu as presented in the Upanishads form the foundation of a South Asian military tradition that could similarly be traced forward. The same could be done for China and east Asia, or Africa. Doing so is beyond the scope of this book; each of those traditions deserves their own in-depth analysis and exploration. They are also regions of the globe that, while I do not lack interest, I have less ability to work in due to languages, source availability, and deep familiarity with the historical-cultural background. Also, this book will not cover military behavior in European colonies directed at indigenous populations. The rules for colonial warfare are highly different than those for noncolonial warfare, especially in terms of the treatment of prisoners of war and civilians. It too deserves its own treatment (see volume two). This book ends as the European colonial push is occurring in the New World and the Indian subcontinent.

Acknowledgments

No book is the work of one person alone, and I received help and support from a number of sources. First, nothing is possible without the love and support of my wife, Robin. I am grateful for her on a daily basis. Üthred and Daisy deserve thanks for daily mental health assistance. I would like to thank the College of Health and Human Services at SIUC for a course release that was essential to the completion of this volume. I would also like to thank Bob Morgan for helping me learn to balance my administrative duties with my ongoing scholarly work. Lastly, I would like to thank the editors at Emerald for their assistance with the project and for their patience with the numerous delays in the delivery of this manuscript.

Chapter 1

The Rules of Warfare

> But in the cities of these peoples that the Lord your God us giving you for an inheritance, you shall save alive nothing that breathes, but you shall devote them to complete destruction, the Hittites and the Amorites, the Canaanites and the Perizzites, the Hivites and the Jebusites, as the Lord your God has commanded that they may not teach you to do according to all their abominable practices that they have done for their gods and so you sin against the Lord your God.
>
> (Deuteronomy 20:16–18)

> Thus says the Lord of hosts, "I have noted that Amalek did to Israel in opposing them on the way when they came up out of Egypt. Now Go and strike Amalek and devote to destruction all that they have. Do not spare them, but kill both man and woman, children and infant, ox and sheep, camel and donkey."
>
> (1 Samuel 15:2–3)

> But when they [the Romans] went in numbers into the lanes of the city [Jerusalem], with their swords drawn, they slew those whom they overtook, without mercy, and set fire to the houses wither the Jews were fled, and burnt every soul in them, and laid waste a great many of the rest; and when they were come to the houses to plunder them, they found in them entire families of dead men, and the upper rooms full of dead corpses, that is of such as died by the famine; they then stood in a horror at this sight, and went out without touching anything. But although they had this commiseration for such as were destroyed in that manner, yet had they not the same for those that were still alive, but they ran every one through whom they met with, and obstructed the very lanes with their dead bodies, and made the whole city run down with blood, to such a degree indeed that the fire of many of the houses was quenched with these men's blood
>
> (Josephus, 2001, pp. 8.404–8.406)

A Socio-Legal History of the Laws of War, 1–18

Published under exclusive licence by Emerald Publishing Limited
doi:10.1108/978-1-78769-857-420231001

Most Nations and Nation-States have found themselves as perpetrators of atrocity violence as well as the victims. The first two quotes show Israel committing atrocity violence at the bequest of their god in the claiming of their "promised land." They are only two scriptural passages in the Judeo-Christian tradition of many that remind us that the original founding of Jerusalem and Israel were bloody, violent events. The Jewish forces intended to occupy the land and decided to remove the current inhabitants to prevent future conflicts or contesting of their claims. As Deuteronomy recounts, people were killed simply for not being Jewish and out of fear that the worship of their deities would be adopted by some Israelites. Josephus describes the behavior of Roman legionnaires engaged in total war against the Jewish people for their resistance to the Roman Empire. While they too were imposing rule on a foreign land, they did not seek to populate those lands with Romans, as the Jewish exodus did. Theirs was a pacification mission, catalyzed by the actions of the Zealots, aimed at ending resistance.

All three examples provided above would be considered atrocity violence by criminologists, historians, and lawyers. Atrocity crime is an umbrella term used to capture a variety of mass violence events, especially crimes against humanity, genocide, and war crimes under a single term and concept. Its use avoids legalistic arguments over the terms "genocide" and "war crimes" and provides an academic over legal conceptual reference point (Holá, Nzitatira, & Weerdesteijn, 2022). All three show genocidal intent and action. The first two examples would be considered legal under Hebraic law as they are presented as direct orders from their God and law-giver. Failing to engage in the violence at the level ordered would be a crime and a sin. If the destruction of Jerusalem by Rome would be considered legal under Roman law or generally accepted by rules of war in the ancient world is a more complicated question. As we will see in Chapter 3, Roman soldiers operated under strict discipline and supervision. Specific standards of behavior and punishments were codified in the army. Such regulations do frequently suggest leaving civilians alone. As mentioned above, the Romans sought to rule the Jewish people in Israel, not empty Israel for Roman settlers. Such motivations typically result in less civilian violence, but here the long terror campaign of the Zealots against the Roman Empire was a critical factor in the order to destroy the city. Zealots did not wear uniforms or have matching tattooed insignia. Rome was facing the problem all nations fighting insurrections face – discerning the enemy from the civilians. Rome chose eradication of all to ensure eradication of the Zealots. Unfortunately, this is a choice many states will make over the eras when faced with populist insurgencies. Under the laws of war shared by most nations in the period, a total sacking was a potential fate of any city lost in warfare. Not pillaging and murdering the inhabitants of conquered cities is often lauded through the period, taken as a sign of the beneficence of the ruler in question. But it was in no understanding forbidden or chastised, except in its most extreme forms, i.e., Rome's destruction of Carthage. The Ancient and Roman worlds placed a fairly low value on human life, especially the lives of Others (non-group members) (Bédoyére, 2020; Coleman, 1918). A thorough burning and pillaging of a conquered city and its people were the expectation, mercy was the exception. Thankfully, in the ancient world man rulers liked to be seen as merciful and just; thus, the pressures of public image could act as a control and limit the amount of atrocity violence engaged in.

Wars are a common facet of human civilization. Scholars place the earliest wars as occurring before written human history. Archaeologists have found evidence of large-scale prehistoric out-group violence in practically every large, settled nation. Twentieth-century ethnologists reported on the war behaviors of tribal peoples globally. Many of the earliest historical records and monuments deal with war. When the typical person thinks of war, images of chaos and mass destruction being carried out by both sides come to mind; most people view military violence as unconstrained and uncontrolled, if not uncontainable and uncontrollable. Yet even in our earliest records of warfare are preserved examples of norms and rules that controlled soldiers and their violence. While the Old Testament depicts the God of the Israelites commanding his people slaughter enemies to the last, the same verses in Deuteronomy also contain proscriptions against destroying fruit trees or despoiling water. Indeed, the Roman army committed many atrocities over the ages, the slaughter in Jerusalem discussed by Josephus and the eradication of the city of Carthage being two prominent examples. Yet, the Roman Legions were the most disciplined, most rule-bounded army in the ancient and classical world. In cases like Carthage and Jerusalem, such rule-produced cohesion catalyzed atrocities (while today, more rule-bound cohesive armies are less likely to commit atrocities).

This book explores the core social, cultural, and legal principles at work behind the conduct of warfare, and the behavior of those who waged war in the ancient world through the early modern era. It will examine how soldiers are governed and controlled across contexts and eras. Warfare presents specific and universal potentialities and problems, especially those relevant to the conduct of soldiers before, during, and after hostilities. How opposition soldiers, civilians, and property are treated during these times is also a universal concern, but how these issues are conceived of and addressed will vary by culture and society. I will explore norms, rules, laws, and penalties used over the centuries that were designed to do what many feel is not possible: constrain the carnage associated with warfare, while keeping warfare as a viable political tool when wanted or needed.

The earliest instances of war show norms and practices which are intended to reduce suffering of both armies. In Mesopotamia, North Africa, and Europe, multiple warrior cultures evolved whose norms inculcated a sense of honor and other internal social controls into troops based on their behavior (or at least their commander's responses to their behavior). As war cultures developed, norms diffuse between nations and combatants. This allows some predictability of the enemy's actions, but it also allows a commander to hold his troops to a disciplinary standard and thus make their behavior more predictable to him and his superiors.[1] For example, a shared culture norm of not fighting on certain shared

[1] I will use the male pronouns throughout when referring to military commanders. This is simply reflective that until the contemporary era, there were few cultures with a tradition of female soldiering (the Scythians are an exception) and few examples of female military leaders. Jean D'Arc and Boudica are anomalies.

holy days reduces violence and warfare by reducing the number of days on which it can occur (see Chapter 4 for a discussion of the medieval catholic church's attempts at this). Ancient Greek armies generally appear to have been satisfied to allow a defeated enemy to escape instead of running the broken army down and destroying it piece meal (Coleman, 1918), reducing the number of fatalities in battle. A losing side could expect to survive as long as they fled. The same has been observed by ethnologists studying warfare among horticulturalists and pastoralist societies (Heider, 1977; Keeley, 1996; LeBlanc, 2003; Otterbein, 2009; Rutar, 2022). From its earliest occurrences, warfare, or violent intergroup conflict in general, has been bounded by cultural norms and expectations. These cultural artifacts change through time and place, though, as we will see, many of the core concerns remain the same. From the fourteenth century, Kings or other Sovereign routinely produced articles of war setting the boundaries for a given conflict, but they were typically only applicable for that conflict. Though, as seen in the articles of English Kings from Richard II through Henry V (see Chapter 5), specific items were recycled from article to article, with changes occurring due to contexts of the war (Curry, 2008, 2011; Martinez, 2017). Eventually, these articles would transform into laws, mostly at the organizational or national-level. International law, what we will eventually call IHL, develops separate from the articles of war evolution. It is driven by civilians, not the military, and places greater emphasis on civilian protections than most national military codes do. Law is the state-level codification of norms; war is the state-level codification of intergroup dispute resolution.

Law, Norms, Institutions, and Values

A typical definition of law identifies law as the codification of prescriptive and proscriptive norms. It is the formalization of a behavioral code that both prohibits and compels individual behavior, which includes detailing of specific negative sanctions applied due to a lack of compliance (typically called substantive law). Further, processes of adjudication are specified (typically called procedural law). Systems of law have both components, even if the latter is simply specified as the exercise of the Sovereign's opinions. A system of laws holds an elevated position in a society's social control institutions as it is, ideally, applied universally and uniformly within the jurisdiction it covers. Conceptually opposed to folkways and other norms, while laws may not bear greater personal or moral weight, they carry specified consequences and established mechanisms for adjudication of accusations and determination of sanctions (Bracey, 2006). They are backed by, and enforced by, the state as an institution. Humans are norm-bound creatures, guided by nonmaterial culture through the interpretation of and interaction with their physical and social worlds. Possessing a unique level of sentience and self-reflection, by our nature we create meaning out of our lives, or acts, and our desires. Hard writ into these processes are norms, base rules for human social interaction that simultaneously address universal concerns and emerge out of historical particularities (Bracey, 2006). To the best of our knowledge, all *Homo sapiens sapiens* have possessed such cognitive abilities and concerns.[2] Violation of even informal rules has consequences, potentially severe. So how are we to distinguish among the various forms of behavioral constraints? How do we tell a norm from a law?

Natural law and legal positivistic views would have us look to extra-social universalistic principles that are understandable via observation but in essence outside of the realm of social creation which follow, respectively, innate natural or a priori logical principles. Such appeals to universality fail to account for the wide variation within and between legal systems in time and place. The approach taken here asserts the fundamentally social and cultural nature of law and thus its constructed nature out of specific cultural-historical processes and circumstances (Bracey, 2006; Harris, 1968; Keeley, 1996; LeBlanc, 2003). This is not to deny a degree of similarity between aspects of procedural and statutory law in various contexts. Similarities are inevitable as similarly situated societies are presented with a similar set of problems to be addressed. As with the natural world, parallel evolution occurs in cultures as well. Some of the oft cited universal particulars of law are a reflection of the more universal aspects of human social interaction and organization. Yes, prohibitions against murder, theft, and the like arise in most all legal systems (as well as in societies without codified law). But, the specified forms and definitions (i.e., the elements of the crime in common law terminology) of these crimes vary widely and are molded by the other social expectations and obligations that are defined with a time and place. How various social groups are defined and what the relationships are within and between these groups are more important shapers of the content of law, driven by the universal social problems of killing, or stealing from, in-group members at the least.

The laws and norms of interest here are mainly those focused on out-group members, often formally defined as enemies by political institutions (via a declaration of war or the like). Law in general is focused on the protection of people within the society through the prevention and punishment of social harm. The laws of war refer to those rules, often internal to a military and/or shared understandings of warfare between belligerent parties while IHL is focused on the protection of those people and places affected by war. National laws governing soldier's behavior have similar civilian protecting functions, but are more focused on maintaining an ordered and functioning military (Jochnick & Normand, 1994). This is part of the general dismissal of the idea of the validity, desirability, or possibility of having laws regulating war often encountered outside military and certain academic circles. As we will see, strong norms, if not laws, guide collective inter-group violence of all forms throughout history and prehistory. They are almost ubiquitously violated in modern conflicts, though at different rates and in different ways (see Mullins, 2011, 2016; Wood, 2006). One sees a similar pattern in premodern warfare, with numerous examples of violations of

---

[2]To the depth that a key question within bio and paleoanthropology is when the appearance of this aspect of culture in human, or primate, history, occurs and whether or not humans are the only creatures that possess such profound reflective and learning capabilities.

the laws of war (and sometimes their punishment) being recorded by chroniclers of the period. While we can't determine prevalence rates and the like for battles in these periods, we can look at what is in the extant record and that record's cultural-historical context to induce a general sense of the laws and rules at work in these periods.

Social scientists who study law argue over the precise definition of law; while there is general recognition of rules bounding conduct outside of the laws of modern nation-states, there is a hesitancy to open up the definition to *any* rule of behavior. The tendency to reify the concept of law as separate and distinct necessitated a rejection of the existence of law in a non-state context, something that did not sit well with socio-cultural anthropologists in the early and mid-twentieth century. The typical counter was to define all rules, norms, and customs as a form of law (see Hoebel, 1954, 1978). Taken at face value this overextends the concept, incorporating not only the identification, punishment, and hoped for deterrence, of behavior deemed wrong or problematic but also all social habits including those of diet, dress, humor, and medical care. Law bears a connotation of an elevated level of seriousness of daily concerns; an off color joke may draw negative sanctions, and such sanctions may reinforce what a given social actor sees as critical values, but such an act is less socially disruptive than a theft or assault. Common law has long held to the criteria of harm as a *raison d'être* of criminal law. Judges in the US have used this rationale repeatedly to strike down laws as unconstitutional as when there is no harm in the behavior there is no public interest in controlling it. *Oberfell* v *Hodges* (2015) and *Lawrence* v *Texas* (2003) are cases in point where an at best center-right court struck down laws prohibiting same-sex marriage and same-sex sexual activity, respectively. Moderate conservatives such as O'Conner and Kennedy joined the more moderate liberals to codify these precedents leading with the argument that there is no harm in these actions and thus nothing for the state to regulate. Still in the twenty-first century, common law adheres to this fundamental principle.

Xymologists, and some Criminologists, have advanced the idea that harm is the true umbrella concept of their discipline, as opposed to a more legalistic violation of criminal statute definition of crime. Seen especially in work done on the offending of elites, corporations, and states the inclusion of "socially analogous harms" with a more typical definition of crime highlights the political nature of law and law-making, while simultaneously being an assertion of criminological control of the definitional aspects of their own field of inquiry (Kauzlarich & Kramer, 1998; Kauzlarich, Mullins, & Matthews, 2003). Within the criminology of war, definitions emphasizing conceptual aspects of the phenomena over legal prohibition is also utilized (see McGarry & Walklate, 2019; Walklate & McGarry, 2015). This reminds us to not solely limit our notions and definitions of law to adjudicable statute. Historically and contemporaneously, this is not the case for the rules of warfare, especially considering the role of custom in modern international law. Even in the contemporary era, much of the laws of war are often referred to as norms even by those scholars who are strong advocates (see, for example, Bassiouni, 2008). Here, as with human rights law, one definitional line is justicability – can these rules, in and of themselves, be brought into a court (of some form, including military tribunals or courts martial) and adjudicated?

A key theme of this work is the increased formalization of the laws of war. This is a topic that inherently exhibits a historical trajectory of increased formalization with a perception of legitimacy and efficacy coming from increased institutionalization and empowerment. The formalization of sanction application and the externalization of said processes are key aspects of a process that we see across the centuries. Militaries tend to implement codes of conduct that they believe will maintain order and discipline in camp, on the march, and on the battlefield. Yet, at certain points in history, various civilian bodies also engage with these rules to reduce the innate harm of military action. For example, as we will explore in Chapter 4, the church in the ninth to eleventh centuries went to great lengths to curtail the violence of the warrior classes of Europe. Through the declaration of the *Pax Dei* and the *Truega Dei*, they attempted to use clerical authority to impose order on a chaotic post-Roman Europe. Many of the ideas were adopted into the warrior code of Chivalry, potentially gaining more influence as the Crusades help thoroughly Christianize European knightdom (Gies, 1984). As feudalism in Europe collapsed, and chivalry faded into the realms of literary tropes, the church's influence on battlefield behavior would also decrease considerably. Large scale attempts to control soldiers would rest solely with the military they served within until the end of nineteenth century. A growing civilian and lawyer-driven attempt to make war safer for civilians as well as sick and injured troops, began to take shape. These humanitarian concerns, over obedience concerns, are first codified in US Army General Order 100, a.k.a, The Lieber Code (Witt, 2012). General Order 100 was the first piece of law as contemporarily conceived. It prohibited a range of behaviors which had long been tolerated if not accepted in warfare, and proscribed specific punishments for war crimes. It only applied to the US Army and was created out of Lincoln's understanding that if the Federals won the US civil war, the South would need to be reintegrated into the nation. This would be easier, he assumed, if the Union army was on its "best behavior" and didn't leave aggrieved and victimized citizens in their wake. In the later nineteenth century European civilian lawyers and rights advocates take up the issue and, slowly, generate what we now see as International Humanitarian Law. After World War II, these principles will be codified into international law as the Geneva Conventions and their four attendant protocols. The end of the cold war will facilitate the development of the long-worked for permanent International Criminal Court, opening the Rome Statute for signatories in 1999 and opening its doors in 2002.

The rules of General Order 100 (Witt, 2012) did not spring forth from Lieber's head like Athena from Zeus'. He drew heavily on extant laws, domestic and international, and custom when drawing up his regulations for the Union Army. The ideas that are codified within it arose and became normalized in certain circles well before the nineteenth century. While we do not know exactly what his direct influences were, it is clear the Lieber was familiar with much of the law and norms we will examine in the book and drew upon the rich tradition of military norms when conceptualizing the military code – both in terms of laws and rules to include and those to exclude.

Even as more formal rules are adopted to protect people and property during conflicts, they are still applied in a fairly ad hoc manner. Officers in the field have great discretion in their use of discipline and victor's justice is still more the rule than the exception. Historical debates over the "victors justice" nature of the tribunals after World War II remain (Minear, 1971). Even a cursory examination of contemporary applications of these laws by ad hoc and permanent courts suggest that, at least in the case of leaders and organizations – those most responsible – are only brought to justice once they are out of power or favor (Lutz & Reiger, 2009; Rothe & Mullins, 2006). This is a nigh across-the-board fact for those adjudicated by ad hoc tribunals in the second half of the twentieth and the start of the twenty first century. When the ICC issued an arrest warrant for a sitting head of state, Omar Al Bashir of The Sudan, little happened that diminished his domestic control. Internationally, several African states, and the Organization of African States, made it clear they would not enforce the warrant. Until his régime fell due to widespread protest and civilian unrest, Bashir had impunity for his actions in Darfur and the Nuba mountains (Totten, 2012). Once he was out of power, he was detained by the new Sudanese régime who have promised a trial.[3] This supranational legal order is still evolving, in principle and in practice, and its roots run deep in Western History.

The Monopolization of Violence

Most social scientists link the development of formal law with the development of states. Both being a product of the increased complexity of high population density and permanent settlement that co-evolve with agriculture, especially large-scale mono-cropping. Such systems create a plethora of new social problems whose solutions lie beyond a family network, but rather require community level solutions – politics in an anthropological sense (Harris, 1968). Horticulturalists, a subsistence pattern dependent on high biodiversity gardening, have mechanisms above the kinship unit of the lineage to solve community issues though they still tend to be kinship-tied.[4] Organizing lineages into clans and clans into moieties, especially where intermarriage is encouraged or, often demanded, creates networks of obligation between individuals across the lines drawn by the upper-level kinship divisions.[5] Here, informal social control powerfully exerts itself, especially as embodied in a corporate kinship system. Elders keep younger kinsfolk in line and negotiate settlements when their kin violate norms. Societies like the Nuer had semi-official dispute resolution agents, the Leopard-skin Chief.[6] If a young (or older) Nuer male would injure another, whether in a cattle raid or a personal

---

[3]As of this writing, he is awaiting trial in Sudanese custody. The UN has encouraged that he be turned over to the ICC.

[4]A lineage is a group of people who can trace their ancestry to a known ancestor. It is often the primary kinship and political unit is foraging, pastoralist, and horticultural societies.

[5]From the French for "half." In a moiety systems clans (groups of related lineages) are collected into two groups who claim a closer set of shared kinship than the opposite moiety.

[6]So-called due to the leopard skin they wore as a badge of office.

dispute, the perpetrator would go to the Leopard-skin chief's compound where they received protection from the male relatives of the offender's victim. Violating this amnesty would bring shame to a lineage, and potentially more serious consequences. It was the duty of the Leopard-skin Chief to go back and forth between the lineage elders and negotiate a nonviolent solution (Evans-Pritchard, 1969). Other nonstate societies had similar social positions or dispute resolution mechanisms that avoided violence between members (i.e., The Inuit song duel, see Hoebel, 1954). Warfare losses can easily compromise a village or lineage's survivability; nonviolent dispute resolution mechanisms are essential for intra-group conflicts, but also inter-group conflicts in low population density societies.

The monopolization of violence by the state (see Weber, 1919/2015), transitions the focus of punishment from the kin-group to the state. As it fully cements itself, the state will ideally establish mechanisms for controlling violence within its borders via recourse to law backed by the state's inherent coercive authority. This centralization of the use of force, of power, under law becomes a keyway in medieval Europe and the English Isles for a king to stabilize and increase their power. The emergence of common law in England is an excellent case in point. Henry II's drive to create a common law of the land for England had very practical purpose – the standardization of law, substantive and procedural, across shires and counties. This unification of English law also increased the power of the throne with the introduction of Crown courts and judges appointed by the king. Anglo-Saxon law was community focused procedurally. Disputes between kin-groups that could not be resolved via negotiation were settled by each side presenting their version of events. The other adult men in the community, the Moot, decided whose case was stronger and how much restitution was due the victim, if any. Oppositionally, crown courts were top-down impositions and usurpations of legal control from local authorities. While some community centered aspects remained (i.e., the jury evolves from the moot), Crown courts made it clear they were imposing the King's justice and power. The courts also inserted themselves into the financial aspects of dispute resolution by take a portion of any wergild assessed on the offender before the remainder was given to the victim or his family.[7,8] Similar attempts were made in France before and after the revolution as a way to unite a land bound only by loose political and cultural ties. It can be argued even today that there is no true monopolization of violence by the state for social control purposes. Black's work is clear on identifying the self-help and social control functions of crime for those unable to access legitimate legal institutions (Black, 1976, 1998; see also LaFree, 1989). Ethnographic work on active offenders has described and theorized these principles in action (see Ammons-Blanfort, D'Alessio, & Stolzenberg, 2023; Jacobs & Wright, 2006;

---

[7]Literally, "man-gold." Those found guilty of harming someone by the moot, would be forced to pay all or a portion of the victim's wergild value depending on the amount of harm done.

[8]I use "his" here, as at this time, women had no real legal rights and an offense against a women was treated until the twentieth century as an offense against the victim's husband or father (if unmarried).

Mullins, Wright, & Jacobs, 2004). Yet, these actions are clearly criminalized under ordinary law and are typically not seen as legitimate in the manner state violence often is.[9]

The Existential Problem of War and Constraint as a Solution

As with the definition of law, the definition of war is similarly a point of contention. Typically, war is seen as product of civilization and historically emerges with the first states in Sumer. Intercommunity violence that takes the forms of raids or individual or small group assaults or thefts, typically referred to as raids and the like, but are seen by many as phenomenologically different than warfare (though raids can be a part of a broader military endeavor). In one sense, this is true. Two score men throwing javelins and firing bows at each other for an hour, after spending a couple of hours in ritualistic taunting, and then departing with little-to-no injuries typically, is a somewhat less intense experience than the clashing of armies composed of hundreds or thousands of men. Yet, archaeologists and anthropologist who study prehistoric combat clearly see it as a form of warfare, just a lower intensity of warfare (see Keeley, 1996; Otterbein, 2009). However such altercations can have a much greater impact on the functioning of a small community of gardeners or cattle herders than modern warfare has on nation states. If even five men a side are injured or killed in the above hypothetical, a village has lost a substantial amount of its subsistence and defensive capability. Five men out of a village of 50 is a significant portion of the adult male population and will compromise the settlement's ability to continue to exist independently. The two 20-year plus wars the US started in the twenty-first century have resulted in the death of 7,015 US service members by combat or other in-theater reasons (accidents, illness). The US labor market and other educational and economic institutions seem not to have been the least bit compromised by the loss of those men and women; more die in the US to homicide every year. The one million plus lost to COVID-19 in the US has had a greater effect on the US workforce than the Iraq and Afghan wars combined. The existential risk of war is greater for smaller societies, with fewer people, and fewer warriors. Larger societies can absorb more losses.

Tribal warfare shows extensive rules that guide their inter-community conflicts which participants seem to adhere to more strictly than contemporary troops. While the relative risk to the individual is the same (injury, mutilation, death), the relative risk to community for smaller societies is much higher, placing strong informal pressure to reduce injury and death to one's opponents as doing so does

[9]Criminologists have highlighted the role of subcultural values in structuring criminal behavior, showing within street networks, violence is, in offenders' minds, a legitimate tool. Similarly, the late twenty-teens has also shown, especially in the US, a rejection of state monopolization of violence by numerous groups of varied political and ideological persuasion (i.e., white supremicists, The Oath Keepers, Boogaloo Bois, and Proud Boys on the right and Antifa on the left).

the same for one's own side.[10] The surplus production and population that exist within a state-level society allows more frequent, violent inter-community events to occur with less direct impact on the societies ability to function.

Violence is a universal problem for humanity, both individual and collective. At both the micro and macro level, violence is a way to solve problems, acquire resources and security, increase or maintain prestige, and to deter future violence. War is a tool, as Clausewitz (1832/1993) famously said, it is just another form of politics. Any society with neighbors is bound to come into conflict them; some of these conflicts will become military ones. If force is a potential solution, some social actors (be they individual or state) will use it. And it is as rule-driven as all other human social behaviors, though these rules vary in time and space.

Collective, organized violence has deep roots in the human family. Our closest biological relatives, *Pan troglodytes*, the common Chimpanzee, have been observed engaging in what can only be described as raiding or warfare between troops in geographical proximity.[11] Initially such observed behavior was seen as an artifact of the provisioning primatologists engaged in when studying Chimpanzee troops in situ. A common interpretation of early violence was that the groups were fighting over the food provided by researchers and would not have come into violent contact without such artificial circumstances. It was the food provisioning which brought the groups into proximity, and thus igniting conflict (Power, 1991). Later field observations have witnessed similar activity unrelated to primatologist provisioning. On occasion, Chimpanzee troops go to war with each other. Raiding to capture (and eat) infants in other Chimpanzee groups has also been recorded, as has similar behaviors directed at other primates in the territories, i.e., Baboons. Yet, even Chimpanzees show that such responses are not inevitable or absolute. Bonobos, *Pan troglodytes paniscus*, the aka pygmy or dwarf chimps, have not been observed to engage in inter-group conflicts and have little in the way of intra-group violent or aggressive conflict. They resolve disputes with sexual activity and grooming over violence and display behaviors.[12] Inductively, we can suggest that intercommunal war-behavior was present in the last common ancestor of the *Pan troglodytes* and *Homo sapiens sapiens.* Bonobo conflict resolution is likely a unique adaption to their local ecosystem, but it shows that the *innateness* of violence in the human species and its relatives is a fabrication, or at best a weak genetic force that can be overpowered by environmental factors. Such would also suggest war or war-like behaviors among earlier members of both the *Australopithecine* and *Homo* genuses. Clearly, war goes deep in human (and pre-human) prehistory. Collective violence is a central human experience.

---

[10]There are also numerous devices for avoiding conflict and resolving conflict before a dispute reaches the stage of inter-community violence in low-density societies, just as the modern world has diplomacy.

[11]The proper name for a group of *P. troglodytes*. Not to be confused with the use of the word "troop" elsewhere in the volume.

[12]*Pan troglodytes* will groom to reestablish social peace in a troop but only after the aggression displays and assaults have ceased.

In most social sciences, violence has been conceptualized as an inter-personal or small group experience. As with most social norms, there are large and powerful distinctions made between how members of an in-group are treated versus how members of an out-group are treated. Drawn from early social psychology (see Cooley, 1901), these concepts are contextually based classifications of social membership that clearly guide and constrain behavior. In-groups are those categories of person which an individual sees themselves has holding a shared identify with, be it on the micro level (family groups), the meso level (neighborhood, community, or work place members), or the macro level (society, culture, nation-state). Out-groups are those individual outside of whatever line is being drawn and are often subject to highly variant treatment and moral reasoning, including being acceptable targets of violence. Current work conceptually aggregates to the level of neighborhood differences, but still focuses on the behaviors of dyads or small groups. Gender scholars are the only group which have presented a fully developed, realized macro-level theory of violence, but here only in so far as macro-level cultural norms translate into individual and small group behavior vis-á-vis gendered norms (see Messerschmidt, 2014, 2018; Miller, 2008; Mullins, 2006; Winlow, 2001).[13] Unsurprisingly, this work has highlighted the masculine nature of violence. Though limited work has been done on female combatants in recent conflicts (i.e., Sierra Leonne, see Mackenzie, 2012).

Defining war is also problematized in historical, political science, and legal literature, especially being focused on the time when a conflict reaches the level of war, as opposed to other forms of conflict or disorder. For those writers who will be of interest later in this volume, defining war was central to a legal project regulating war, a concern that drives the evolution of the Geneva conventions in the twentieth century and is still manifest today in debates over application of extant IHL (see Bassiouni, 2008). War is the aggregation of interpersonal violence. It is violence between two or more large corporate groupings of individuals. It differs from raiding in scope and objectives, though raids are a tactical tool drawn upon in war. It differs from terrorism in that it tends to be more symmetrical and the violence typically targets opposing belligerents, not citizens or other third parties (though exceptions exist in every conflict).

War not only constitutes a major disruption of the activities of the participants, it is a disruptor of society itself. Functioning societies are grounded on peaceful interactions between their citizens and with their neighbors (Durkheim, 1893/1984). Some debate if peace or war is the natural state of humanity (Hobbs, 1651/1985, Rousseau, 1762), this begs the question of war's socially disruptive nature

[13]Macro theories of crime, such as Messner and Rosenfeld's (2007) Institutional Anomie theory (IAT), or Bonger's (1916) Marxist criminology do exist. Yet, neither of these, or other macro theories, do a decent job distinguishing what is likely to produce *violence* over general offending. Even when they do statistically predict violence, they don't explain it. For example, IAT has been repeatedly shown to accurately predict homicide, but doesn't explain why the response to anomic institutional conditions is homicide over robbery, burglary, or drug use. It also does a poor job of accurately predicting non-homicide criminal events.

and the need for it to be rule bound and rule bound in a specific fashion. The norms of war obliterate the norms of peace, with the latter being turned on their head. Simply, in war humans have to act differently than they do in non-military interactions. Proscriptions against killing and harming people and property are inverted. For millennia, military officers have had to teach their troops not only the ways and whys of war, but the different ethic which guides behavior – Clausewitz's (1832/1993) grammar of war. The forces of physical and social destruction embodied within a military are existentially dangerous to a society. The norms of the soldier cannot replace the norms of the citizen and see a given society survive in its current form. It has to create and maintain a separate socio-cultural space to prevent total disruption of all human endeavor. Starting war means the eradication of daily norms, schemas, relationships, and meanings. Not just what society is built upon, but society itself. War requires the creation of a liminal space to avoid contamination of the mundane (Durkheim, 1912/1915).

War is liminal – a state of transition outside of normal cultural space that must be demarked and contained to prevent damage of the broader social order. Hence, for the ancient Greeks, legal declarations of war were highly ceremonial and ritualized (Coleman, 1918; Garland, 1975, 1984; Lanni, 2008; Pritchett, 1971, 1974, 1991) to demark the creation of a different social space with different rules and expectations. The Greeks felt the need to physically, temporally, and geographically isolate war into its own socio-geographical space. This could be a result of the lower comparative population densities between Greek city-states and current nation-states, but more likely a function of the need to separate or compartmentalize the lives of citizen soldiers. Early on, the Greek Polis' population was also its army. When called, farmers would trade hoe for spear and join the ranks of the phalanx. Once the summer campaign ended, the spear was traded for a scythe and harvest time. Not an unusual practice in the ancient world, this limited the amount of time a commander has for a campaign, including a siege if decided upon. Allowed or not, the men will leave come autumn as failure to harvest their fields means starvation for them and their family. Thus, the ritualized onset of war highlights a clean break from citizen to soldier life and from the prior political relations that existed between the respective parties. This is a formal declaration that a new set of norms are in now in place; the ritualized closing doing the reverse: reminding the soldiers they were standing down as warriors and returning to their other lives, duties, and obligations.

During war, relationships, rules, etc. all change, especially within the geographical territories seeing combat. Declarations and armistices are both functional and symbolic, they attempt to constrain in time and place the conflict with formal markings of beginning and endings of the applicability of war norms to guide behavior over ordinary norms. Such ritual constraints become normative constraints; behaviors appropriate to the liminal space are not allowed in the mundane world. Entry and exit into this space must be clearly demarcated, as must participants and nonparticipants to ensure a shared definition of the situation among social actors (see Goffman, 1959).

The Idea of the Laws of War

Before we explore some different sources and types of laws focused on conflict or its aftermath, we need to establish that there are really two different bodies of laws here. The first, typically called "the laws of war" over the centuries, are those norms developed within and applied to militaries and soldiering. Their codification, if they are codified, tend to take the forms of Articles of War or later, domestic legal codes. These Articles lay out the various rules, expectations, and punishments for the conduct of troops in the field. Often, these declarations are as much about military camp construction, marching order, fire control, and the like. Often, there is little mentioning of treatment of the enemy or civilians. In the 1779 *Regulation for the Order and Discipline of the Troops of the United States* (Steuben, 1779/1786/2019), civilians are only mentioned once. In Chapter XV, which is focused on camp construction, there is a single sentence: "The suttlers tents are to be between the kitchens [*sic*]" (p. 74).[14] Suttlers were civilian merchants who followed the army; they have been a standard fixture of army camps since at least the late middle ages, when they are first mentioned in Articles of War. Today, essentially every modern military has codified rules of conduct for their troops. Most of these rules focus on maintaining good order in camp and the ranks. Yet each is individualized to the military of a specific time and place and only covers the soldiers of that nation.

The second body of law is International Humanitarian Law (IHL) and International Criminal Law (ICL) as created by the Rome statute. It's earliest expression is the 1864 "Red Cross Convention," or more officially the "Convention for the Amelioration of the Conditions of the Wounded Armies in the Field." This is the first major international agreement concerning the behavior of soldiers, here, protecting the sick, wounded, and surrendered.[15] IHL evolves through the nineteenth and twentieth centuries, reaching its apex in the Four Geneva Conventions and their Attendant Protocols. It is further refined through the adjudication processes of the various late twentieth century ad hoc tribunals (i.e., the International Criminal Tribunal for the former Yugoslavia).[16] In the twenty-first century, with the opening of the International Criminal Court (ICC), it is supplemented by ICL as codified in the Rome Statute of 1999. These laws differ from the "laws of war" in that they are multi-lateral in nature and largely built by civilians, not militaries. It represents an attempt to make warfare more humane through *externally imposed* constraints on numerous types of violence's and targets. It codifies some of what we find in Articles of War but is not interested in factors such as camp or general order maintenance. IHL focuses on how noncombatants are treated by combatants. It tends to see anyone who, either by

[14]When quoting manuscripts which typeset *f* for *s*, I have transcribed them into standard English usage, i.e., "Futtlers" is written here as "suttlers" no mater how the source was typeset.

[15]It was heavily influenced by the Lieber Code (aka General Order 100).

[16]Though the ad hocs, drawing on customary international law, have utilized the laws of war and not just IHL in their legal and judicial reasoning.

virtue of being a civilian, voluntarily through surrender or involuntarily through injury, is no longer able to participate in hostilities as a non-combatant and thus not a legitimate target of violence or other ill treatment. It covers civilians as well as soldiers unable (or unwilling) to fight. It is driven by civilians, with civilian interests fore fronted, unlike the laws of war which are created by a military and forefronts military concerns. The two often don't agree on the finer points of legal soldering.

In and of itself IHL is not justiciable – as written it can't be taken into a court and used to charge a person or state with wrongdoing. It is a set of treaties and compacts that nations have promised to follow. It is not until the twentieth century that one sees courts emerge to hold states, or key state actors, responsible for their misdeeds. The International Court of Justice (ICJ), often the UN deemed clearing house for interstate disputes, only accepts cases between states and its decisions are not binding as it has no coercive power. Some ICJ precedent has worked its way into the jurisprudence of the ad hocs or the ICC, but it has otherwise had little direct impact on the way war is waged. Even in its ruling in one of the few military cases it has heard, *Nicaragua* v *the United States*, went ignored by the offending power. With the exception of the collapse of Yugoslavia, few IHL issues have reached the ICJ. Rather IHL requires a state to incorporate its tenants into their domestic law and apply it through such channels. Or it requires the creation of an ad hoc tribunal, typically under the auspices of the UN Security council. Each tribunal has had its own charter outlining how substantive and procedural IHL will be used. Since the opening of the ICC in 2002, states that are under ICC jurisdiction have an additional mechanism for pursuing justice for mass atrocity events by trying responsible individuals on criminal charges.

This book focuses on the development and eventual codification of the laws of war. It will examine IHL concerns and highlights how these principles emerge overtime, but the time frame covered by this volume ends just before we see the growth on an international peace movement and the drive, led by the Red Cross, to develop IHL as a separate set of laws and create a set of independent courts to adjudicate.

Key Areas of Concern

The typical nature of military conflict raises some almost universal concerns for the behavior of soldiers in the field. These concerns are easily categorizable into four major areas: behaviors toward combatants, noncombatants, property, and cultural sites/artifacts. Rules surrounding conduct vis-à-vis these concerns are as historically deep as warfare itself, being recorded as early as the Peloponnesian wars. Combatants are typically those adults who are actively engaged in the military endeavor.[17] They are attached and integrated into a military and fall within a chain of command.

[17]Child soldiers are the exception here. It is a key concern of the Rome statute and has received ample attention by the ICC. Yet at what age one eligible to join a military varies by state and not all member states are in compliance with the Rome statute's delimitation of 18 as the appropriate age of majority, i.e., the UK and Ireland allow enlistment at 16.

Noncombatants are individuals who do not participate in hostilities and are given a separate space within such contexts. Yet there are often sub-categorizations in terms of potential hostility. Those who are deemed not current but potentially future combatants, non-serving men and older male children, will potentially face harsher treatment due to the potential threat they pose. From Carthage to Srebrenica, men and boys are often separated from other civilians and slaughtered. Such mass killing is unfortunately not rare and accepted into the pre-modern era, and after, in colonial European territories.

Women's treatment, historically and contemporaneously, is a thread that this volume will repeatedly return to. Sexual violence and abuse appears to be part and parcel of women's experiences in armed conflicts. Its ubiquity has been acknowledged by scholars and the real questions rest in understanding its variation (Mullins, 2011, 2015; Wood, 2006). Even in antiquity, there were oppositional norms and treatments, with women simply being seen as adjunct to the property being looted after a city's sacking, to commanders issuing express orders to not harm a single civilian and severely punishing those who did. The medieval rules of chivalry put noble women on a unique pedestal of reverence, but countless women of lower birth will be raped and killed in the aftermath of sieges throughout the period.

Children present a separate set of issues. They are potential future combatants, especially male children. Hence, they are often targeted with adult men in genocides and other atrocity events. The relatively young are malleable and can be enslaved or adopted into one's own group, a common practice found from pre-Columbian Americans to eighth-century England on down to today (though prohibited by the 1948 Genocide Convention and the 1999 Rome Statute of the International Criminal Court). Females are more likely to experience this than males as they are often not seen as a military threat and provide potential domestic labor and reproductive value.

Property, destroying it or taking it, is a central target of war. Through the early modern period, loot (the property of the defeated and sometimes the defeated themselves) was an expectation of soldiers. Through early medieval period loot often served as pay, as military service obligations were the core of feudalism. It will not be until the thirteenth century CE that armies begin to pay troops on a regular basis for their service, often with the expressed intent of reducing looting from enemy civilians. Regular pay is part of the broader enlargement and bureaucratization of military forces. Adjunct to the questions of private property are questions of places and objects seen as commonly owned: such as cultural or religious artifacts and sacred places. The Greeks had strong norms against the destruction of religious sites (Coleman, 1918). During the middle ages, the church issued decree after decree calling for the protection of church property and people from military predation. Sandholtz (2007) shows how during the Napoleonic wars the idea of art as a public or cultural resources emerged as a key concern of the allies in the aftermath. Instead of simply replundering what Napoleon had plundered from all over Europe, the allies tried to return *objects d'art* to original owners if known. If repatriation wasn't possible, the nation was given other works of a similar cultural and monetary value as replacement. This substantially redefines the norms of plunder, ending a practice unquestioned since ancient times.

The Plan of the Book

From here the book will examine the evolution of the laws of war from antiquity through the eighteenth century. It will trace key themes in laws of war, their changes, and the sociopolitical and socioeconomic forces behind those changes. Chapter 2 examines the rules and rituals that guided warfare in the classical age, focusing on the rules guiding conduct of soldiers in Mesopotamia, the early Levant, and classic Greece. This is the period which sees the formation of states and clearly recorded inter-state disputes of a large scale: we see armies taking the field against other armies, not raiding bands stealing cows and pigs. It marks the origin of what most would recognize as warfare. Chapter 3 examines the Roman military and its world. Rome's army was the largest, most complex, and rule-bound force to date. These rules, and the contexts that produce them, change over time through the Republican and Imperial periods.

Chapter 4 examines the early medieval era, from secular codes, such as the Visigothic code (634/1910), to the Catholic Church's interventions, and finally the socio-literary code of Chivalry. This period sees more concentration of power – martial and economic – in the hands of a small elite group of landowners (who became landowners via warfare). Armies get larger, better organized, more diverse in troop-type, and weapon technology steadily improves through the period – especially armor and fortification building, and later, gunpowder. Early in this period the Church attempts to directly control aspects of warfare via the *Pax Dei* and *Treuga Dei*. While these edicts were not fully integrated into the aristocratic mindset concern warfare, these pronouncements stimulate and form the core of a key set of martial values that will be central in the period: chivalry. It closes with the socioeconomic elements that brought about the fall of chivalry. Chapter 5 explores the articles of battle issued by late medieval/early modern kings and princes. Its focus is on those of the Hundred Years War, examining how by the thirteenth century Kings are issuing written orders and rules for their troops and securing their obedience. It comparatively examines the evolution of these codes in the period: their content, role, and effects.

Chapter 6 examines the early modern period and the Age of Reason. The Age of Reason saw a rationalization and refinement of the idea of law binding the behavior of nation states, including during armed conflict. In the international domain, there is a general trend of dismissing earlier notions of Natural Law in favor of rationally deduced principles based upon careful analysis of current actions and behaviors, an early version of *realpolitik*, often referred to as Positive Law. Not only does this period see the development of a new outlook vis-à-vis law and law formation, it also brings the behavior of nation-states under the rule of law, and also attempts to do so with inter-state violence. This is the era of the earliest framing of "laws" of war in the writings of Grotius and Vattel, as well as the work of Hobbes. War is disentangled from justice and an individualized conception, in favor of a framework that defines war as a condition. Limitations of the means of war also begin to surface. Many key concerns of contemporary International Humanitarian Law emerge as law is rationalized, as is the state. Law, including the laws of war, become folded into a new positivist world view with an empirical and scientific drive during the seventeenth and eighteenth centuries which reaches its apex in the nineteenth century. While a framework for governing the war-making behavior of states develops in this period, the fundamental ideals of sovereignty work against the development of a "community" of nations, with rules binding them to acts. Rather, following the laws of war is voluntary and any sanctions for violating them are at best informal and at the whim of other nation-states. Yet, as seen in numerous conflicts, such whims are often backed by military force, reflecting the penultimate belief of the period: that might still makes right. This won't begin to be undone until the Treaty of Westphalia (1648) and the end of the Thirty Years War.

This volume now turns to an examination of humanity's earliest experiences with warfare and attempts to constrain it in such a way as to reduce the destruction inherent in war and reduce the amount of human suffering experienced by war. While such values are not uncovered in the archeological record of early warfare, the ethnographic record is rich with studies of indigenous warfare. It is clear that inter-group conflict is an early aspect of the human experience. We will see as societies become more sedentary and complex, warfare norms and practices begin to shift with belligerents fielding armies over warbands and seeking real destruction over symbolic victories.

Chapter 2

War in the Prehistoric and Ancient Worlds

> All warfare is an exception to the humane standards of law and justice, even so it has quasi-laws. . .of its own: a truce. . .may not be broken; heralds must not be put to death; a man who has placed himself under the protection of a superior opponent may not be visited with punishment or vengeance.
>
> Diodoros (30.18.2) as quoted in Pritchett (1991, p. 203)

Accounts of war and wars appear in our oldest historical and scriptural documents and other artifacts. It is clear that around 10,000 years ago, shortly after the first permanent settlements were founded, they became fortified (Ferguson, 2013; Keeley, 1996; LeBlanc, 2003). As the building of fortifications is a difficult, resource-intense process, it is unlikely to be done for aesthetic or other nonmilitary reasons. One builds city walls in response to a perceived threat. It is a project that requires large scale attainment and coordination of labor and resources. Similarly, around the same period (and in the same places), archaeologists begin to find signs on conflict and conflict-related death in their excavations: cities clearly burned, skeletal remains with embedded projectile points, patterns of injuries which suggest a violent demise, i.e., slashes or breaks in forearm bones are indicative of someone protecting their head/face with their arms during an assault. Evidence of blunt force head trauma and/or head removal are also frequent skeletal indicators of conflicts (Ferguson, 2013; Keeley, 1996; LeBlanc, 2003; Rutar, 2022). Our earliest historical writings from the era also show a rise of large-scale warfare in this period.

Warfare emerges with the development of permanent settlements. Living in the same location year round amplifies the level of investment people have in a given place. Agrarian lifestyles require the production and storage of large amounts of food. As it is less of a time investment to steal or take by force grains and livestock (or other surplus production), motivation for raiding neighbors arises. As villages evolve into cities and city-states (and later early Empires), territorial acquisition becomes a prominent motive for conflict. Hence fortification of cities. The social forces that shape cultures as they become sedentary also encourage the development of writing, typically initially for trade-accounting purposes, and creation of monuments marking what a given leader considers an important event, often a military victory. The historical record of war emerges with these cultural innovations. However,

A Socio-Legal History of the Laws of War, 19–38

Published under exclusive licence by Emerald Publishing Limited
doi:10.1108/978-1-78769-857-420231002

warfare didn't begin with the founding of cities in Mesopotamia. It dates much earlier in human prehistory.

This chapter looks at the development and evolution of warfare and its structuring rules and norms from our earliest examples through the Classical Greek world. It thus focuses primarily on Sumeria and the Mediterranean and Aegean world. The period sees the emergence of the first states and legal codes, along with a transformation of intergroup conflict from localized raiding and feuding into large-scale conflicts between massed forces. Within this context, there is little in terms of codified law regarding any sort of interstate interactions. Each period and regional geography had strongly held customs that guided warfare – its timing, its causes, its conduct, and its consequences. This new form of conflict would generate a new system of interstate relations, a new set of norms and customs to frame the war and peace as different states of being, and the development of norms designed to coordinate and control the behavior of soldiers. While there is a lack of international *laws*, there are state domestic laws which do regulate the ability of state leadership to engage in war, whether it is seen as a the right of a sovereign, or the collective will of a portion of the population as embodied in the decision of a representative body.

Earliest Warfare

When the "first" war happened is dependent upon one's definition of war and warfare. Here, war is defined as hostilities between two or more sovereign states or a sovereign state and an organized resistance group within the state's territory. This conceptualization is at the forefront of many norms and customs concerning war. Organized intergroup violence, however, predates *Homo sapiens sapiens* in our evolutionary lineage. There are clear quantitative and qualitative differences between warfare and other forms of organized intergroup violence such as Nüer cattle raids (Evans-Pritchard, 1969), street gang wars (Jankowski, 1991, Hagedorn, 1988), or terrorism disconnected from wars of liberation or similar conflicts (Bassiouni, 2008). The line where a style of conflict becomes *war* over something else is far from precise. Wars are traditionally conceptualized as state-led disputes when other attempts at resolution fail or are discounted (Clausewitz's politics by another name). Yet, smaller-scale organized intergroup violence is not uncommon in substate level societies – historically and prehistorically. While states may increase the probability or presence of warfare, they are not a necessary condition for intergroup violence. A form of political institution is requisite, as intergroup violence requires at least social hierarchy to organize and orchestrate organized, group-based violence. Such intuitions exist in all human societies, even small groups of food foragers or young adults on a street corner. They vary in the amount of persuasive and coercive pressure they have to elicit participation in hostilities, but culturally recognized reasons for hostilities, war-leaders, and associated rules of engagement are found in all conflicts we have records of.

Evolutionary psychologists and physical anthropologists have argued that violence is endemic to human society as it is endemic in that of our closest known living biological relative, *Pan troglodytes*, the common chimpanzee. Field primatologists have witnessed organized out-group-directed violence among groups of mostly young male chimpanzees. This behavior is qualitatively different from the predatory behavior of chimpanzees observed in the field directed at infant baboons and the like. Based on number of participants, the closest human equivalent is a gang fight, using the term gang loosely to refer to a set of individuals who have banded together for a shared goal, through parallels to more organized youth street gangs are not unwarranted due to dominance hierarchies in chimpanzee society which provide social organization. Our focus here isn't the origins and development of warfare overall, but rather those norms and rules that guide warfare. While primatologists have observed complex social and tool-making behavior among our closest biological cousins, they have been unable to derive any rules or normative structures that guide their out-group-directed violence.

Much archaeological evidence of conflict from across contexts has been unearthed. Walled cities appearing in Mesopotamia ca.10,000 years ago are the first sign of large-scale conflict, or rather, clear attempts to protect oneself from it. Most excavations of city walls in this period are associated with other evidence of conflict: broken gear ranging from stone projectile points to bronze helms and swords. Archaeological sites on all continents save Antarctica have uncovered signs of group violence and violent death. The earliest public monuments record military losses and victories. As Keeley (1996) discusses, the "myth of the peaceful past" often proffered by archaeologists and ethnographers is just that: a myth. He shows group conflict is a common feature of the human experience and extends deep into our prehistory. Though 10,000 years ago the fighting is a low-intensity event, with few combatants and often highly ritualized scripts for combat (which serve to reduce the damage caused to participants). The ethnographic evidence is also rich in showing that violence is neither limited to the industrialized nor normless. Ethnographies highlight the role the violence, ritualized and real, played in preindustrial societies (see, e.g., Hoebel, 1954). For brevity, we will quickly look at the type of warfare and the rules which guided it for the Grand Valley Dani and the indigenous peoples of the North American plains.

For the Grand Valley Dani of Papua New Guinea, war far was an almost constant aspect of their lives. "Every Dani alliance was constantly at war with at least one of its neighboring alliances. Every individual Dani was touched by war" (Heider, 1977, p. 95). Conflict between Dani alliances was endemic; both raids and field battles with rivals were common occurrences. Raids consisted of few men either seeking to ambush an enemy villager or steal pigs. Battles were larger, formal events with up to hundreds of participants. Participation was neither mandatory nor was lack of participation scorned (Heider, 1977). A novice observer would see a chaotic swirl of arrows and javelins launched, with individuals or small groups occasionally coming into melee contact with longer spears. Injuries and deaths are not uncommon, but many of the norms and practices guiding these battles serve to reduce the suffering and loss of life.

Heider (1977, p. 104) notes that the Dani never utilized volley fire by their archers. Each shot was made singularly, and thus more easily dodged or otherwise evaded. Heider claims to never have asked the Dani why, afraid they might adopt a far more lethal use of missile fire. It is doubtful that the Dani hadn't realized volley fire was possible; it is adopted by any army fielding large numbers of archers. It would have been far more accurate and deadly, which was why it is avoided. Further reducing the lethality of missile fire, Dani arrows were not fletched and thus less accurate when shot. The Dani used feathers for ornamentation in other contexts, so it was within their technological abilities.[1] The Dani went into battle with weapons that were less deadly than they could be and were used in a manner which also reduced casualties. In addition, western observers report no ascertainable leadership on the battlefield. While the Dani had "Big Men" who were often the ones who called for a raid or battle, on the field itself, these Big Men had no formal leadership role. Men seemed to advance to the front, launch their missiles or attempt to stab an enemy according to their own will and plans, even if a "Big Man" attempted to direct the battle "no one was obeying" (Heider, 1977, p. 104).

It wasn't that the Dani had strong cultural prohibitions about killing. Raids were common affairs, consisting of small groups of men who attempted to ambush people in enemy villages with the intent, and result, of killing others. This is where the bulk of the killing (and looting) was done; large battles appear far more ceremonial in intent and purpose. Designed as a symbolic show of strength and courage, and not driven by the primary intention of ensuring opponents are no longer capable of offering resistance – the modal goal of battle. It is also suggested that they did not seek to make their warfare more lethal. For example, Heider's field team had several firearms with them that they used to hunt. The Dani were very impressed with the technology but never suggested firearms be used in battle. The inference is such weapons would be too lethal and that was not warfare's main goal for the Dani. What were the key pressures in Dani society which produced these two different forms of intergroup conflict?

The Dani etic view of warfare was that it was necessary to appease ghosts, the remnants of the dead who were seen as staying around the same geographies they knew in life. They can be helpful, as they are sometimes summoned the nights before battle with the hope of gaining their assistance the next day.[2] The ghosts of those who died in battle or raids would demand revenge be taken for their deaths. Ghosts were also seen as highly dangerous and a reason to not go outside at night. It was feared a ghost would throttle anyone found outside after dark; ghosts were also said to enforce the violation of taboos, such as that against incest (Heider, 1977), thus serving a key social control function.

Dani battle also highlights the liminal aspects of warfare. Here a battle is an engagement with another, sacred space.[3] The ritualization of battle creates a space for the ghosts to be placated, for revenge to be had, and for a wrong to be righted –

---

[1]Heider (1977, p. 104) mentions that no New Guinea Highlands peoples fletched their arrows.

[2]That they believed ghosts were only active at night goes unremarked on by the ethnographer here.

[3]Per Durkheim (1912/1915).

for social order to be restored. As mentioned, ghosts were thought to be on the battlefield helping their living peers. Practices seen in large battles were not seen elsewhere. Raids could be deadly and downright brutal in attacking not just men, but women and children who are culturally defined as non-combatants. Even men who left the designated battlespace were no longer considered appropriate targets, unless they return to the field. This focus on targeting only current combatants will be theme throughout war norms examined in this book, a theme that will be paralleled by concerns of prisoner treatment. This highlights that the battle was not just an activity bound by rules, but one of those rules was space – battles had fixed areas where the fighting would occur. Rarely would it spill out of those bounds. Socially, these behaviors while necessary and meaningful had to be constrained to a specific time and place. A liminal space between life and death; between civilian order and chaos.

Many tribal groups on the Great Plains before and at contact could be described as having warrior cultures or a warrior culture embedded within a broader set of values and beliefs (i.e., the Crow, the Cheyenne, the Comanche, the Sioux). Many ethnographers of the Plains describe an area driven with constant war between numerous groups and shifting alliances that becomes more chaotic and complicated as eastern woodlands groups are pushed westward by white settlement and the growth of the US (Hoebel, 1954, 1978; Kehoe, 1989, Oehler, 1997). Much of the conflict among the Plains groups was the result of indigenous groups moving westward by forced or pushed by European colonization. Not counting English (Germanic), there were three different language families extant on the Plains in the 18th century and scores of individual languages. Increasingly new arrivals began to tax the ecosystem, while the northern prairies had ample resources, movement onto the high plains sees a reduction in biodiversity as you move into highlands desert. Competition for resources is growing in both areas by the time Europeans, in the form of French fur traders, reach the area in 1738. This was quickly followed by a major change for all prairie and plains tribes in 1739: the introduction of the European horse (Hoebel, 1954, 1978). Almost all tribes embraced the horse as a beast of burden and transportation. Some tribes, like the Cheyenne and the Crow, fully embraced the horse, becoming Bison following nomads.

The Cheyenne, as well the Comanche, Crow, and other tribal groups, adopted nomadic warrior cultures that emphasized and cultivated the same skills one used in hunting bison could be turned against other men. These cultures are marked by honor and courage displays in combat, which provide more social accolades from allies than kills on the battlefield. A core element of establishing an adult masculinity in these societies revolved around success in warfare and hunting. Of the Comanche, Hoebel (1954) writes that the male sense of self is only achieved through "war honors, horses, and women" (p. 131). Horses and woman could be obtained via raids and warfare. Gendered selves among the Comanche and other tribal groups were borne out of and depended upon inter-group warfare. For the Cheyenne, "[w]ar is necessary ... [for self-protection] ... and to permit individual self-expression of the male" (Hoebel, 1954, p. 143). As it is typically seen as the purview of men, it is not surprising to see manhood explicitly linked to warfare and soldering. This occurs in most contemporary societies with militaries generally being viewed by social scientists as hypermasculine organizations, providing masculine capital for members and acting as a frame for masculinity among civilians (Connell, 1995, 2002). In these warrior cultures, as we will see with the nobility during Europe's Middle Ages, war is an essential part of the normative life cycle of the community, with adult masculinity only fully attainable through the collection of battlefield experiences and honors. Such social pressures would increase the frequency, if not intensity, of intergroup conflicts as the men in several Plain's tribal cultures had to prove themselves in battle to marry and enjoy the other privileges of adulthood. To reduce fatalities, which as we have noted are highly problematic in a low population density group, specific cultural norms emerged and diffused across the region.

For many, the point of combat was not killing or victory in the sense of subduing people or land, but the gaining of honor, prestige, and distinctly masculine social capital. On the plains, the practice was referred to as counting coup – the act of touching or striking an enemy with a hand, short stick (called a coup stick by the Crow), or weapon and then riding off. Coup could also be counted for other laudable war deeds such as rescuing a colleague or being the first scout to find an enemy encampment. Its importance however was paramount, per Hoebel (1978, p. 77): "War has been transformed into a great game in which scoring against the enemy often takes precedence over killing him" and "Public glory is the ever-present reward the man who fights bravely and well. Public ridicule and scornful songs sung by the women drive on the young men" (Hoebel, 1978, p. 75). Through shifting one's military aims from the killing/wounding of enemies to counting coup off your enemies, the number of injuries and fatalities are lessened, and as Hoebel says above, the combats were as much about winning individual prestige than achieving war objectives important to the community.

By no means does this mean these conflicts were not lethal; killing and scalping were common place but did not convey the same amount of honor as counting coup. It should also be noted that along with the horse came the rifle, a weapon Natives did not shy away from using. Yet, unless used to strike an opponent with the butt, the rifle was not a weapon that used to count coup. Successful raids were those where no Cheyenne died, unless they had counted coup before their death. Such raids were celebrated with the Scalp Dance led by the *hemaneh* (halfman-halfwoman), a berdache role containing associations with fertility and virility (who often accompanied the warriors on raids). Berdache is an anthropological term that refers to a man who assumes the dress and some of the social role of a woman, yet also has strong magical associations with fertility due to their dual status as men and women, while being neither and both at the same time. By their natures, berdache's are liminal figures. Here their liminality helps them mark the closing of the social space of war and a return to regular social order. While the scalps taken in battle are artifacts used by the *hemaneh* in the dances that follow, the symbology (and surface meaning) of the dances are focused on sexual/romantic partnering not directly reflective of the events which stimulated the dance in the first place.

Coup practices reduce fatalities and serious causalities among combatants as the chief goal of each combatant is to earn honor by showing courage and the willingness to get close to their enemy and touch them, but not badly injure or kill them. Such carnage reduction norms are understandable in the eighteenth and nineteenth-century plains context – large influxes of indigenous groups from the eastern woodlands, new technologies (horses, firearms), and the constant, growing pressure of US westward expansion kept tensions high and potential conflict ubiquitous. Coup practices allowed tensions to play out into hostilities and gave young (and not so young) men a nonlethal path toward adulthood, as well as honor and respect as a warrior. They allowed groups to develop and maintain warrior cultures while reducing the negative effects on the group's population (early deaths and debilitating injuries). As mentioned above, small populations cannot afford to lose large or even moderate numbers of combatants in a conflict. A killed warrior is one less hunter, reducing the group's chance of further survival. Coup mediates these tensions by providing nonlethal solutions to honor awarding, which becomes a secondary aim of war.

The integration of the *hemaneh* both in battle and the ceremonies afterward highlights the role of liminality in battle here. The *hemaneh* is seen as holding special powers over virility as they are sexually liminal – both man and woman while neither at once. This is the essence of liminal conditions – boundaries between places or states of being filled with power due to their dual nature. It makes sense to be accompanied by a liminal figure in the hope that their "magic" helps the warriors; it is also logical for the *hemaneh* to head the ceremony that redirects the aggression of the warriors into courtship and romance which will, literally, recreate the group in the next generation.[4]

Anthropologists and archaeologists with a cultural materialist approach (see Harris, 1968) would context such decision within an economic utility framework. Where sparing captives gives material benefit, we are apt to find non-combatants, especially women and children, taken as family members (i.e., wives and adopted children) or servants/slaves. Keeley (1996) argues that as states develop, this utility becomes ubiquitous, and we see the development of "formal surrender and widespread official distaste of killing noncombatants. . .express[ing]. . .this interest" (p. 87). The point is well taken; economic value often guides the development of the earliest laws in both peace and war. Yet, as history clearly shows, other interests and forces often override potential economic gains and result is wide scale slaughter not only of those who seemingly constituted a real or potential threat (males and male children) but of all civilians in a city or territory.

Evidence for warfare in the archaeological, ethnographic, and ethological literature all reinforce its ubiquity but also its rules bound nature. Formal and informal practices limited casualties, especially fatalities. In low population density societies, this makes social and ecological sense. People (men) are individually more necessary to the success of a community than in more population

[4]Magic, sorcery, etc. are seen as being more powerful or accessible in liminal times and places and by liminal peoples.

dense societies which can more easily adjust to the loss of a portion of the population (see Europe after each World War). When population densities increase, it is not surprising to see emerge what we traditionally think of as ancient warfare: massed ranks of troops which close to melee and attempt to break the opposition. We will now turn to examine how early sedentary lifestyle and associated social structural elements transform and mold warfare from highly ritualized affairs with relatively few participants (and fewer casualties) into affairs involving hundreds or thousands of troops that exhibit higher levels of casualties and begin to flow over into civilian lives and geographies.

The Chariot War Period and the Beginning of Massed Warfare

Earliest records are economic in nature, not surprisingly. Writing itself grew out of trade practices in Mesopotamia. Some of the earliest public records include monuments or other public displays recounting war victories and losses. Scriptures of key religions also provide some insight into period norms, though have to be read differently than monument inscriptions. By the third millennia BCE, military organization had reached a level of sophistication implying strict rules, if not laws, guiding operations of armies and of troops within armies. Large standing armies developed, and some states used conscription (Parker, 2020). Large aggregations of individuals would seemingly necessitate many aspects of military organization that are well known to us: chains of command, smaller, unit level organizations, various ranking of officers, and code of conduct to maintain order on and off the battlefield. However, little of this survives in the historical record. Much of what we know comes from preserved religious scriptures or inscriptions on monuments erected to commemorate victories. The former do provide some insights into what were seen as undesirable behaviors for soldiers in the field, while the latter provide us knowledge of conflicts, outcomes, and often treaty stipulations.

In general in this era, which we will refer to as the Chariot Wars period, battles were either one of two types: pitched battles or sieges.[5] Pitched battles contested between two armies on a field, often away from a city or other dense human habitation. City sieges, surrounding a city to cut it off from supplies or a relief force in an effort to force capitulation. They were often accompanied with raids on the surrounding country-side – both to support the besieging army and to put pressure on the city to surrender. Pitched Battles were a more desirable event for a commander and were deemed more normative, exhibiting the courage expected of a warrior class. The issue could be settled more quickly than a siege and with less loss of life to both violence and disease. Refusing open battle while tactically or strategically advantageous, was often declared, at least by the attacking forces, to

[5]A large number of terms are used to describe this period, and many are culturally specific (i.e., referring to the period as "Biblical"). I use the phrase Chariot Wars as it is named from a common military unit that generally passes out of use after this period (save for certain places like the British Isles) and thus distinguishes this period of warfare from others.

be cowardly and unbecoming of a true warrior. It also moves warfare from a liminal space directly into the heart of domestic space.

If an invaded people refused to give battle on the field, the aggressor army could, and often did, besiege a major city. Sieges were also common when an army had been defeated on the field, but the state refused to concede to their aggressors. Sieges were a fundamentally different type of conflict, with their own rules and consequences. Instead of attempting to defeat the enemy force by reducing its ability to function the battlefield, sieges were designed and carried out to cause hardship to all those within the city's defense: military and civilian alike, with the aim of bringing starvation and disease within the city to a point where the controllers capitulated. Surrounding lands were often ravaged and denuded of crops and dwellings; a punishment for "making" the belligerent power besiege your city instead of standing for a pitched battle. The use of siege engines and mines were utilized to destabilize walls and other fortifications, allowing the attacking army into the city itself. The consequences of a siege were typically much worse for the defenders than those defeated in a pitched battle. Cities were typically offered surrender first, an offer typically taken if the attacking army was large enough; if the territory was more than a city-state, city mayors or leadership who were less tied to those who claimed dominion over their area would surrender their towns in a blatant change of alliance. Much of this was driven by the desire to preserve the population from atrocity. Cities that surrendered received better terms, and their citizens' better treatment, than those who held out and had their walls and gates breeched by artillery or sappers. If a city refused surrender, it produced a situation "causing unnecessary casualties, then no mercy need be shown to the inhabitants" (Bartlett, 1995, p. 55).

Written records do establish treaties and terms of peace were codified and preserved. Public monuments and interstate correspondence records the terms and intents. Thus, there is clearly a set of rules for the defeated and the victor, and their framing in the legalistic language of treaties emphasizes their perceived importance. Overall, these post-defeat demands were for transportable wealth, land, and people (via marriage or servitude). For example, a treaty between Rameses II and the Hittites established peace, the exchange of valuable minerals in the form of tribute from the Hittites to Egypt, and the marriage of a Hittite princess to Rameses. Additionally, the compact bound current and future heirs to the treaties terms, including a mutual defense pact and promises to extradite political opponents and fugitives. It also bound both sides to humane treatment of returning fugitives, promising "and let not his house be torn down, nor his women and children(dispersed); let him not be executed; let no injury be inflicted on his ears, eyes, mouth, or feet; and let no criminal charges be raised against him" (Bell, 2007, p. 110). This is significant as, at least in recorded military history of the period, it was a rarity to demand or offer such protections for civilians. As we will see below, the opposite typically occurred. Religious overtones added additional severity by inviting divine blessing on those who abided by the treaty and curses upon those who broke it.

Enslavement of civilians in a territory was normative, as was deporting captives back to one's home nation as slaves. This was one way in which empires were built. When a sovereign is defeated, he loses the right to his possessions and his status, unless he can negotiate them back after the battle. The people in a geography were as much possessions of a King as the gold or the cattle. It was deemed lawful, and merciful, to take captives as slaves, whether captured on the battlefield or during the sacking of a city. The alternative was typically banishment or slaughter.

Several narratives from this period discuss the elimination or total destruction of one people by another. Such genocidal behavior was not uncommon in ancient warfare, though how common and how extensive is unknown. Inscriptions (and translations thereof) are not always clear. Eradication adds risk for one's troops and destroys valuable human capital. Enslavement, tribute demands, and other outcomes are more beneficial to the victor than genociding a city-state. Some of the worst outcomes were reserved for cities that rebelled against their ruler. For example, in the midst of a profitable summer campaign season, the Assyrian king Ashurnasirpal ordered atrocities visited upon a city in rebellion, despite the city offering surrender before hostilities began (Bradford, 2001). The king wrote "I took the city by assault and skinned alive all of the leaders of the rebels and built a pillar which I covered with their skin. . ..some I impaled on the pillar and others I tied to stakes around the pillar. . .I burned. . .captives alive. . .Many I took alive. I cut off their noses, their ears, and their fingers; I put out their eyes. . .I burned the young men and women alive" (as quoted in Bradford, 2001, p. 42). He left the rest to die of thirst in the desert. As Bradford (2001, p. 43) points out, the "Assyrians ruled by terror. . .they ravaged the Near East. And they gave nothing in return." This form of post-battle atrocity was not limited to the Assyrians.

The *Old Testament* lists numerous nations and peoples eradicated after losing to the Israelites. The Book of Deuteronomy specifically mentions killing all men and enslaving women and children if Israel's armies are resisted. If the opposition force surrendered and submitted to Israeli authority, they became slaves. In the case of ancient Israel, treatment of enemies appears to have been harsher the more geographically proximate they were to Israel itself. The land that became Israel itself was cleared of others by Israel's armies. It is not rare for the god of the Israeli's to demand they invade and destroy a neighboring people; it is how they acquired their kingdom to begin with. However, while Hebrew scripture contains numerous injunctions to slaughter a neighboring people in their entirety, it also lays out specific prohibitions the Israeli troops must follow. Israeli law demanded the preservation of physical property and agricultural resources, specifically fruit trees (see Deuteronomy 20). Such rules are common when one intends to inhabit the land being conquered. Olive trees take 4–5 years to mature for their first fruit bearing season. While the ancient Israeli rules of war were less concerned about the fate of defeated peoples, they were very concerned about the condition of the property won.

Until very recently, plunder was considered a right of military victory. Land, resources, and people were all plundered in the wake of a victory. It is unclear from sources whether or not the armies of their period were directly paid for their service. Most service was demanded from the King. Loot and plunder served for many armies for many centuries as a soldier's pay. This is an innately poor motivator of behavior, as it strongly encourages theft and looting not only of a city after it falls but of any small village marched passed along the way. Most armies of this and later periods that rely on plunder have strict rules concerning its division. Typically, it is all seen as the rightful property of the Sovereign (as it was his army which won the battle and collected the spoils), but often highly specific rules for breaking the loot down from King to footman. It was desired that such rules would lead to soldiers turning in all (or almost all) the loot they found and would be less motivated to stash items for themselves, as a soldier knew he would be getting about as much of the take as other men in his position. It isn't known how much "personal stashing" the rules prevented, nor what the punishment was.

Such spoils taking could extend to religious artifacts as well. When Assyria took Uruk in 692 BCE, statutes of the principle deities of Uruk and Larsh were removed back to the Assyrian capital. This is a form of looting that is also destruction (or at least removal of) cultural artifacts and patrimony, something deemed illegal under current laws. Taking the statues of a defeated people's gods adds cultural insult to the physical and financial cost extracted from the defeated. It shows one is unable to protect that which is most holy and revered by a people. By commandeering what is held sacred by a people, a victor displays their total control over the war's outcome and thus the defeated is disgraced. Such humiliation can intend to send a strong message of deterrence of future hostilities but can just as easily generate motivation for future conflict.[6]

One of the earliest known codified law systems, The Code of Hammurabi (~1700 +/− 20 years BCE), lists 282 specific prohibitions and remedies. Eight of those pertain to warfare, and seven relate to prisoners of war. Interestingly, these laws are placed in the context of laws about robbery and property theft, not warfare.[7] The first addresses a common practice into nineteenth century, that of hiring someone else to take one's place when called to muster. The law forbids withholding the mercenary's pay, with the consequence of death and transfer of one's property to said substitute. Similarly, if a man sends a mercenary in his place, yet later withdraws that substitute, the hirer will be put to death. Three address what happens to a man's possessions back home if he is captured. If the soldier has a son of age, the son assumes his father's position as head of the household and property (and obligations including debts). If the son is too young, a third of the lands are given to the mother to raise the child. Finally, if a prisoner of war returns home to find his land occupied by another, he is allowed to retake possession of it.

If a captured man has his freedom bought by a third party, that party cannot claim the man's physical property (field, house, or garden) in return for the

---

[6]This is also seen in inter-personal and inter-gang street violence (see Katz, 1988). Humiliation and its rectification motivates a large amount of violence, especially in the West.

[7]There are laws in the code which allow for abandoned land to be occupied and worked, with the person doing so attaining ownership rights after a period of non-contested use. About half of these laws are directed toward preventing, or remedying, the situation if a prisoner of war's land is claimed by another.

ransomed soldier's freedom. Rather, if the soldier himself has the funds to buy himself free from the merchant, he is allowed to do so. If he lacks the means, the community temple will buy his freedom. If the temple cannot do so, the court will do so. This emphasizes the importance of property to citizenship and to survival in the period. A landless man is destitute; a large number of such men freshly returned from war is a security issue, not just an issue of patriotism giving due respect to military service. Maintaining order postwar required a reimposition of the prewar order, including property ownership. The other law addressed order in the military organization by shoring up the power of the chain of command: anyone who harmed a captain or took his property faced a death sentence.

The lack of much in the way of discussion of warfare in Hammurabi's code suggests a separate set of rules or laws covering that behavior. Enslavement and selling of prisoners are alluded to, as is the right to buy one's freedom if capable. This tells us some norms of prisoner taking existed at the time. Further a rank system is clearly alluded to in rule #34 which specifically identifies the rank of "Captain." One would expect an internal discipline system as well. With war as a liminal space and experience, it is not surprising to see it referred to sparingly in a code of civil laws. With peace and war being separate spaces and states of existence, separate codes of law would be understandable. If so, the military regulations did not survive to the present day.

The Chariot Wars period sees the fielding of large, coordinated forces, which often have some functional differentiation between how certain formations are used or fight. For example, most armies in this period had a core of infantry, some use of missile fire be it archers or slingers, in skirmishing or ranked formations, and some form of cavalry, be it light or heavy cavalry or chariots (or some combination thereof). Such conflicts were larger and more organizationally complicated than that recorded in the ethnographic literature, and it is a complexity that is supported by both the historical and archaeological records. Though not preserved in written form, we can assume the existence of organizational norms simply due to the size of groups involved. Warfare requires coordination, norms are the primary way in which humans coordinate their behavior. Soldiering requires discipline, which implies a set of norms and sanctions to inculcate and enforce. We don't know if discipline was frequent or harsh. We don't know the procedures in place for determining and administering punishments if they existed. The tendency to end conflicts with genocide (population eradication) appears to be more frequent and normative during this period, though that could be an artifact of which events were historically recorded in a manner which survived. Larger, more consequential events were more likely to be commemorated by monuments and the like; thus, we may simply be unaware of many lesser battles and wars. It also can't be said whether genocide held the same meanings 5,000 ya as it does today.

As the Chariot Wars period begins to wane, the infantry man takes a more central role in battle. The next civilization we will discuss relied heavily upon infantry to compose their forces, with cavalry of any form being decidedly less central. The Hoplite phalanx dominated battlefields until it was either kept at pikes length by the Macedonian variation on the phalanx or faced the triple lines of the Roman Republic's legions. We have much more documentary and artifactual evidence to help us discern the rules of war followed by the Ancient Greeks.

Greece

While there is a tendency to think of Ancient Greece as monolithic culture and society, until the modern era, Greece was divided into small polities, that in the ancient period cooperated as much as they entered conflicts with each other. They shared a language, religious beliefs and practices, other cultural elements, including a similar approach to warfare that relied on citizen-soldiers mustered only during campaign season (Bradford, 1984, 2001; Coleman, 1918; Garland, 1975, 1984; Pritchett, 1971, 1991).[8] An incredible amount of ritual, religious, and legal thought and action surrounded warfare in Ancient Greece. War was seen as a dangerous force to be constrained and bounded like other liminalities. It was a site of chaos and violence: a breakdown of the peace time social order. It was a locus of transformation: to hero, to corpse, to slave. It is here we find one of the early instances where there are clear and deliberate steps taken to differentiate states of peace and states of war. This establishes war not only as a specific realm of action but a specific realm of redress of perceived wrongdoing, of justice. This notion will be more strongly expressed in post-Roman Europe through the middle ages.

Coleman (1918) claims the Greeks drew a "distinction between private morality and public conduct, on the ground the rules of justice were to be observed between individuals, but that considerations of expediency … should preponderate in matters of public or interstatal character" (p. 96). Spartans were well known for the subordination of the individual to the state and state needs. Lysander, commander of the Spartan fleet, exemplified this strongly in his embracement of an ends-justifies-the-means philosophy, "no matter how cruel, deceitful, or unscrupulous they were" (Coleman, 1918, p. 97). Deceit and trickery were seen as being as valuable in battle as force and sound tactics, as long as the state's needs were met. While the Spartan view was an extreme position of norms generally held by Greek military commanders, others embraced such tactics as well. The Greek literary hero Odysseus is known and praised for his trickery and wiliness. And of course, it is deceit which bring about the fall of Troy. Praise for such behavior, at least in Greek sources, seems reserved for those Greeks who were successful in their use of such tactics. Enemies which drew upon them were deemed dishonorable and unjust (i.e., the Persians at Thermopile). However, the religious nature of much of the Greek's laws of war meant that non-Greek enemies were not expected to follow such rites, nor were Greeks obligated to

[8]There were exceptions. Over time in Athens, elites came to dominate the ranks, as they did the officer ranks in Macedonia. In Sparta militarism was a year-round focus. When there was pressure to field large armies, immigrants or native forces in occupied lands were utilized, as were mercenaries (Garland, 1984).

follow them against outsiders – not an uncommon situation where belligerents have disagreements about or different sets of rules of war. Despite this cultural appreciation for creative response to military situations, there were many norms and laws which framed how Greeks thought about and practiced warfare. As Pritchett (1974, p. 147) discusses: "fighting seems to have developed a certain fixed code, an etiquette of its own. War was by no means a scramble in which 'all is fair'." Rules bound behavior of all sorts concerning hostilities. Most were grounded in, or at least legitimized through, a religious framework. This meant that one would find mutual observance of such rules only between city-states in Greece proper; outsiders were neither expected to receive the benefits of or confirm to the demands of Greek ideal of war. Views of outsiders as inferior and barbaric, of being unable to understand and appreciate law and Greek custom were common. This is common exception found in the laws of war, Christian military law did not apply to Saracens, and vice versa, in the crusades.

The state of open war (*phaneros polemos*) was clearly defined and delineated as beginning when an army crossed political borders without mutual agreement, an act of direct aggression (Alonso, 2007, p. 215). Open declarations were expected. Ceremonies were also held before the neighbor's border was crossed, initiating this transition of the state of the relationship between polities also indicated a shift from the laws of peace being replaced by the laws of war. Many of the Greek laws of war had their roots in a shared religious system; as many of these were the product of shared religious worldview, war against non-Greeks were not as severely proscribed and saw much greater latitude given to the wagers of war to engage in destructive tactics and outcomes. The laws of war were in force only in conflicts with other organized and sovereign states – this excludes general banditry and piracy but also conflicts against those the Greeks saw as barbarians. Violence used against such group need not be constrained or limited, the fighters not given the benefits and protections of law (Coleman, 1918). This is representative of the strong line drawn between violence in war and violence in peace, with the latter being a crime and a violation of the ordinary order and the former a tactic of state power and social control.

Ideally for the Greeks battle was sought on flat plains far from cities, identified by mutual agreement, with the hope of reducing the harm to civilians and civilian property (Alonso, 1984, 2007; Coleman, 1918; Garland, 1975, 1984). Alonso (2007) postulates these norms were the product of Greeks viewing war as inevitable and these rules restrict the space (and people) affected. It also ensured the scattering of a defeated force, instead of a retreat into a walled city. The cultural norm was for the single hoplite battle to settle what ever issues had emerged between the belligerent city-states. This physical separation of space also speaks to the liminality of war, especially in the eyes of the Ancient Greeks. It was a dangerous and potentially contagious violence than needed to be isolated to be controlled. Although not even the Greeks observed such practice in all cases. Cities were fortified for a reason.

The Greeks, at least for intra-Greek city-state conflicts, held strong rules against cutting off or fouling the water supply of a besieged city. Such behavior would been seen as an intemperate assault on the citizens of the town, not just the armed forces holding the town. Yet, blocking water and a general policy of scorched earth was acceptable against non-Greeks. Coleman (1918, p. 30) points to a general sense of racial superiority held by Hellenistic Greeks and the uniting factors of shared religion. This shared religious framework seems to be one of the strongest sources of, and motivators to follow, the laws of war. Such rules came from the Gods themselves and violations of them required due appeasement of the same. This is seen sharply in the prohibitions against violation of religious or otherwise sacred places and objects, such as graves, temples, and the like. If damages occurred, reparations were expected. Such protections were backed by human and divine law, with violations bringing – at least according to the work of chroniclers of the period – madness or other calamity upon the military leader or their family. Just punishments were believed to be handed down by the gods themselves.

Stemming from a religious root, respect for the bodies of the enemy's dead was a key norm. Honorable leaders returned the bodies of the dead and struck truces for the collection and burial thereof, even amid hostilities. Preventing the bodies of one's enemies from being collected or otherwise intentionally preventing their burial is cast as one of the worst offenses of the time, second only to cowardice in the phalanx. Mutilation or disfigurement of the bodies was similarly taboo; such violence was unnecessary to the Greek war aims.

In Ancient Greece, soldering was a citizen's obligation. When called, they were expected to serve for the campaign season without pay for their labor. As Michell (1940, p. 361, quoted in Pritchett, 1971, p. 3) explained "[w]ith regard to military expenses...down to the outbreak of the Peloponnesian war, the armed forces for the state we composed of civilians who provided their own equipment and maintained themselves while on active service...[i]t is quite possible for the state to bear little or no expense." Not only was soldering a citizen's obligation but a form of taxation as the hoplite had to provide his own weapons, armor and other gear, saving the government expense. Thucydides refers to solders receiving payments using the term *misthos*, it is not clear if this is a reference to the providing of an allowance typically given to the soldier by the state for provisions while on campaign, or whether it served additionally as compensation for service. The confusion arises from divining the exact meaning of several Greek phrases that refer to money or payments (see Pritchett, 1971, Ch 1, for an in-depth discussion of the terms used and their potential meanings). Despite translation arguments, it seems clear that through the fifth century BCE most Greek hoplites received little financial renumeration for their work, and what little they did receive was intended (and used) for campaign provisions. This is not an unusual situation in the period and helps fuel the drive for plundering one's defeated enemies. Generals (*Hegemons*) were paid for their work but were also criminally liable for failure, often facing execution for failure. As common throughout the ancient world, the rights of plunder – of land, property, and people – was the right of the victor in Greece.

Typically, plunder was divided in a strict fashion: 10% was given to the Gods in sacrifice, a portion was given to the state itself, and the rest was shared out among the soldiers but not in an equal fashion. Captured territories were often offered up to city-state citizens to colonize (Coleman, 1918). Milder treatment was not uncommon, with tributes and ransoms being demanded instead of the whole sale taking possession of the people and property of a Polis. Whether or not the city voluntarily surrendered, versus being taken by force, typically influenced the terms offered. In the latter case, subjugation was often total, involving the slaughter of males of age and the enslavement of the rest. Plunder was essentially total and the emptied city often turned over for settlement by citizens of the victor's state or burned to the ground.

Captives, sometimes viewed as part of plunder, received mixed treatments depending on who they were captives of (Coleman, 1918; Garland, 1975, 1984; Gillespie, 2011a, 2011b; Lanni, 2008). Despite Diodorus' injunction at the chapter's beginning about not harming prisoners of war, this was not a view shared by military actors across the region or period. There does not seem to be a clear standard applied across polities. After a war between the Eleians and their allies the Arkadians versus Eleian exiles and mercenaries, the victorious Eleians and Arkadians divided up some 4,000 prisoners or war between them. The Arkadians sold theirs into slavery, a common fate of both military and civilian captives. The "Eleians cut the throats...of their part" (Pritchett, 1991, p. 203), which was their right and another not uncommon fate of prisoners of war. At times, killing prisoners was a product of expediency (Luban, 2013). The victorious army simply would not, or could not, maintain security, food, etc. for the captives. Or the more total eradication of a foe was desired. Pritchett (1991) identifies 65 civilian massacres between the sixth and second centuries BCE, with 46 different perpetrating militaries. More common was the killing of male prisoners and the enslavement of women and children, or the enslavement of everyone. Such incidents are typically mentioned in the absence of discussions of trials or other forms of justice, thus assumed acceptable. Two incidents which did produce trials and the invocation of law to punish atrocity committers are discussed below, but these cases are the exception and not the rule.

For all armies, a key concern is order in the ranks and the discipline required to create it and keep it. As we will see, a multitude of rules and punishments utilized by the Roman army have survived; unfortunately, there is little such material for the Greeks. Some surviving orations indicate the typical expectations for soldiers in battle, with desertion and cowardice being mentioned not only in public oratory but being used politically to soil an opponent's name. Thucydides records in Argos, the traditional norm was to hold a public court outside of the city before allowing the soldiers to return home. Here, crimes which occurred during the campaign would be adjudicated before allowing the men to go their separate ways. As, especially for the Greeks, war was a liminal space/force, adjudicating potential wrong doings *before* the city is entered maintains the separation of peace and war. Once the army has returned, they are citizens again, not warriors. They have returned to domestic space. To prevent the problems of war from disrupting civilian space, the city of Argos at least ensured all aspects of the war experience, including postwar justice, were resolved outside of that sacred, communal space to avoid polluting it.[9] It also serves as a strong symbolic reminder to the men that they are home and no longer soldiers; such rituals assist in shifting between social roles and positions. This suggests the existence of an entire slate of norms and rules that supplant those of civil day-to-day life in warfare. Adjudication implies rules or laws. Further, conducting these "trials" outside of the city further suggests a set of rules applicable to activity outside the city rather than within it. Unfortunately, most of the sets or rules or details of their adjudication related to warfare were not systematically recorded to be examined as in other eras.

As with commanders today, some Greek commanders were harsh disciplinarians. Xenophon admitted to beating troops who failed to maintain good order in the ranks, whether it was running ahead to get to loot before others or those lagging behind slowing the march. Xenophon claimed such acts were not done out of cruelty but as pedagogy, "I struck such a one [a straggler] with the fist in order that the enemy might not strike him with the lance." While an astute criminologist will recognize the neutralization of an appeal to higher loyalty (See Sykes & Matza, 1957), the pragmatism of Xenophon's approach was likely shared by many commanders of his day and after. Outside of Sparta, *hegemon* were elected by their troops and had an incentive to be fair in their use of discipline if they wanted to maintain their position and their public honor. Unusual, but not unknown, troops electing their own officers provides a social control check on potential abuses of power by leaders.[10]

We do have records of Generals who faced trial at home for military failures, and the mentioning's of individual soldiers being disciplined in various historical and literary sources, we only have a couple of examples of what can be considered full war crimes trials – trials not brought about simply by the outcome of the battle but held due to the problematic actions of leaders and soldiers in the fights.[11,12] Two key Greek examples, which bookend the Peloponnesian war, are illustrative: Plataea and Aegospotami. These two incidents highlight the core laws of war that guided the interaction of armed forces with opposition solders and of civilians. Other keys aspects of these rules are also brought into sharp focus – the lack of their application to outsiders (non-Greeks) and the needs of expediency outweighing strict legal doctrines.

The first of these occurs in the aftermath of the siege of Plataea (429–427 BCE), an incident regarded as a key trigger of the Peloponnesian War. The city of Plataea was an ally of Athens in the years leading up to the conflict and the only city state in Boeotia not a member of the Boeotian league. Thebes, a dominant force in the Boeotian league and a Spartan ally, dispatched a small force of 300 men to invade the city in 431 BCE, hoping to take the city by surprise and without

---

[9]In the Durkheimian sense.

[10]For example, in the US troops elected their officers up to and into the US Civil War of the 1860s.

[11]Not an uncommon practice which is still practiced by some forces today.

[12]Save Thucydides (2009) mention of the practices at Argos, though he gives no details of crimes or procedures used.

violence. A larger force followed behind, in the hope of evading detection and arriving to fully secure control of the city. Agents within Palataea who sought an alliance with Thebes opened the city gates and allowed the initial force entry to the city, which established itself in the central marketplace. City leaders initially acquiesced to the Thebian demand for surrender.

When the townsfolk realized the small size of the invading force, they rose enmasse at night against the army, killing 120 and capturing 180. The larger force arrived in the morning, the Palataeans sent out a herald and negotiated an agreement whereby if the Theban force would withdraw, they would release the prisoners. Thucydides indicates accounts of this agreement differed between Theban and Palataean narratives about when and how the prisoners would be released. That said, the prisoners were executed but the bodies were released to the Theban forces. The Palataeans showed proper respect for the dead by returning their bodies. The Theban forces withdrew. Shortly thereafter, Athens supplied the city and equipped a small garrison force.

The Plataeans were quick to protest Spartan military aggression, reminded them that their city fought with the Greeks against Persia and in the aftermath their city was promised freedom ad protection if attacked. They invoked the specifically religious nature of the oaths sworn in the city by Spartan military commanders in Zeus' name. Archidamus invoked "all you gods and heroes who possess the land. . .be our witness now that from the start it was with no wrongful motive. . ., but because the Plataeans had first broken our communal oath. . .[thus] grant then the punishment of those who first did wrong, and vindication or those who lawfully seek to impose it" (Thucydides II:72). This emphasizes the fusion of political and religious norms within the laws of war and highlights the key bond of religion between Greek city states. It is also illustration of an often used metaphor of war as a form of justice – similar to that which would be dispatched by a court (with all of the substantive and procedural law implied) but writ large.

The Spartans promised to respect Palataea's independence if they would remain neutral in the conflict between Athens and Sparta. Palataea responded that they needed Athen's permission to do so, emphasizing that Athens held Palataean women and children as hostages. Sparta allowed messengers to depart to Athens. Then, in preparation for hostilities, they told the city to enumerate their property: "pacify the boundaries of your land, the number of your trees, and anything that can be quantified" (Thucydides II:72) and offered to hold material in trust until the end of the war whereupon it would be returned to the city, a proposal that was rejected. Messengers returned from Athens with the promise that the city would not be abandoned and to reject the Spartan demands. Sparta sieges the city, ritualistically invoking the Gods, establishing the war as a form of justice to punish the Palataeans for breaking their oaths. The religious justification is not only symbolic but verifies the lawful nature of the conflict (despite the lack of need to do so, as their target is not a Greek city, but a Boeotian one). Sparta could not initially break through the defenses. They set up blockade, built two walls around the city and settled in for a long seige.

After two years, the city fell. Once the Spartans realized their assault would be successful, that the city's defenders were too weak to defend themselves, they ceased the attack and refrained from storming the city. While an act that provided some measure of mercy to the citizenry, the main goal was shaped by their agreement with Athens concerning the conduct of the war. If they took the city by force, it would be returned at the end of the conflict. If the city surrendered voluntarily, it would remain in Spartan (or Thebian) control. Sparta offered to refrain from sacking the city if the Palataeans agreed to surrender the "guilty" for trial, meaning those responsible for killing the Thebian solders and for violating past oaths. Palataea agreed.

As recorded by Thucydides, the public trial was simple in structure. Five Spartan judges were appointed, they brought no specific legal charges or allegations but asked the assembled citizenry "if they had done anything to the benefit of Spartans and their allies in the current war" (Thucydides III: 72, p. 155). After making procedural objections to the trial's form – there were no clear charges laid against them and they were not convinced the Spartan judges were indeed neutral parties – they provided an account of the history of treaties they had entered into and that they saw as currently binding their obligations. Specifically, they had been loyal to Greek interests in the Persian wars and afterward were bound by obligations made to Athens, which they could not forsake simply due to Spartan demands in the wake of the Theban aggression that started the conflict. They reminded the judges of the law: "piety . . . recognizes that we gave ourselves up to you freely, with our hands outstretched in supplication 'Greek law prohibits the killing of supplicants'" (Thucydides III; 58, p. 158). Further, they noted that they had tended to the graves of Spartans killed by Persians and buried in their lands, thus showing honor and friendship to Sparta.

Failing to protect supplicants became a specific charge leveled against Plataea by Thebes in their response to the Plataean speech. While acknowledging a legal right to fight and kill the soldiers during the night-time ambush, they claimed that under the laws of war the killing of prisoners was an atrocity that ran counter to the oaths the city had given – oaths which Plataea claimed it had never made. Note the issue is not that the prisoners were killed per se, but the killing was supposedly done in violation of a prior oath. The crime is breaking the oath, not the slaughter of soldiers. Thebian speakers called for the judges to make an example out of Plataea in the name of broader Greek law. The Spartan judges then called individual Plataeans, and Athenians who had been in the city, before them one by one, asking them if they had done anything during the war to benefit Sparta. Those who answered "No" were executed. More than 200 Plataeans and 25 Athenians were put to death; the city's women were sold as slaves. Afterward, the Spartans handed the city over to the Megarians, who razed it a year later.

There may have been greater attention given to legally framing aspects of this case, especially in establishing a Spartan justification for sieging and capturing the city. Plataea is the trigger event in the onset of the Peloponnesian War; while there are numerous of other incidents, forces, and conditions that produced the conflict, this was the incident that belligerent parties framed as the key treaty violation which catalyzed a transition from peace to war. Legally justifying war – with both the religious and political connotations – was crucial, especially from the Spartan perspective. Hence, at the resolution of the siege a legalistic frame was called for to legitimate the war itself.

Another example comes from the end of the Peloponnesian War: the atrocities committed at the naval battle at Aegospotami in 405 BCE.[13] In response to Sparta capturing Lampsaque, Athens dispatched a fleet of around 180 triremes. After several failed attempts by the Athenians to lure the Spartans into battle, the Spartans surprised the Athenians while most of the fleet went ashore at night. The attack captured all of the unoccupied boats and most of the troops ashore at the time of the attack. After the battle, the Spartans discovered two key actions committed by Athenians they considered atrocities in need of legal punishment. The first of these was the result of a meeting among the six Athenian admirals previous to the encounter. The group had voted 5-1 to remove the right hand of every enemy captured in the ensuring battles, a direct violation of prohibitions against despoiling the bodies of the slain or of captives. Only Adeimantus opposed this potential course of action. During the action, one of the Athenian admirals, Philocles, had ordered the crews of two captured Spartan triremes thrown overboard. Both acts violated basic principles of the Greek laws of war. Mutilation of captives was unwarranted and dishonorable, the execution of whole crews of captives even more so. A trial, of sorts, was held by Spartan allied military leaders, led by Lysander. That the killings were intra-Greek, emphasized by Lysander, made them violations of the laws of war, reiterating the legal lines surrounding appropriate behavior between Greeks and between Greeks and non-Greeks. Had those killed not been Greek, it would not have been a violation of law per Lysander. Jurisdiction here was clearly ethnically based. Philocles and 4,000 Athenians were executed and refused burial – an especially damning punishment (Pausanias 1989/2013 Bk IX 32. 9) and a war crime itself.

Ancient Greece as we think of it was a geographically proximate group of city states who shared language, religion, and culture. Yet were each independent politically. Alliances and confederations were built and collapsed. Economic and political competition between polities abounded. No unifying power center arose and all Greek warfare was essentially "local" warfare, either against another Greek city-state or a bordering people encroaching on Greek lands. This kept warfare a small and limited affair, especially early on and especially in comparison with other states of the period. This context created a specific set of rules that were reinforced by both shared religious and legal culture. Within the shared Greek vision and rules of war, we find the Greek solution to the near-universal problems presented by warfare. The next case examines highly different solutions to the same questions. Roman military laws and norms address similar problems, often differently, as well as addressing problems. As well as problems unique to the Legions as Rome became expansionistic.

---

[13]There are two key narrative versions of this incident that survive: Xenophon's and Diodorus'. Investigating and reckoning differences between these accounts will not be attempted here; see Strauss (1983) for such a discussion.

Chapter 3

The Roman Republic and Empire

> Writing in the early second century CE, the historian Florus stressed that until the reign of August Rome had been almost permanently at war. Until 29 BCE, he said, the doors of the temple of Janus had been symbolically closed only twice to make times of peace.
>
> (Bédoyére, 2020)

So far, we have discussed military forms and rules that have largely come down to us piecemeal from artifacts, obelisks, and other archaeological discoveries. What we have been able to say about the laws of war with any surety has been limited. With the Greeks, surviving literature gives us a look at many of their rules and regulations, but each city-state had varied resources to draw upon. There is clearly a broader culture surrounding Greek warfare that they themselves saw as distinctly different from, and not applicable to, non-Greeks. Yet, these norms come down to us not directly from military manuals or writings, but secondarily from historians, geographers, and poets. This is not the case for the Roman army. Many manuals and guides survive from the period, providing solid insights into how the Romans organized, used, and controlled their forces. These guides will be translated and published on their own (i.e., *De Militaria*) or will be subsumed into other volumes of military tactics and discipline (i.e., Grotius (1625/1971)). Roman disciplinary practices will particularly find a home in armies, and especially navies (see Napier, 1837; Singha, 2016) into the twentieth century.

There is no monolithic form the Roman army takes that spans the nation's history. The early armies fielded against early hill tribes looked and acted like most other armies of the period (i.e., the phalanx which dominated military organization and tactics at the time). During the Republic, the army would adopt its famous manipular structure (aka the Polybian Army), best described to us by the Greek historian Polybius. The manipular army spurred the mass rank and file style phalanx. Instead, the troops were groups into maniples of approximately 120 men that were deployed in three lines: the *hastate*, the *principes*, and the *triarii*.[1] The

[1]This is the "paper" strength of the maniples. The actual numbers no doubt varied by context.

A Socio-Legal History of the Laws of War, 39–49

Published under exclusive licence by Emerald Publishing Limited
doi:10.1108/978-1-78769-857-420231003

experience level of the troops varied with the line they were assigned: new recruits were put in the *hastate*, those with some experience in the *principes*, with the senior veterans placed in the *triarii*, who were kept as a reserve force as needed. Another innovation is the rotation of men in the files, where a group would fight until the Centurion called for rotation, where the man in front would make his way to the back rank of his file in the maniple, and the man behind him would step up to the front line. This kept soldiers from exhaustion and was designed to pit a fresh line of Romans against an increasingly battered and weary line of their opponents. The army was reorganized by Marius and then again under Octavius I. Over time, the Imperial army would rely more and more upon non-Romans to make up their ranks, both of auxilia and legion. The Roman army also saw innovations in weapons (the pilum and the gladius) and armor (segmenta). It was an army that, in its various formulations, conquered the known world and held most of it in their Empire. Compared with the Greeks, the Romans faced a wider variety of enemies in a wider variety of contexts that other nations to that time. The need to organize, standardize, and keep account of such a large army produced ample written records.

Rome had a much more formally organized military apparatus than Greece or other ancient civilizations. Rome's military structures lasted longer and grew larger than any prior military. Such a complex organizational endeavor requires greater levels of structure, including norms, rules, and laws. Consequently, our understanding of legal issues as they relate to the military is richer and more detailed. Ruffus produced his *Military* Law, Emperor Maurice's *Strategica*, and Book 49, Title 16 of the Civil Law dealt directly with military affairs.[2] The Civil Law explicitly draws a line between civil and military law, dictating "[a]n offense is specifically military if it is committed by a person in his capacity as a soldier" (Brand, 1968, p. 172) and simply would not be possible to complete unless that individual was a soldier. Such a clear delineation of types of law and when to draw upon one over the other is the sign of a complex and intricate legal system. It is further recognition of the social distinction between states of existence and appropriate behavior therein. This is the liminality of war being constrained by a separate set of specialized laws; the creation of a separate set of rules is reinforcement that war demands different behaviors during its conduct strong socio-legal lines between war, and those who engage in it, and the rest of society were seen as necessary.

Rome was an expansive power from its early days, seeking to gain territory, peoples, and property. From its early struggles with its neighboring hill tribes through the third century CE, Rome was intent upon growth by any means. This is no better reflected than in one of Rome's founding myths: the rape of the Sabine women. In order to grow, in population and power, Roman leaders invite their

[2]The precise provenance of this volume is unknown. In the late sixteenth century, it was translated from both Greek and Latin versions. The initial presumption was that the Greek was the original text, with the Latin a translation. But as Brand (1968, p. 148) points out, and as we shall see in the subsequent pages, the laws seem more Roman than Greek, as does the author's name. This suggests the translation of a Latin text to Greek in the Byzantian period.

neighboring tribes, including the Sabines, to festivities celebrating Neptune Equester. During the festival, the Sabine men were murdered, and their wives taken by the Romans as wives. When the Sabines later sent an army to liberate their women, it was the women themselves who intervened, placing themselves between the armies to avoid the bloodshed of their husbands and their male blood relatives. It is reasonable to assume that the women had accepted their fate, had birthed "Roman" children, and to some degree considered themselves Roman. Rome wouldn't stop at the absorption of its closest neighbor, it would eventually conquer most of the world known to it, with an empire spanning from the Levant and North Africa to the English Isles. Central to this colonial enterprise was the Roman army, which was used to acquire and maintain the empires holdings. While estimates and counts provided by ancient chroniclers vary widely and are largely untrustworthy, it is clear that Rome's army was the largest and most ethnically diverse standing armed force in the ancient world. It was also one of the rare standing, professional armed forces in the ancient world (Bédoyére, 2020).

The questions concerning what constitutes a legal, versus an illegal, war that will plague international lawyers through many periods have their roots in Roman legal and political thought. Here we find the first usage of the term *iustus bellum*, or "just war." While earlier periods, including the Greeks, had distinct ideas about what had to be done to legitimate the violence of a war, and even contained a core idea about war as undoing wrongs committed against a state or a people, we find a fuller expression of this idea in Roman military law. A just war was one that followed necessary laws, that was a response to a weighty grievance that demanded a weighty response, and was at its core a demand for satisfaction in the face of an offense. Coleman (1918, p. 182) lists the following as main causes for war among the Romans: "violation of a treaty, desertion from an alliance or confederation, offense committed against allies, violation of the sanctity of ambassadors, unjustifiable refusal to receive embassies, denial of neutrality, infringement of territorial rights, desecration of scared places, unjust refusal of *deditio*, or extradition of a person or persons guilty of these and other offenses."[3] Apart from the obvious allowability of fighting a defensive war due to territorial infringement, much of these rationales involve rejections of treaties and other international agreements between states or the treatment of those practicing diplomacy or international relations – here, following Clausewutz (1993), we clearly see Roman warfare as an extension of politics in almost all cited reasons. The Romans are thinking of warfare in a way similar to ideologies of war in the medieval period. War is a form of justice, the way to right a wrong done against one's people. It is also a highly political endeavor not only framing protecting of its own lands a just cause for war, but extended this to the attacking of allies or a denied request for neutrality in a conflict. The refusal to receive embassies is a seemingly odd rationale for armed conflict. Neither then nor today is there an established expectation or right to send

[3]The literal translation of *deditio* is surrender or capitulation. In the Middle Ages, it referred to a ritualistic surrendering to a monarch. Here it likely refers to states that refuse to show fealty to Rome.

or refuse embassies. While embassies are central to maintaining political ties between states, they are also known centers of espionage and other covert information gathering. Here Rome is flexing its power on her neighbors by claiming the right to establish embassies under threat of war (Bédoyére, 2020; Brand, 1968).

One rationale for war is unique in this context that arises repeatedly through the ages: ill treatment of sacred spaces. Protection of sacred or cultural sites is a common prohibition in modern warfare, both in the laws of war and IHL (Sandholtz, 2007). Here though, instead of being a war crime, it is a reason for war itself. Romans also went to war to dominate their region of the world. Vegetius (2019) reminds Emperors and military leaders that Rome's material wealth and success was not the source of respect or fear from their enemies but rather, "[t]his can only be effected by the terror of our arms. . .in war, errors are fatal and without remedy and are followed by immediate punishment" (pp. 12–13); hence, discipline should be fast and if not harsh, proportional. He later blames the army's decline on sloth and lax discipline which led to troops not wearing all of their armor in battle, especially helmets and cuirasses, which resulted in the expected defeats, especially when confronted with missile fire (pp. 15–16).

It is with the Roman army that we get the first surviving fully realized sets of rules directed to the behavior of soldiers on and off the field of battle. The Roman army, from the days of the Republic, was a large, bureaucratic organization which required a plethora of rules to guide it and those within it. Like many states, it was not an independent entity but did the calling of the Senate during the republic and the bidding of the Emperor after Octavius. We have ample archaeological, documentary, and literary evidence to draw upon when examining the Roman rules of warfare and what happened to those who failed to do so. Polybius (1889, VI. 37 and 38) also establishes the existence of courts martial during the Republican period with the Tribunes holding the court.

An overriding concern of Roman military regulation is focused on maintaining good order in camp, on the march, and in battle. Commanders were told "to keep up so strict a discipline as to leave them no room to harbor any thoughts but of submission and obedience" (Vegetius, 2019, p. 51). A common tactic was to keep the Legions too busy to abuse the locals or contemplate mutiny. Hard labor (felling trees, digging ditches, repairing roads, etc.), drill, inspection, and martial practice consumed a legionnaire's day. Such practices were simultaneously effective social control and good physical conditioning for soldiers.

Known criminals were prohibited from military service on the reasoning that their innate lack of discipline led them to a criminal lifestyle makes them unsuited for military service and likely to cause problems within the ranks.[4] Ruffus (in

[4]Even in contemporary times, one can move from a jurisdiction one has been criminally punished to a jurisdiction that doesn't share information with the one that punished an individual. Before the twentieth century, it was easy to move after such sanctioning (in Rome it was often required). The new community (and jurisdiction) would not know of your past offenses unless the society practiced branding or other mutilation of convict's bodies (one purpose of such behavior), which was not uncommon through the Middle Ages in Europe (see Chambliss, 1964).

Brand, 1968) makes this clear in his *Military Laws*. Anyone who enlists to escape punishment or other legal problems and conceals the fact is eligible for execution. Otherwise, the man faced exile for life. This is another practice that will be abandoned until the modern era (and not completely followed then); many Medieval and Early Modern armies had few qualms about allowing prisoners into the ranks, assuming their status was known. The Free Companies that will run rough shod over France during the Hundred Years War period were little more than brigands when not contracted by a given Sovereign. As late as the Vietnam conflict, US judges offered armed services enlistment as a form of probation to offenders who were young and largely nonviolent. There is a logic in recruiting those who are skilled in or predisposed to violence – this is what you are expecting the man to do once battle commences. It is a common tactic for genocidaires (i.e., Arkan's Tigers in Serbia, The Janjaweed in the Sudan) or other political principles seeking agents to do "dirty" work on their behalf (Mullins & Rothe, 2008; Rueda & Tanner, 2016). However, for a professionalized standing army, such individuals are more trouble than they are worth. Very little of a soldier's time is spent in combat itself, even if it their most critical function. Most is spent in camp, on the march, or based in a controlled geography. Idleness and other aspects of daily military life bring ample opportunity for property and violent crime commission. Romans, like many others, believed offenders in the ranks would lead to disruptions, conflicts, and disorder. Further, it would diminish the pride and honor of the legion to have known criminals in their ranks. Ironically, soldiers being lauded for victories, including the mass slaughter of civilians (for example, after the destruction of Carthage or Jerusalem), were essential examples of "Roman *virtus*, which meant honorable courage, manliness and heroism all dressed up in a semi-religious veneration of violence" (Bédoyére, 2020, p. 207. Italics in original). In the minds of Rome's military leaders, allowing criminals in the ranks would sully the honor of the legion and those in it and secondarily the honor of Rome and all Romans. As the size of the army grew as the Empire grew, the probability of a felon entering the legions was higher than before, as it became easier to escape a sullied reputation in one part of the Empire and join the army or auxiliaries in another. Also, as with modern forces, as demand for soldiers grew, exceptions were often made to rules.[5] Also, the Roman Empire is famous for its use of Auxiliary troops to supplement the legions. These, often ethnic-specific commands, were a significant force multiplier for the empire, but the conditions for recruitment were not as stringent, almost ensuring former offenders in the ranks.

Not surprisingly, numerous rules manuals focus not just on order, but on obeying the chain of command and proscribe the results for infractions. Death was the penalty for plotting or attempting mutiny, and for threatening or assaulting one's superior. Malingerers, those who flee to the enemy but return,

---

[5]As the US wars with Iraq and Afghanistan exhausted the supply of qualified volunteers, entrance standards, including those surrounding criminal convictions, was loosened. This was also seen during the Vietnam era.

and those who reveal secrets to the enemy can also expect capital sentences.[6] Such actions undermine the foundation of military order and many armed forces still hold the death penalty for similar behaviors today. By their nature, armies are complex hierarchical organizations, requiring clear and obeyed chains of command to function at all, much less in the field. This requires obedience to your superiors and clearly communicating your superior's orders to your subordinates. It was recognized that lower officers held the responsibility of ensuring compliance. Per Rufus, those who disobey an order through "ignorance of the order, the decurion shall be chastised for failure to instruct him in the first place" (Brand, 1968 p. 153).[7] Save for the most serious and rebellious acts, soldiers would be publicly beaten or flogged.[8]

Another common punishment carried out against the man, but not the man's body, was reduction in rank. Essentially, this is a change in the branch of service. For example, a cavalryman given this punishment would be reassigned to an infantry battalion. Such punishment is highly shameful, as cavalry received their elevated military position due to their higher social position. They were drawn from the ranks of landowners and other elites who could afford the horses and gear. To be reduced to a legionnaire would be humiliating and a removal of the privileges of their socioeconomic status until they returned home. An infantry soldier would be transferred to a labor battalion. These were essentially penal units given the most menial, back-breaking work and awarded the least esteem. A more rarely proscribed punishment, discharge from service, was used in cases where the soldier had not committed a capital offense, such as striking an officer, but whose actions suggest that he is not fit for further service or is more troublesome than he is worth in the battle line. Such a fate awaited to those who lead disorderly gatherings which were short of mutiny, injured a fellow soldier with a stone, injured himself to avoid duty, or attempted suicide (Brand, 1968). Recipients of a "dishonorable" discharge would lose whatever had been promised them for serving (i.e., citizenship, land, etc.). Throughout the Republican and Imperial era, soldiers were offered various incentives to sign up for what would become increasing longer terms of service (from 3 years in the early Republic to 25 years in the late Empire). When terms were short, i.e., 3 years, there was typically no incentive waiting at the end of one's hitch save one's freedom. As the terms that legionnaires served lengthened, these incentives varied due to both Imperial whim and resource availability. The *Corpus Juris Civilis* lists three types of military

[6]Soldiers who fake illness or the like to avoid fighting or other duties.

[7]Decurion's were cavalry officers typically in charge of 30 men. The term also has a civilian meaning – a member of a town council. In this context, it appears Decurion is being used generically to refer to mid-rank commanders. It literally translates as "leader of 10 men." Elsewhere, Ruffus refers to the quincurion (literally – leader of five men), specifically that they would be chastised for opposing their Decurion, which suggests its use here is not limited to cavalry officers.

[8]Ruffus uses the specific term *castigator*, which was translated in my source as "chastise." The contexts of usage suggest chastisement was a physical discipline, often delivered with the commander's vine encircled rod of office.

discharge: honorable (the soldier completed his term of service in good standing), discharge for cause if the legionnaire is deemed unfit physical or mentally for service, and dishonorable discharges resulting from crime commission (ordinary crimes and military crimes). Dishonorable dischargees not only lost whatever incentives were offered for service, but were banished from Rome itself (in Brand, 1968).

In general, theft in camp was punished by the offender paying back double of what he stole. If he stole weapons, he was to be beaten with cudgel or whip and reduced in rank. Such theft, while common in military camps, reduces morale and generates ill will between soldiers. This weakens the army. Hence the harsh punishment being reduced in rank was the most severe penalty short of execution or dismissal from service. The value of what was stolen also mattered, as reflected in the intensity of punishments. Stealing beasts of burden or transportation was cause for having one's hands chopped off, indicating their greater value to the military. While not a death sentence, such a soldier would be reduced to begging for the rest of his life unless natal family members took him in.

In addition to keeping order in camp or on the march, it was of utmost importance to keep discipline on the battlefield. Roman military law provides the first detailed list of violations that undermine unit cohesiveness. Roman battle tactics rested on the ability of the legionaries to stay in tight formation and fight as one, as did the phalanx. This disciplined formation was one of the keys to the success of Rome against her neighbors; it is the hallmark characteristic of the Roman army. Deployed as heavy infantry, disrupting the formation – breaking the line – reduced their effectiveness both as a unit and individual soldiers. Not surprisingly then, it was forbidden, to break ranks and pursue a fleeing enemy. Fleeing the line of battle was punishable by death, with the offender's property being transferred into the community share of the Legion.[9] Later codes added to this stopping to loot the dead, or hasty disorganized pursuits as well as entering an enemy's baggage train or camp. If units retreated in the face of the enemy without "justifiable and manifest cause," the sentence was decimation carried out by other Legions.[10] Decimation involved the public killing of every 10th soldier in the offending unit (determined randomly). Such rules highlight the need to maintain order in the ranks and keep a unit under command until officers are sure the hostilities are over, as well as revealing the strong lure plunder and loot have on troops.

Discipline and battle-readiness extended to the health and readiness of the troops. Vegetius calls on Centurions and Tribunes "to take care that the sick soldiers are supplied with proper diet and diligently attended by the physicians" (p. 47). This recognizes that illness is often a greater foe to any army than its opposition. The epidemiology is not complicated. Large numbers of people in

---

[9]This was the portion of the legions that financial resources used to bury its dead and send payments home to the deceased family.

[10]Rufus lists other legions carrying out the decimation, other writers record decimation was committed by the disgraced legion itself, and those chosen were executed by their own century mates.

small spaces, living in less-than-sanitary conditions, exposed to the elements and exhaustion are prime targets to be infected by opportunistic illness vectors. Disease has been a march companion of all armies, but this is the first historical record of rules designed to address the issue. Discussion of camp sanitation will not reemerge until articles of battle issued by the Tudors. Rules for digging latrines are covered as well as providing doing so as a punishment. Specific discussions of officers providing the best available care to the sick will not be seen until von Steuben's 1775 rules manual for the US Colonial army. While these commands do not extend to those that were captured, the Roman drive for slave-taking led to less lethal civilian-directed violence as well as taking prisoners on the battlefield.

In addition to rules for battlefield conduct, the army also imposed a series of regulations on garrisoned troops designed to reduce their contact with local populations. Crimes committed by legionnaires against civilians during peace were forbidden and, in cases, harshly punished. For example, per Rufus, if a soldier raped a girl, his nose was to be cut off and he was to surrender one-third of his property to her. Nonsexual assaults and theft are not specifically mentioned by that author. During the Republic era and after, soldiers were prohibited from engaging in a host of economic activities within the territories they were posted to. Military code forbids troops from farming, being a merchant, or owning land (with family estates being an exception). Such prohibitions are driven by a few concerns. First, such activities inevitably interfered with or took away from a soldier's ability to complete their military duties. They were a distraction at best. Second, this prevents active-duty troops from making local social and economic attachments that might make them hesitant to deploy to another area.[11] Also, while the close social ties that develop from being integrated into a community might help military-civilian interaction during times of peace, they would be a definite hindrance in times of war. Soldiers might be hesitant to deploy violence against peoples with whom they have socioeconomic (if not familial) connections.[12] It is difficult to psychologically otherize a population one has casual or intimate ties to, which makes it more psychologically problematic to enact violence upon them. They are no longer out-group members and thus not subject to suspension of norms of violence which prohibit in-group violence (criminal laws) while allowing out-group violence (raids, war, etc.).

[11]Archaeological evidence from the UK suggests officers and potentially enlisted soldiers stationed in further flung area of the empire were accompanied by their Roman wives and families.

[12]This is a problem of social structure and who is an allowable marriage partner. In many clan-based societies, clan-feuding tendencies were tampered down by marital rules that made one marry into another clan or the opposite moiety if one exists (some clan-based societies divided their clans into two groups, termed moieties by ethnographers), thus reducing the likelihood of intra-group conflict arising out of clan disputes, as going to "war" with a clan in one's opposite moiety would entail fighting biological relatives and in-laws. Such social structures pressured for informal resolutions to conflicts which arose.

Almost all of the extant Roman army regulations are focused on soldier behavior in relation to their actions toward or their ability to work with other members of the legion. In the discussion above we mentioned a prohibition against civilian rape, but this was in the context of garrison life in peace time. In terms of prohibitions limiting violence against civilians or property during battle or sieges and their aftermath, the will of the consul leading the army was the primary determinant of how the civilians would be treated. In 209 BCE, when Scipio took the city of Nova Carthago (New Carthage, aka Cartagena), he ordered his troops to kill all life found in the city: humans, livestock, dogs, etc. His actions were lauded back in Rome, as Bédoyére simply says: "He was a hero; someone to live up to" (2020, p. 209). This is only one of many atrocities committed by the Roman army throughout its history. Brutalizing one's enemy and promoting such actions were long standing Roman army norms (Bédoyére, 2020). As with the Greeks, the Romans did not consider outsiders worthy of the same treatment as insiders. Rather, through deed and word, the army built an image of itself as a harsh and brutal foe, one not to be roused to battle lightly. The Assyrians at the height of their power similarly used their army as a generator of terror with anticipated deterrent effects. Brutalizing a defeated enemy not only ensures that army will not be faced again on the battlefield, but the state that fielded it should be wary of crossing Rome again. Such atrocities also served as a lesson to other peoples in the area to be afraid of Rome and her ire. When terror is one of the goals of a military event, like the storming and destruction of Nova Carthago, rules that would limit carnage and bloodshed are of no use, or ignored if they exist. Rome's leaders knew the value of discipline and controlling their troops in camp and limiting the harm they would cause in peacetime. But when it came to unleashing the violence that a Roman legion and its auxiliaries could produce, there was little if any attempt to limit it.[13] As much of post-Roman European social structures are built on the ruins, literally and figuratively, of Roman norms and structures, total war as often practiced by the Romans was not uncommon in the early Middle Ages in the wake of the empire's collapse. The Roman army provides a record of how large armies, especially standing armies, create a large organization which requires systematic and universally applied rules to maintain order and coordinate activity. Rome was not the first state to have a standing army, or something close to it (Keepie, 2008).

The Ancient and classical periods saw the development of mass warfare and the first sets of rules which governed it. War evolved in conjunction with and as a part of the broader development of civilization as we recognize it today. Population and population density increases, large-scale monocropping, centralized political governance, coercive governmental authority, increased political and economic interaction with neighbors, development of law, emergence of writing

[13]A famous counterexample is Marcus Claudius Marcellus' order that Archimedes be spared in the sacking of Syracuse. The order wasn't given out of beneficence though, but from the realization that Archimedes could prove useful to the Romans. Ironically, during the attack, Archimedes is killed by a Roman soldier, unaware of the man's identity, who didn't take kindly to being told to leave the scholar alone while he worked.

and currency, and advances in metallurgy all accompanied the rise of warfare as we know it. The shift from raids and skirmishes between small groups of related combatants to centralized polities using mass violence as a political tool against rivals both drives and is driven by changes in other social institutions. It is doubtful that even the best modeled regression equation can parse the contributions of each on the other. All 12 of these factors feed into each other during societal growth and evolution. Larger populations drive the need for and provide for large-scale monocropping, which tends to require a centralized political authority to organize.[14] Increased commerce is driven by and drives contact with other communities, writing, and law. Advances in metallurgy are made possible through the trade of items and ideas among peoples, as well as the sedentary lifestyle that city living and monocropping bring.[15] As wealth of people, items, and the like become aggregated into urban areas surrounded by worked land, it can seem easier to take what you need than make what you need, be it people, grain, or iron. It is this constellation of factors that generated and drove war in the ancient world, and also drove the rules that guided it. For most armies of the period, the main concern was good order in the ranks during battle, followed closely by keeping an orderly camp and ensuring that soldiers do not either wander away from their post for the night or go AWOL from the force entirely.[16]

There is little concern expressed for civilians, rather they are typically classified as part of plunder and any effort to keep them alive is due to their possible enslavement. Ancient warfare, as far as we know, was also less concerned with rules protecting enemy prisoners of war or the sick or injured. Few of what will become the major concerns of IHL are present in this period (Gillespie, 2011b). There is little expressed concern for the treatment of one's enemies or their property. Societies drawing their circles of humanity often did so solely around themselves, expressly excluding neighboring peoples and other foreign aliens. As expected, different rules are applied to different populations, with in-group/out-group dichotomies being strong. This is before the development and transmission of Enlightenment norms that see every human as having a fundamental value and thus fundamental rights.[17] Life was cheap in the ancient world, and this was reflected in the behavior and treatment of the period's soldiers.

When needed, the Romans had no compunction about engaging in what we now call total war – a conflict where the only military rules that matter are a soldier's obedience to his officers. Nothing need be spared if its destruction

[14]In the anthropological sense of an organization focused on solving problems larger than a given kin-group. It might appeal to secular or sacred authority.

[15]It is resource intensive to build a forge capable of melting ore and not something seen until people are living in permanent settlements. Beating copper into weapons, armor, or decoration is a separate set of skills and knowledge.

[16]Absent without leave. Book XLIX, title 16 of The Civil Law provides a lengthy discussion on how commanders are to treat AWOL soldiers who return (or are returned) to camp based on the reasons for the soldier's absence.

[17]Of course, most of these Enlightenment authors meant male citizens when they discussed "humanity" and human rights. Christian writers were speaking of and to the faithful.

brought the Roman army closer to their military objectives. Such war was waged everywhere in enemy territory and there were few-to-no attempts to reduce or otherwise constrain the violence used by the army – be it against women, children, or animals. Polybius mentions the sacking of Nova Carthago even dogs were cut in two and body parts of other animals littered the streets (Bédoyére, 2020; Polybius, 1889). Rome did not shy away from militaristic brutality when lead officers and politicians on the ground found it expedient or useful. Terror, directed specifically at a given enemy and its civilians, was a key objective of such slaughter as well.

Some of the fundamental principles of the laws of war do arise in this period, mostly the same problems faced by all large fighting forces. As armies grow and campaigns lengthen and become more complex, rules arose within the military to ensure efficient functioning of the institution. Logistics issues become more central. The power of the chain of command was reinforced with punishments for those who violate the orders of their superiors. Early elements of what we now call command responsibility emerge in some armies, as we saw with Roman junior officers being punished if their men failed to understand an order (and thus improperly execute it). The aim here was successful military action, with the rules and punishments directed toward order maintenance.

The collapse of Rome in the west reverts much of western European life to more locally focused concerns. Communication and interactions over longer distances become rarer. Polities find their geographies smaller, at least in Western Europe. In the absence of Roman control, local rivalries emerge between warlords which become military engagements. These wars, or raids, bring land under the control of a warrior who had built a band of followers. This will begin the evolution of complex network of relationships between warlords-cum-nobles, the state, law, the church, and each other. The development of Feudalism will create clear lines of power and obligations in the military sphere. It will also facilitate warfare as a normative solution to inter-group conflict. The rise of opposition to this life and social order by the Church in the ninth and tenth centuries leads to the creation of specific canon laws concerning warfare, but also catalyzes the development of the normative-literary complex known as chivalry to attempt to reign in and control the excesses seen in the early part of the period. The next chapter examines these changes in depth and how they led to new rules limiting warfare's practices both within an army and between armies. Roman military codes and norms will resurface in the Middle Ages and hold strong influence through the early modern period. Surviving Roman tracts on military law or military organization and training get translated and redistributed where they are studied and implemented by commanders. The neoclassical fascination that strikes Europe during the Renaissance extends to methods and rules of warfare as well as art and literature. Disciplinary rules and practices are the main aspect of Roman military thought, which will survive the longest. Punishing the body of the soldier becomes a central fixation in the Roman military that will last into the twentieth century. The practice of flogging specifically will be used extensively in post-Medieval armies and navies, not garnering much critical attention until the seventeenth and eighteenth centuries (see Hurl-Eamon, 2022; Napier, 1837; Underwood, Pfaff, & Hechter, 2018).

Chapter 4

The Early Medieval World

> [W]e must beware treating the law of arms as if it were modern international law. Though its rules and signs had legal significance among men of different nations, it was observed by them because its regulations were rules of honor, rather than for any rational of humanitarian element.
>
> Keen. *The Laws of War in the High Middle Ages* (1965, p. 108)

The Middle Ages, at least in Europe, are the fulcrum from which many of our modern concepts and practices of law emerge. The laws of war are no exception, though the quote from Keen above reminds us to be careful of context and attend to the emic views of these rules held by soldiers at the time and not uncritically apply the concepts of contemporary law or war. There is an emergence of legal scholarship in the period (Aquinas, 1485/1947; Augustine, 1950, 1958) mainly focused on when a war is or isn't legal – when does a leader have the right to go to war? The easy answer in post-Roman Europe is: whenever he wanted to. The concepts of war and justice are fused to the point that war is seen as the equivalent of criminal justice between sovereigns. War was to be a response to a wrongdoing or injustice which corrected that wrong. It was justice administered on a large scale that held citizens guilty of the "crimes" of their sovereign. Both nobles and clergy wrote extensively about just wars and proper versus improper triggers for warfare. While some of this legal history is relevant here, there is a voluminous body of writing of this topic (Aquinas, 1485/1947; Augustine, 1950, 1958; Bonét, 1949); however, it will not be the focus of this chapter, but this arise as relevant to understand our focus, the control of soldiers themselves. While not the main focus of scholars of the time, there were numerous innovations in thoughts about the laws of war especially as it pertained to the behavior of soldiers on the field of battle. This discourse would reach its apogee in the chivalric manuals, like Bonèt's *L'Arbre de Batailles* or De Charney's *On Chivalry*, and literature of the later middle ages, such as Chaucer's *Troilus and Criseyde* and *The Knights Tale*, *Roman de la Rose*, or the work of Chrètien de Troyes. While idealistic and literary depictions, the idealized values of the warrior code are reflected in all aspects of these works and can be excavated from these aspirational literature. As can examples of failures.

A Socio-Legal History of the Laws of War, 51–74

Published under exclusive licence by Emerald Publishing Limited
doi:10.1108/978-1-78769-857-420231004

The tenth to fourteenth centuries see large changes in law itself, in its codification, in its attachment to secular over church authority, and in its standardization. It also sees violence moved out of the process of case adjudication, limiting it to the actions that bring one to the court and what the court does to the convicted afterward. Trial by combat was staple during the middle ages. If wronged, and the dispute was limited to the testimony of only two participants, it was theologically believed that a combat between the two parties could decide the issue of who was telling the truth, as God was seen as always backing the truth. In the medieval mind, God's hand was at work daily in all things. Yet, by the end of the period, even writers of chivalric manuals begin to reject the practice. For example, the first question addressed in Bonèt's Part III of *L'Arbre de Batailles* is the justness of trail by combat. This is significant as the third book is when he begins his explorations of contemporary-to-him legal issues. His first reason for opposition to the idea is straight forward enough: "that it has often been experienced that the man who had right on his side has . . . lost the battle." Bonèt notes that this is Canon law, but acknowledges the *realpolik* of the situation in admitting that "royal custom and temporal lordship" saw "such combat is due where the matter calls for it" (p. 117). This is not the only point of contention between the religious and secular authorities of the time. As we will see in this chapter, the church attempts to regulate war and ordinary violence begin in the ninth and tenth centuries and continues to do so throughout the period. The *Pax Deus* (Peace of God) and *Truega Deus* (Truce of God) being central examples. The influence of the teachings of these church decrees becomes the foundation for Chivalry – a code of behavior applied to nobles designed to curtail their excesses and abuses of those in lower statuses. While infused with Catholic teaching, Chivalry is a secular ideology and creates secular social structures but with an acknowledgment that this is a secular social system firmly grounded in Medieval Christian Theology. In the tenth and eleventh centuries, we begin to see more systematic codification of laws in post-Charlemagne Europe and especially in the attempt of Henry II of England to forge a "common law" for the British Isles. Ultimately, the Church lost the overall struggle for legal control over Europe and the jurisdiction of Canon law declines through the centuries, eclipsed by local, secular law. Chivalry envisions an international brotherhood of knights, bound by specific obligations and possessing specific rights, separate from the political loyalties and boundaries of the day. This chapter starts by examining early legal codes that emerged in the wake of the Roman Empire's collapse (i.e., Salic law, the Visogothic code), at least those aspects that dealt with military matters. It will then look at the Church's attempt to curb violence with the *Pax* and *Treuga* and how these efforts evolve into the normative and literary system of chivalry. It provides a thorough discussion of the cultural aspects of chivalry and examines chivalric manuals written to promote and teach these ideals.

Post-Roman Europe

In the wake of the Roman Empire, what would become Europe was divided, localized, and save for settlements where direct control could be exerted, anarchic. The third–fifth centuries CE were no stranger to warfare, it was such a common occurrence that whether peace or war was the natural state of humanity was a central theological debate (Augustine, 1950, 1958, 1961). Unfortunately, we lack the written and archaeological evidence to accurately estimate the amount of inter-group violence occurring. Most peoples of the period had enforceable normative codes, whether codified or not. If the region had been conquered by Rome, Roman law (and Roman military laws) provided a scaffolding for indigenous law making, which many elements of the former Empire did, as the social elites who largely adopted Roman lifeways during occupation found themselves without the legal and military protections of Empire.

With the collapse of the Roman Empire, record keeping was not as prominent. Charlemagne based his laws on old Roman codes, though issued new ones as needs arose. For example, he forbade the export of swords, *brunia* (mail shirts), and *baugae* (arm guards) from his lands. His primary purpose was to reduce the chance he would face his own weaponry and armament on the battlefield, to ensure his troops were better equipped than the enemy. Frankish swords were highly valued across Europe and highly expensive. They are noticeably rare in grave goods assemblies; the general interpretation is that these weapons were being handed down family lines instead of buried with their owners (Hampton, 2011).[1] While the specific law focused on trade, the intent of the law is clearly war-orientated.

Codified ca 634 CE, the Visigoth code (634/1910), one of the many derivations of Charlemagne's *capitularies*, contains many important precursors seen in contemporary law such as establishing the equality of all before the law (or at least giving the less powerful a voice). It also shifted testimonies from an emphasis on character-based testimony of friends to accounts provided of the crimes by witnesses or victims – a key characteristic of any criminal law where the act is center of the legal discourse, not the character of the person. Visigoth law is focused on what law codes typically are: the mundane wrongs that people do to each other on a frequent basis, especially those involving property. As settlements get more permanent, in both membership and geography, the need for law, often codified law, grows stronger. In part, it is a simple function of population density: more people means more disputes, law is a way to adjudicate these disputes. Whether it is justified by divine right, the existence of natural law, or a modern legal formalism, complex communities require solutions seen as neutral, or at least generated or empowered external to the community itself. Visigoth law is mostly concerned with trade (Book V), land rights (Book II, Book V, Book X), family and inheritance (Book II title V, Book III, Book IV), theft and fraud (Book VII), and the resolution of intra-community inter-personal violence (Book VI, Book VIII).

It does contain certain concerns for military actions and military organization. Most are in Book IX, Title II. A key element of concern is organizational

[1]Modern TV and films have strongly mischaracterized the frequency of the sword-armed warrior in this period. In the early middle ages, the most common armaments were a spear, dagger, and shield. Only the wealthiest could afford mail and swords.

operations and actions. Refusal to serve, be it a refusal to show for service at the ordained time or leaving a theater of service earlier than ordered, is criminalized (Book IX Title II). Robbery by soldiers is forbidden, being punished with fourfold restitution of what was stolen, and/or upto 50 lashes (Book VIII, Title IX), as are a host of other forms of theft and property appropriation and bribery (Book IX, Title II-1, II-2, II-5–II-7). This highlights that humanitarian concerns, not just discipline and good order, are driving some of the laws of war from early in European history. Here we find troops being punished both bodily, the lash being a common Roman survival, and financially. This will characterize much of the law of the period and after.

The code utilizes command responsibility to punish officers for the misdeeds of their men. A Roman model of army organization was adopted in-part, at least the division of men into decimal units. A *tiuphadus*, an officer in charge of 1,000 men at paper strength, was responsible for the behavior of his men and their families, be it on or off the battlefield. Similar responsibilities fell on those officers at each level. For example, if an officer allows a soldier to leave for home or refuse to force them to leave home when mustered, he is fined depending on the number of men under his command (the fewer those under him, the smaller the fine). This is on top of the fine (ten *solidi*) and a public beating given to the solder in the town-center.

Special attention is given to corruption of officers, both in recruiting and in the field. Many of the articles in Title II mention various forms of bribes officers might encounter and their punishment. To follow up on the example above, if the officer allows a soldier to leave without permission he is fined by the army and the funds redirected to the soldiers (II.I). If he is bribed by said soldier, "he shall pay ninefold the amount which he received to governor of the city" (II.I pp. 399–400) where the troops are currently garrisoned.

Unlike the later Middle Ages, Visigothic law assumed every able-bodied male was to respond to a call to war or village defense. "[I]f any enemy should attack our country, *all* of our subjects, whether they be bishops or other members of the clergy…" (694/1910:325 emphasis added) are expected to turn out in defense if within 100 miles of the incursion. The only "out" for the clergy under the law was to pay the damages incurred by the invaders; otherwise, he will be exiled. Punishments differed by rank. Nobles who refused the call to service were enslaved and given to whomever the king wished (327–328). Similar fates awaited the non-nobles, but they would be publicly lashed and scalped before being enslaved.

The inviolability of holy ground is also protected by the law as it enshrined practices of sanctuary; violence was not allowed in churches or other holy places. One had to remove one's arms upon entry if sanctuary was sought, and the individual was only able to be harmed if he attacked others. Otherwise, it was illegal to forcefully remove someone from a church, unless they were fleeing debt payments. Outside of verified infirmity, sanctuary was the only way out of one's martial obligations.

The code also ignominiously contains the seeds a legal justification of the later Spanish Inquisition's pogrom against European Jews (Book XII). Jewish residents are heavily constrained in their behavior, largely prohibited from conducting their rituals, prohibited from owning Christian slaves, and are not allowed to keep the sabbath and their holy days but are forced to cease labor on Sundays and to honor Christian holidays. All social control of the Jews was handed over to the clergy. While adjacent to our major concern here, this is remarkable due to the extensiveness of the control placed around Jewish people and their lives. It clearly carves Jews out their own legal and civil space, which will catalyze, if not passively approve, many atrocities committed against Jews in Europe, from this time period through the Holocaust.

The large, standing armies of the Roman and other Empires was not a facet of Visigothic (or other Germanic peoples) life in that a professional, salaried corps of soldiers and officers were at the ready when called upon or occupying frontier lands (despite their borrowing Roman military organization). Until the age of Charlemagne, a given war lord, whatever he called himself, didn't control enough land to warrant large, standing border protection forces. Since every able-bodied adult Visigoth male was expected to provide military service when needed, there wasn't a need for an army as a separate social institution. It is merely another set of communal activities, like the early Greek Polis. Thus, key concerns are addressed and responses codified, but we do not see the density of law as we did in the Roman empire. This is, in part, a feature of the lower population densities seen, both in a territory overall and within a given settlement. With the collapse of Rome in the West and the return to a comparatively very localized control of political matters, military forces got smaller with less territory to administer, and fewer enemies of concern.

Post-Roman Europe and Briton held on to many vestiges of Roman life and culture, including law. The Visigothic code is just one example of the types laws used by Germanic, Celtic, and British peoples. Much is derived from the Roman model, but local influences remold the laws over time, especially on the British Isles. While the uniting features of the Roman Empire were lost, the Catholic Church began to grow and become a trans-national institution which didn't replace the empire but became a uniting cultural and political institution with the ability to exert social control over secular rulers. Such power derived both from the worldly power and wealth of the church and from the spiritual control the church exercised over adherent's souls (i.e., excommunication). The growth of the influence of the church is where we now turn, as they take the next step in attempting to constrain military conflicts and their harm.

A New International Order

The tenth and eleventh centuries are a time of essential social transformations. With the death of Charlemagne, his land was divided among his heirs who saw their power dissipated, along with the social order and legal order that it brought. It saw "kingdoms fracturing progressively into principalities, counties, then. . .into castellanies" (Bisson, 1994, p. 6). Out of this absence of structure and social control, what would become classic feudalism emerged.[2] Local warlords

[2]While important, I am avoiding the argument over the "feudal revolution" (see Barthelemy & White, 1996; Bisson, 1994, 1997; Reuter & Wickham, 1997). For the purposes of this project, that we see a form of feudalism present by the tenth century is what matters, less so the intricacies of its evolution to that point.

consolidated power, both political and economic. The power was rooted on control of arable land and those people living on it. Warlords reinforced the loyalty of underlings with grants of land in exchange for military service. Raiding and warfare grew some polities and subsumed others. The amount of such violence is impossible to know, but it was extensive enough to be viewed as a key problem by the clergy of the period. A problem they attempted to resolve.

The Role of the Church

In the absence of a secular push to control the excesses of the martial class, elements within the Church began a concerted push to encircle warriorhood within religious and social constraints. Later, as the international brotherhood of knighthood developed, such norms would become embodied within the institution of chivalry, but in the tenth century, the primary concern was simply bringing the warrior classes under rudimentary control and shouldering upon them a base level of responsibility for peace and the well-being of the people on their lands.

There is no denying the power of Christianity in shaping the medieval era. Between the fall of the Carolingian dynasty and the rise of nationalism in the wake of the 100 Years War, the Church stood as the most stable institution in Europe which wielded a great of what we would think of now as international power. The logic of the scripture (at least as interpreted by the clergy) place the Church above local, secular political structures. Barons, Dukes, and Kings might control their lands and their vassals, but the Church held authority over their souls and their experiences in the afterlife. Theological and legal arguments arise over "right" or "wrong" wars, examining when the uses of military force are warranted and viable and when they are merely predatory. Eventually, these ideas will become central pillars in the *jus bellum* debates that still rage today (see UN Charter Article 24).

The nigh anarchy of post-Carolingian Europe presented a series of clear threats to public well-being and social order. Sanctioned and unsanctioned violence grew, threatening commerce, travel, and the Church's control of its lands (with the church itself not a rare target). While there was still social order in so far as the daily institutions of life continued – people worked, reproduced, etc., but the ability to do this in peace and safety was threatened by the lack of political authority and the lack of secular powers to monopolize violence. While a definitional aspect of the modern state (Weber, 1919/2015), violence monopolization here meant controlling those underneath you in the feudal system. With law often embodied in a ruler and not an external code (or at least administered as such), the ability to control a geography by monopolizing violence within it was often the product of one person's ability to bribe, convince, cajole, and/or threaten other warriors in their area with fewer resources. A leader's power extended as far as their wealth and troops could take it and enforce it. Warfare frequently disrupted the peace and the biggest check on a leader's power was the power of their neighbors. Between, and sometimes within, these communities anarchy reigned with, more often than not, might equaling right. It is into this chaotic landscape that the Church tried to exert its authority and bring peace and order. This is not done out of a lack of self-interest. As said, churches, abbeys, and monasteries often found themselves victims of pillage and murder (and not only along the Eastern coast of England). This is not the first time the Church or Church thinkers turned their writing toward war.

Early Christianity

Within the Christian tradition, the just war debate begins with Augustine of Hippo (Augustine, 1950; Keen, 1965; Neff, 2005) and continues to this day. Augustine fuses the concept of justice, of righting a wrong done to you, with war, thus fusing law and war. War becomes just another tool (along with courts) to dispense or obtain justice. War driven by righting a wrong, brought in response to harmful actions of another state, was a *just war*, and allowed under canon law. Wars brought for other reasons were deemed *unjust* and illegal in the eyes God. Church logic saw the rulers appointed by God and obligated to follow His commands. Waging an unjust war could result in excommunication (and not only for the King) – and thus eternal damnation. Teachings held that in a dispute only one power could be "right" and thus wage a just war. By definition, one belligerent was just in their cause and the other was not. At the level of the individual soldier, Augustine deems killing acceptable if it is done in the context of a just war and it is done without rage, revenge, or other emotional catalysts. As early as the fifth century, the church is trying to limit the harms of war and constrain the violence that occurs within. Augustine takes two types of war-violence off the table. First, that done against innocents. A key characteristic of a just war is not simply having a just cause, but one must wage war in a just fashion, which includes not harming noncombatants. This prohibition survives to this day in numerous ways within the laws of war and international humanitarian law. Second, violence done for revenge or glory are also prohibited, as they are driven by the sin of pride (Hartigan, 1982, pp. 28–30).

Aquinas in the *Summa Theologica* (1485/1947) follows Augustine in separating just from unjust wars, and thus framing some wars as right and just and thus acceptable in the eyes of the Church, quoting Augustine's framing of war as punishment for the sinful and unjust. In fact, both argue being on the losing end of a just war is a good thing for the soldiery as it strips them of their sin: "it is good for him to vanquished, since nothing is more hopeless than the happiness of sinners." Aquinas proposes three characteristics of a just war: the command to war must come from the political sovereign, it must be just in cause, and the belligerents "should have rightful intention, so they intend the advancement of good or the avoidance of evil" (40.1). That the war derive from the will of the sovereign is a clear reflection of the Catholic political theology which saw Kings as in charge of the public weal and, as Roman's 13:4 commands, Kings are to act as "God's minister, an avenger to execute wrath upon him that does evil." The concepts of evil, sin, and injustice are fused in this worldview. There is little perceived difference in legitimacy between what we would think of as criminal justice and what we would think of warfare: here all are acts ordered by the sovereign to right wrongs done. During the medieval period war became to be seen as the penultimate form of "international" criminal justice.[3] It was the tool for righting wrongs done by those from another polity. The only difference between punishing a burglar and a neighboring enemy is the number of people needed. Kings had the right and obligation to pursue justice for their people, thus Aquinas concludes that not all war is sinful. Only those without just provocation.

The Pope would cast his call for crusade in this framework: Jerusalem and the rest of the Holy Land was "unjustly" occupied by Moslems. Their occupation was seen as unjust as Israel was the spiritual home of Christianity and its occupation by "heretics" a wrong to be righted. It is clear from the actions and rhetoric of the crusading armies that once they left Northwestern Europe, everyone was considered a non-Christian who did not enjoy the privileges of protection of the law – military or otherwise. An unknown number of European Jewish communities were destroyed by enroute crusading armies; the Crusader's violent sacking of Jerusalem in 1099 is well known (Allen, 2017; Asbridge, 2005).

Just because a just war itself was not seen as evil or sinful *a priori*, it doesn't mean killing during the war was sinless. Medieval penitential manuals deem killing during war to be a venial sin, and while requiring penance, it is much less than would be required of a murderer. For example, a penitential attributed to Bede from the eighth century proscribes the following time-lengths of penances for murder: seven years for killing a clergy member, four years if the murder is done with malice aforethought, three years if in a quarrel or other heated context, one year if by accident, and 40 days if the killing is done in war.[4] The only shorter penance for such a deed is for striking a man with intent to kill (but failing to do so) at 21 days (McNeill & Gamer, 1990). In addition to requiring penance for violence committed in war, soldiers also had to do penance for their looting as well. For example, The Penitential of Theodore, dating to the seventh century, required 40 days of penance for taking "Of money which has been seized in a foreign province from a conquered enemy…the third part shall be given to the church or to the poor" (McNeill & Gamer, 1990, p. 190). The 40-day period is justified as "it was the King's command" (p. 190) which provoked the sin. Thus, while the church saw a need for a war, and made numerous theological allowances for warfare of various sorts, it still recognized violence against people and property as sinful, just not to the same degree as it is done under the command of the King, whose divine right to rule doesn't nullify the scriptural rules broken in war (killing, stealing, etc.) but does lessen the culpability of the solider who commits these acts, as the troops were ordered by those whom the soldiers are obligated to follow due to the demands of the feudal system or the articles of

[3]To an extent the notion of an international law binding separate sovereign nations together in a shared system of social control is stronger. In the tenth century, the Church's ownership and control of the most widely shared cultural system of Europe could be stronger at compelling behavior.

[4]The exact term used is "De occisione," variously translated as killing, murder, slaughter, etc.

battle drawn up for a given conflict. This is similar to canon law's take on sexual intercourse. Augustine (1950) reduced it from a cardinal to a venial sin as long as it was done in the context of marriage and for the purposes of reproduction. A position still canon law today. It is a rational response to a contradiction between practical behavior and theology. Pragmatism was driving Augustine here on both topics. War is going to happen, and the church needed to adopt rules on violence if it hoped to gain a key a grasp on Europe. The practical thing to do is recognize the social inevitability of the action and attempts to put constraints about it. Thus penance for killing and looting if ordered, is lighter than that for murder and robbery. Similarly, the early church realized evangelism alone would not maintain a church whose members were chaste. The easiest way to ensure another generation of Christians is to birth and raise them, not convert them, hence the allowance for marital reproduction.

It is in this context that certain Bishops within the Church begin to take an active, public role in attempting to limit and reduce the harmfulness of inter-community violence. Debated and pronounced at several councils, the first result of this intervention was the *Pax Dei* – the Peace of God grounded in the declarations of multiple bishops and shaped and pronounced at numerous councils throughout the region. There were at least two separate Pax movements in post-Roman France (Aquitianian and Auvergnatian) (Head, 1999, p. 674), if not more specific declarations. While there are minor differences between the movements and their proclamations, they are similar enough, and aimed at the same social issue, to be discussed as a single social force. Cowdrey (1970, p. 44) lists a dozen councils between 975 CE and 1025 in the Aquitaine region alone. The *Pax Dei* sought firstly and foremostly to protect the people and property of the church and secondarily to extend such protection to farmers and other peasants. At Le Puy in 975 CE Bishop Guy "sought to enforce an oath to respect the goods of the church and of the *pauperes*" (Cowdry, 1970, p. 43. Emphasis in original). The church, not surprisingly, forbade attacking or robbing churches and clergy. With increasing amounts of wealth, churches and abbeys were long judged by raiders as easy targets. One need look no further than the Anglo-Saxon chronicle (1954) to see the fear generated by Norse raiders in holy houses along the English coasts. English abbeys were not the only targets of these raiders; Norsemen made their presence felt from the North Sea to the Mediterranean (Roesdahl, 1987). Later, protections such as these would be extended to serfs, the poor, and other disempowered groups. Such protections were enforced outside of battlefield situations, with protections of women in part being a direct attempt to counter sexual assaults of peasants, both in the country lands and at courts or estates. While the ecclesiastical threat of excommunication gave the pronouncement real teeth in that the church could imperil the fate of an offenders soul, Bishop Guy quelled initial resistance with the martial assistance of the counts of Brioude and Gévandan.

Head (1999) notes that at Charroux in 989 CE, the main driver of the conclave was: "the abuse by secular magistrates of their traditional vicarial rights, as well as the rights they enjoyed as lay abbots...[and] forceful expropriation of church property" (p. 667). The council of Charroux was specifically addressed at the behavior of one leader in particular, William Iron Arm. William took an oath of peace, and generally abided by the agreement for five years, until his forces went to the defense of his brother-in-law Odo II in 994 CE. That year saw another conference at Limoges among the Aquitanians. In addition to relying upon the threat of excommunication, the Bishops at Limoge were careful to sacralize the proceedings. Prior, bishops had negotiated with political leaders in secular space. Here the council held in the synod, was preceded by fasting, and the "bishops orchestrated. . .[a] ritual drama surrounding the use of Saints relics" (Head, 1999, p. 676). While secular military leaders had flouted church rules and commands with martial force, Limoge was designed to remind them of the sacred power behind the Church and its pronouncements. This was necessary as the Church's punishments, in the medieval mind, are rooted in their power as the representatives of God on Earth. The sacred power wielded by the church was flaunted by such displays. While excommunication was still the harshest punishment the church could levy, at Limoge other punishments and penances were added to make excommunication the last resort and provide intermediate spiritual sanctions (Bowman, 1994). Of course, these sanctions are only as effective as the power of the church – be it symbolic power wielded vis-á-vis reference to divine grace and power, economic power derived from the Church's massive wealth, or political power exerted on other nobles and nations to comply with and enforce divine will. If the destructive behavior of the military classes were not an issue, the Church would not likely have developed such a specific and sustained message, especially when realizing that many of the peace council were held independent of each other, though are correctly seen as part of a broader social movement of the period. Simply put, organizations don't spend great amounts of resources on things they consider "non-problems." And in the early middle ages, the church and the nobles were definitely at odds over the proper behavior of soldiers on and off the battlefield.

While embraced by some nobles who took the oaths of peace demanded by the bishops, martial depredations on the church and its property and on civilians did not vanish with the declaration of the *Pax*. Rather, the *Pax Dei* was the first attempt of the church to insert itself into the laws of medieval European warfare, not the last. Continued chaos and carnage pushed church authorities to further articulate means by which the harms of warfare could be limited. This takes the form of the *Treuga Dei*, The Truce of God.

Treuga Dei

The *Treuga* was a broader and more extensive set of restrictions on warfare, confirmed at a council in Clermont in 1095 (Watkin, 1942, p. 289). It grandly "declared permanent peace for all churches, and their grounds, the monks, clerks, and chattels, all women, pilgrims, merchant and the servants, cattle and horses and men at work in the fields. . .[for warriors] truce was required throughout the Advent season, the Lenten season, and from the beginning of Rogation until eight days after Pentecost" (Watkin, 1942, p. 298). Later councils will add Saint's and feast days, as well as prior prohibitions against fighting on the holy days of Wednesday and Sunday, and even later Friday. By the twelfth century, a truly observant King had less than 80 days a year to wage war. Many contemporary concerns about noncombatants are highlighted in the *Treuga*; the church is attempting here to limit those exposed to the direct violence of war by setting as "off-limits" all save those serving as soldiers. It presages the birth of the civilian or noncombatant as being a central figure in the laws of war, and IHL. It also attempts to limit the extent of warfare by removing chunks of the calendar in which a just war could be held, though the traditional summer campaign season was less impacted by these restrictions (which were more prevalent in the Winter and Spring, times few battles occurred).

Attempts to restrict the days warfare was allowed ultimately failed. By the mid-thirteenth century Aquinas (1485/1947) and others allow fighting on holy or feast days for the purposes of defending the realm or the common good. This is essentially the definition of a just war – defending the public well-being, either proactively or reactively. Thus, he undermines the *Treuga* more severely than it would appear at first glance. Aquinas is also acknowledging the reality that Kings are not following the *Pax* and *Treuga*; they fight when they want to, with whom they want to, in the manner they wish. Polities are becoming more organized, some are beginning to centralize power and authority, and coming into conflict with each other. States, if we can use the term here even loosely, are becoming larger in population, territory, and ambition. As this process occurs, the church's direct influence wanes. Even though they wield large amounts of soft power, it is often not enough to bring Europe's warrior-nobility to heel. The counter forces of developing feudalism and kingdom growth work against the church's violence reduction attempts. One might be tempted to discount the *Pax* and the *Treuga* as historical curiosities which ultimately failed. However, the ideas at the core of these declarations are the central pillars of a value system the church helps develop and assists nobles in inculcating in the upper class. While feudalism created a politico-economic structure, it's only guiding ideology was loyalty to one's feudal lord. Drawing upon early medieval theological concerns, both clerical and lay authors produce a series of manuals designed to guide the nobility through their daily life, on and off the battlefield. The value system construct here is, of course, chivalry.

Chivalry: Controlling the Warrior Caste

The value system of chivalry emerged in the context of feudalism and more precisely defined the duties and obligations of knights to those above them in the social order and to those below.[5] Feudalism as social structure also produced an ad hoc army in each fief, ready to be called to service at their liege lord's will. Charlemagne expressly tied any land ownership, no matter how small, to military

[5]I am using the term "knight" here to represent a warrior with of some degree of noble lineage who obtained the title by birthright or was awarded the title as a battlefield honor. Until the Hundred Years War, these men composed heavy cavalry units. Later, as the longbow and pike become effective counters to a heavy cavalry charge, knights start fighting dismounted, though still with superior arms and armor than the rank-and-file.

service, in effect establishing feudalism as a political-economic system. "Every freeman, at the call to arms, had to report in full military equipment to the local count and every noble was responsible for the military fitness of his constitutants" (Durant, 1950, p. 463). This wasn't a Frankish convention alone, the Saxon fyrd was structured the same way. Feudalism organized land ownership, shaped access to the means of production, and categorized individuals into one of three castes: peasant, noble, or clergy. Each caste has specific rights it expected of other ranks and explicit obligations to those same groups. Feudalism, as a political economy, was grounded in land ownership and warfare. The political system was little more than an elaborate system of peonage with vassals owing service to those who bequeathed them fiefs. Kings enfifed Dukes who enfifed knights. Vassals owed their lord taxes, portions of the production of their lands, and military service, often a specific number of days per year. Serf tenants owed rents to the landlords, paid by working the noble's land or giving a portion as their own produce as taxation. Both laws and norms undergird the system, with numerous demands mutually held by the parties tying them together in a social web of obligation. At its best, feudalism was a creaky system that survived as long as the primary duty of the first caste was to fight, supposedly, defensive wars. Chivalry was the normative glue that tried to hold the system together and managed to do so through the Hundred Years War.

The word "chivalry" carries with it a plethora of modern, and historical, connotations. While its contemporary meanings are far removed from its historical origins, it codifies a set of norms that simultaneously elevate women and children as an object of protection and nigh veneration, while subjugating those people to the same authority held by the purported protector. Much of what is at the core of the "chivalric ideal" was originally formulated and promulgated by the Church in the previously discussed Peace and Truce of God declarations. It is difficult to ascertain how much influence these ideals had on the conduct of the warrior nobility of Europe; chroniclers like Froissart (1968) provide accounts of knights seemingly embodying all of these ideals and accounts of those presented as de-based villains who ignore God's law for their own aggrandizement. Apart from those held up as paragons of a given ideal, the daily routine of enacting and abiding by norms is rarely commented on or highlighted in the historical record. By the mid-fourteenth century, chivalry had evolved, thanks to the literary work of Chaucer, the Gawain poet, Chrétien de Troyes (1970) and others, into a set of literary tropes over a guide to daily life for a knight or squire. However, the extant chivalry manuals address real problems faced by those inhabiting, and controlling those who inhabit, the warrior strata – both on and off the battle field. Numerous period tomes survive giving us some sense of how medieval nobility viewed chivalry and their obligations under it. Most were written by knights themselves (i.e., de Charney's *De Chivalry* or Ramón Lull's *Le Libre del Orde de Cauayleria*), though others were written by clergy (i.e., Honoré Bonét's *L'Arbre des Batailles*).[6]

[6]In the Anglophone world, Lull's work was better known from Caxton's (Caxton, 1485/1926) published Middle English translation.

Despite difference caste positions, both knights and clergy borrowed extensively from each other's work producing a nearly homogenous set of values. Gies (1984) points out that chivalry was "a code perhaps violated more often than honored, but [it is known for] exercising incontestable influence on the thought and conduct of posterity" (p. 2). One of these "incontestable influences" is its effect on the laws of war.

Chivalry emerged to address one core problem of early medieval society: uncontrolled warriors using violence to accomplish their goals in a state of nigh anarchic anomie. With no legal apparatus, public opinion and internalized values were basically the only social control on warrior behavior – on and off the battlefield (see Duby, 1978). Gies (1984) describes there early "knights" as "living largely by violence, uncontrolled by a public justice that had virtually disappeared." In the ninth and tenth centuries, decentralized or nonexistent political power and institutions had very little reach or actual influence. Through most of Europe, the only uniting factor was faith, and it was the Christian Church that attempted to address and curtail warriors' violence in multiple contexts as we saw in our earlier discussions of the *Pax Dei* and *Treuga Dei.* By investing these ideas with the authority and legitimacy of the church, threats of excommunication and peer disapproval from fellow Christians were marshalled to at least polish up the rough edges of these violent men, if not prevent their depredations on the public, especially those ill-equipped to protect themselves (i.e., serfs and clergy).

Ideas within the *Pax* and the *Treuga* form the core of much of chivalric thought, but it is clearly religious thought as seen via a military lens. Later chroniclers and other authors frame the existence and empowerment of the landed nobility to have been a deep historical event directed by God himself to establish peace and control over lawless and uncontrolled lands and people. Thirteenth-century knight and author, Geoffroi de Charny (N.D.) describes the process as such: "the reasons for which they are made and the manner in which it was accomplished were very good, holy, and just. For those persons who were the most suitable in body and the most perfect in good behavior, elected by all their people, were chosen and given power at this time and from them have come and still come all the emperors, kings, and princes of the present day" or/and "when the princes were chosen the people selected from among themselves those who had strong and well-fashioned bodies and who were able to endure pain of all kinds and to work hard for the good government of their people both in war and peace" (pp. 47–48).[7] Bonét's (1949) version is similar: "asked about the origin of jurisdiction and lordship. . .according to the decretal it comes by ordinance of God. . .[God]allotted to men reason, sense, and discretion, that they might live reasonably. . .all just and true jurisdiction comes from God, and by man's election" (pp. 114–115). Such rhetoric gives a historical legitimacy to the values expressed in these manuals and to the notion of a brotherhood of international knights bound not by country or liege but by adherence to chivalry. Further, the placement of placing these origins in the distant-mythical past adds legitimacy.

[7]This is obviously a fictionalized version of the rise of nobility in Europe and England.

Courtly literature presented idealized visions of this life, most strongly captured in epic poems like *Le Roman de la Rose* or as the era unfolds, forms as a crucible for the critique of a noble class that seems aimless and having lost its moral way, such as Chaucer's *Troylus and Criseyde* (817 CE/1989). In the *Troylus*, Chaucer takes his Homeric source material and refashions it into a story of how courtly love and chivalry-as-literature's obsession with unavailable/unrequited love (i.e., *Le Roman De la Rose*, Castiglione's (1528/1959) *Book of the Courtier*) leads to the downfall of a knight, the titular Troylus. Once smitten with love for the daughter of his enemy, Criseyde, Troylus is unfit to fulfill his duties as a warrior. He sulks, whines, and naps his way through the siege of Troy, when he should be winning honors of the field of battle. While Troylus' behavior clearly fits the literary tropes of love and its induced actions prevalent during the period, it also runs counter to everything chivalric manuals of the period teach.

Gawain, in the Gawain poet's *Gawain and the Green Knight* ca. 14th century also fails to uphold the tenants of chivalry when he first lies to the Green Knight about what he "won" while the Green Knight was out hunting. His major failure is that of courage. He wears the belt given to him by the Green Knight's wife that will supposedly make him immune from the ax blow Gawain is due. A proper knight should not fear injury or death and definitely not resort to trickery in a contest. This is intensified as Gawain is acting as a representative of his King, Arthur, as he accepted the Green Knights challenge in the King's name. Unlike Troylus, Gawain is redeemed when he admits his failure of courage and attempted trickery after the Green Knight reveals the challenge was a ruse to teach humility. This mirrors much of Arthurian literature of the period (and after), knights (and Kings) face challenges, fail, and hopefully learn from their failures. Some do (i.e., Gawain), some do not (i.e., Lancelot and Guinevere), but this is how literary devices work. Characters become exemplary of various strengths and failings as defined by chivalric values and ideals. This serves as a key source of narrative tension, but also highlights the frequency nobles were exposed to chivalric ideals and values. Such literature presents dilemmas the reader or listener of the period would recognize and might face themselves.[8] Thus, an evening's post-dinner entertainment is likely to include inculcation into or reinforcement of chivalric values.

Of course, it would take more than stories to prevent young nobles from assaulting peasant girls and young noble women (especially when some of the characters in the stories have problems doing the same). The chivalric manuals are as clear about the treatment of women (and other innocents) as the *Pax* and *Treuga* are. While it contains echoes of the courtly love sentiments seen in *La Roman De la Rose* or *The Book of the Courtier* on the subject of women De Charni writes "I firmly maintain that these very good women ought to be honored, served, and loved and other women as well who thus do good things and

[8]Most courtly literature, which includes the various Arthurian cycles and the work of Chaucer, was written to be read aloud. Literacy rates were still generally low among all except the clergy.

make men become good knights and soldiers" (p. 9). The first group of women de Charni refers to are the noble women, whom he uniformly sees as good and virtuous. He extends his praise to lower ranked women who "do good things," implying that this does not refer to all women. Nowhere in his writing does de Charni reject being chivalrous toward peasants and others below their rank; he rather insists upon it, as authors of similar manuals did.

De Charni's *De Chivalerie* focuses on all aspects of a knight's life, be it martial, domestic, or spiritual. He is most concerned with outlining and lauding what he deems the best personal, and personality, characteristics a knight can possess and should demonstrate. Geoffry is known from history more as a warrior than a philosopher or literary figure. Froissart calls him the flower of French chivalry. He carried the Oriflamme for both King Philip IV and King Jean II. Geoffry, bearing the Oriflamme until his end, dies at the battle of Poitiers (1356).[9] While he is buried locally, King Jean II paid to have the body exhumed shipped to Paris and interred in the church of the Celestines, a high honor.[10]

Geoffry's fame and honor gave credence and weight to his writings on knighthood and appropriate behavior, which is no doubt reinforced by the praise heaped upon him by various chroniclers. In terms of battlefield behavior, while defeating the enemy is paramount, *how* one defeats the enemy and acts in the aftermath defines a knight's character. Some things should be sought more readily than others. Geoffry is critical of knight's focus on pillage, "A good soldier should set his heart and his intention more on acquiring honor which lasts forever than on gaining booty which one can lose in a single hour" (p. 12). Creating a good name for one's self is more important than wealth that can be quickly frittered away. Loot and booty were a clear draw for soldiers, landed knights included. Geoffrey, however, instructs warriors entering battle to seek reputation – glory from feats of bravery and skill – and not wealth. Later, he links desire for wealth to a fear of death, one thing he feels a knight should not possess (recall Gawain's failure). "The more wealth a man has, the more he hates to die...the more honor a man has, the less he fears death, for goodness and honor will remain with him always" (p. 27). In other words, rather than trying to cling to wealth and the rewards of the present, one should be more concerned with one's reputation, which might live on long after one's death. The New Testament roots of these ideas are clear.

Geoffry's manual is directed at all of the Nobility, but especially the younger sons of Lords who will likely inherit little to nothing of their father's estate or power. Such men are the main of those who composed the ranks of knights during the period. First sons were inheritors of their father's position, second sons were often sent to the clergy, the rest were idle when not on campaign. Maintaining

---

[9]The Oriflamme was the French battle-standard that indicated no quarter was to be asked or given. Carrying it into battle was one of the greatest honors the French King could bestow on a knight, and one of the most dangerous.

[10]Wilson (2021) has suggested that *On Chivalry* and other works attributed to Geoffry were actually written by his son of the same name. For our purposes here, the point is moot.

them in good behavior was a chore, of which the ideals of Chivalry were one of many attempted solutions.

Henri Bonét's *L'Arbre des Batailles* is less concerned with courtly graces and the condition of a warrior's soul and is more concerned, at least is part, with laying out and exploring the numerous and nuanced demands that govern the choices and behaviors of the warrior class. Often addressing the necessary minutia of law (i.e., can you imprison a knight who has lost his mental faculties and if he is cured can he be imprisoned after – Chapters XCI and XCII), showing an evolution of both military manuals and law. While most of the chivalry manuals of the time were focused on instilling virtues in knights and knights-to-be, Bonét's work is much more a law treatise. Written for French King Charles VI, parts III and IV especially focus on how the general legal obligations between liege and vassal work in countless contexts. It is the work of a scholar not a warrior and attempts to collect and systematize law undergirding feudalism, which by nature includes warfare and soldiering.

De Chivalerie is a book focused on norms and virtues, persuading the warrior classes to adopt and exhibit the tenants of chivalry as a cultural system of beliefs that guide action. *L'Arbe des Batalles* is a collection of legal arguments extrapolated from fundamental principles that Bonét lays down. The former is intended as a moral guide to life for all nobility, the later a law manual for a sovereign or scholar.

A Confederation of Cousins

A fact often lost on a modern reader, use to contemporary conventions and structures of war, was the tightly interrelated nature of noble families on the continent and in the British Isles. Due to generations of political and economically driven inter-marriage, knights could, and did, find themselves in opposite battle lines than their cousins or even siblings. This created obvious tensions and contradictions. Unlike other warfare that sees family members participating on opposite sides (i.e., some civil wars), which are acute instances, this confederation of cousins controlled Europe and warfare for centuries. The social-familial relationships between the top echelons of the medieval military world undergirded the complex system of ransoms and hospitality that governed the end-game of any battle. This is a distinctly medieval evolution, as ransoms as seen here are rare both before and after the period. The tradition of parlay will become part of the laws of war; hospitality expectations will find themselves reshaped into POW treatment regimes. These three features changed the nature of warfare and were a distinct response to the fusion of family, politics, and war.

During hostilities, either belligerent could request a cessation of fighting to engage in parley. While cease-fires to negotiate armistices are very common throughout the history of warfare, medieval parley often had different goals. Parlay was indeed be called to seeking terms of surrender. But in this era, it had much smaller applications, which were more frequently invoked. For example, it was not uncommon to call parley so two cousins could exchange letters between their respective mothers or something similar. Parley was as much about maintaining social relations as it was resolving a specific military encounter. It is a reflection of the courtesy of high social position and the need to acknowledge and maintain ongoing relationships despite whom a given knight might currently be in the service of.

Ransom was another innovation largely driven by the tightly interrelated nature of medieval European combatants. Ransom changed the nature of warfare, especially for nobles on either side of a conflict. As discussed earlier, taking war captives as slaves was seen as the norm for much of military history to this point; it was codified in Roman law. Taking the defeated (and their families) as slaves was also common in the British Isles and Nordic lands. This process begin to wane in the ninth and tenth centuries directly in parallel to the rise of Christianity as an institutional power. Christian teaching at the time forbade Christians enslaving other Christians (non-Christians were a different matter entirely). This necessitates tactical changes in how one approaches the battle. Slave taking discourages killing of the defeated, rather making their capture profitable. As Europe Christianizes, leaders in Europe and the British Isles find themselves opposing other Christians in their military endeavors. Enslavement is off the table. This reduces pressures to limit carnage, fatality, and atrocity in combat; there is no social or economic value in allowing enemies to live. Ransoming prisoners of war changes that, at least for the nobility.

If captured on the battlefield, a noble could (and would) be held captive until his family/estate paid the demanded price for his freedom. This changed the objectives of a knight during battle and shaped the manner in which a potential target was approached on the field. A noble, especially one whose heraldry indicated a wealthy family, would be fought to be subdued and captured, not killed. According to Froissart and other early chroniclers, it was not uncommon to have multiple knights attempt to claim the same valuable prisoner. Once bested, if a knight gave his word in surrender – a simple "I yield to you" – he would be spared and ushered from the chaos of the melee to safer ground. He was no longer a combatant to be defeated; he was a payday to collect. This meant that there was competition on the field for the most valuable hostages. Also, the chaos of the battlefield could lead a man to surrender to several different knights in succession if his safety and security was not ensured after his oath was given. Which oath prevailed was a legal question. Keen (1965, pp. 165–166) discusses the case of a dispute between the Edward, the Black Prince, and the Earl of Salisbury, over a hostage that apparently gave his surrender oath to several people during the battle, firstly to a squire of the Black Prince and lastly to a man pledged to the Earl of Salisbury. Salisbury and the Prince took the case to the courts, where the confusion and complexity inherent in the question was acknowledged and definitive rules established for knights to follow in judging whom a captive belonged to. The first man to receive a soldier's surrender was the one ransom was owed to, but, the courts established clear steps to be taken to establish this. Once a verbal oath was obtained, a knight was to take his prisoner's right gauntlet and then place his right hand in the prisoner's right hand. This establishes one man as a captive of the other. In addition, though, the captor must also ensure that their captive is protected for the rest of the battle, often by being escorted behind the captor's lines. Failure to observe either criterion legally voided one's claim to a prisoner. After the battle, those taken for ransom would attest more detailed oaths to their captors. These ideas find themselves codified in the late medieval articles of battle (see Chapter 5).

Ransom severely reduces the lethality of war, for nobles at least. Peasant foot soldiers, archers, or mercenaries were not captured and ransomed. They were often killed after the battle, being run down by cavalry after their lines broke. If initially spared, they still faced abuse at the hands of their captors. For example, a Welsh or British archer captured alive by the French or Flemish (or a Free Company) could expect to have his forefinger and index finger cut off the hand used to draw the bow string: an injury both symbolic and practical: it embodied the hatred many knights and foot felt for the longbow men, and it meant that man would never draw a longbow again. They may or may not be allowed to live afterward; release was justified as the man in question would never fight in the line as an archer again. Both Catholic Christianity and Chivalry demanded mercy be shown to those unable to fight. Yet, peasant soldiers could not count on the Christian mercy their foes would show the nobility.

Echoing church decrees, but also presaging modern IHL, both Bonét and de Charni castigate those who abuse or otherwise injure noble prisoners once they have surrendered as dishonorable and as against the tenants of chivalry.[11] If unable to pay immediately, the prisoner would be taken to the captor's estate where he would be treated as a honored guest of the manor's lord, which, in effect, he was. He shared the same bonds of noble birth and the chivalric oath as his captor and was expected to uphold his knightly vows and obey the conditions of his confinement. Keen (1965, p. 157) quotes Paris of Pozzo explaining, "When a man surrenders, and his victor accepts him as a prisoner…then he makes a *contract* with him, that he shall be a captive and shall not be killed" (emphasis added). By framing surrender as a contract, the law and law's enforcement of contracts is called forth to add weight to the oath given. Prisoners would even be paroled and allowed to return to their own estates promising to send the ransom later. While on parole, which included an oath to not fight in current hostilities, a paroled knight could move freely through the countryside and expect not to come to any harm from any belligerent party as he wasn't a combatant for any side at that point if he carried the appropriate pass.

Hospitality rules intended to be applied generally to all other nobles visiting one's house were even more salient when the recipient of said hospitality was a ransom prisoner. Good lords were to provide adequately for the needs of their households and their guests. Guests especially were to be treated with the care and respect due to them, with hospitality norms suggesting that if it was in his power, a Lord should refuse no reasonable request. Those held under ransom were rarely treated as prisoners, typically they were treated as any other member of the court – which they essentially were. One would be allowed to come and go as one

[11]Neither has anything particular to say about the abuse of peasant soldiers, especially the hated archers.

pleased, within broad limits. This could include travel away from the estate in which they were "imprisoned" for extended lengths of time.

Ransom was a means of economic gain outside of pillage and looting. It provided an alternative path to make warfare lucrative for the participants. At least those of noble birth. It also reduced the potential lethality of battle for nobles, changing a warrior's logic to one that in some ways parallels the melee of a tournament over the carnage of war. It reduced lethality by making lethality costly to the killer. However, it only applied to the noble combatants. Peasants typically had nothing to offer as a ransom and were not spared. Similarly, the peasants were not bound by the rules of chivalry. They were not seen as constitutionally capable of it (if so, the logic went, God would have made them nobles to begin with). This caste-based standard locked the battle logic of the peasant warriors into a simple kill-or-be-killed that soldiers have always faced. This division in some cases catalyzed atrocity violence events during and after battles. Agincourt (1415) is an excellent example in point.

Due to weather and terrain, the battle of Agincourt was a remarkably lopsided victory for Henry V's smaller English forces over a much larger French army, similar to the English victories at Crécy (1346). English archers reaped a deadly harvest of French noble and peasant alike as units got bogged down in mud pit that was the battlefield. The initial advancing Genoese crossbow men were routed by the English longbow men (Bartlett, 1995; Callister & Whitbread, 2022; Keegan, 1976; Keen, 1965). While such fighting might have offended some chivalric sensibilities about courage and honor (the longbow was considered a cowardly and dishonorable weapon by the French nobility, despite their heavy use of Genoise crossbow men during the Hundred Years War), it violated no laws of war. Unlike French forces, which at one point in the battle raided and slaughtered those present in the English camp. The aftermath was a different story. The English archers roamed the field of battle, stealing anything they could pocket and unceremoniously finished off any wounded survivors encountered, actions decried as criminal and cowardly by chroniclers and other commentators.

Geoffry de Charni's death at Poitiers is, in a way, accidentally symbolic of the death of high chivalry itself. By the time the Hundred Years War ends, the days of the knight as heavy cavalry is over, canons and handguns are appearing on the battlefield which reduce the protection offered by metal armor. Military technology was making the mounted, armored knight a thing of the past. As a system of thought and values, chivalry produced a number of key themes and tropes that still thrive in modern warrior ethos and began to address key concerns that will become central in the development of international laws of warfare. Treatment of prisoners is a case in point. Chivalry embodied the notion of amicable and humane treatment of PoWs, especially officers. In this period, that distinction is meaningless, nobles fought in separate units as shock cavalry or heavy infantry and were not in minute control of peasant combatants. However, as warfare evolved in Europe toward its more modern forms, nobles became officers *ex officio*.

While killing and looting in war was the self-claimed purpose of medieval nobility, it was still a sin under canon law, be it venial and not cardinal.

Penitential manuals make it clear, through comparison, that violence during a *just* war carries the least guilt and has the least demands for penance. Surviving penitential manuals show multiple clerical authors setting the penance demand at 40 days for killing done in war. Most other forms of intentional and malicious killing warrant seven to 10 years of penance (see McNeill & Gamer, 1990). Canon law's acknowledgment of war-borne violence as less sinful and thus in less need of penitential correction recognizes the nature of war itself but simultaneously highlights early attempts to lessen its presence and power. Putting it on the same level of sin as reproductive marital intercourse, shows the Vatican has recognized war as a necessary evil in the world that should be managed to reduce its worse affects. This is the same logic behind marital sex being sinful – early Christianity strongly encouraged, if it didn't demand, celibacy, and chastity among all of its adherents. Early congregational resistance and the simple fact that the best way to increase the number of believers is to raise people in a faith from childhood, persuaded the church to downgrade marital sex from a Cardinal sin as long as it was for reproductive purposes. A necessary "evil." As such individual sanctions are rarely recorded, we don't know how priests dealt with soldier's confessions of killing on the battlefield or if they even confessed such as sin, much less completed any penance given them.

One of the few records we do have of knights admitting their guilt to "war crimes" are the extant plea rolls from Edward I's of England's Scottish expedition. It lists hundreds of offenses. The exact crimes are not always listed, especially when the records indicate an informal agreement between victim and offender was reached. Most of this is disputes over lodging, property, or business transactions. "Trespass" is the modal offense recorded. Most of the crimes seemed to occur during the occupation and not during hostilities.

The 100 Years War also advanced considerably the perceived need for laws governing military behavior. The Free Companies and *chevauchees* of multiple belligerents in the countryside highlighted the need to control otherwise uncontrolled soldiers. The ideals of chivalry were designed to do just this, but the conflict laid bare the problems with the system and its practice. The Free Companies are an example of how the loyalties of many military companies shifted frequently during the course of the prolonged conflict. Free Companies were mercenaries and "professional" soldiers. If they were not in the employ of a Sovereign on campaign, they lived by raiding the country side. They were a special scourge on the French country side. National powers did little to stop them due to past and future business relationships. Further, there was little desire for pitched battle against the Free Companies among the military leaders of the Hundred Years War.

Keeping men under arms year-round becomes an important change in European warfare in this period. Especially toward the end of the century plus long conflict, belligerent parties kept more forces active and more maintain standing forces led to the need for more rules and administration specifically to maintain a loyal, peaceful garrison where needed. More people to order and keep ordered creates a need for more proto-bureaucracy to track enlistment and payment, if nothing else. Which is exactly what we see in England and her holdings in France.

A muster system was designed requiring all serving members present themselves at specific times and places for counting (and payment). Those absent were left off the payroll and faced other potential punishments. Such a pay system was, in part, designed to reduce the lure of pillage and looting in the wake of Agincourt and similar incidents (Newhall, 1940). It also ensured soldiers remained at their garrisons.

A main concern, especially in occupied Norman and French territory, was troop loyalty. In England we see an "[I]ssuance of orders restricting the garrison to Englishmen and to non-Norman subjects of King Henry, and forbidding members of garrisons to reside and do business in the town where they are stationed... with no more than half of the lances (mounted troops) be French and all archers be English, Irish, Welsh, or Gascon" (Newhall, 1940, p. 116). Recall, Roman soldiers had similar constraints placed upon them while stationed in frontier areas. The English are using similar logic. It is not wise to develop ties to a community of people you could be ordered to kill at a moment's notice. Extended interactions might bring disloyalty, where troops see themselves as more a part of the community instead of part of the garrison. Further, we see the emergence of a nationalism in Henry's thinking about who would be loyal (English, Irish, Welsh, Gascon – those areas solidly under Henry's rule) and thus limiting enrollment in the expeditionary force to those deemed manageable and unlikely to turncoat in the field.

The Decline of Chivalry

The days of chivalry as a set of social norms were numbered. Chroniclers show us while there was lot of talk about Chivalric values, their application on the battle left a lot to be desired. Froissart's discussion of the debacle at Crécy in 1346 is a good example. When confronted with an English siege, the townsfolk insisted on meeting the English in the field and the local Constable agrees. Seeing the English advance "in three solid, close-ordered divisions...they were so filled with dismay that nothing in the world could stop them taking to their heels" (p. 74). The Normans retreated in confusion and chaos, but the English pursued, "killing as they liked without mercy...sparing none" (pp. 74–75). Froissart (1968) makes it seem as if the atrocities were only committed by the archers, especially by paralleling the telling of that story with that of Sir Thomas Holland, who saves the Count and Constable of the city by taking them prisoner. Sir Thomas' chivalry and honorable behavior is extended to his men, which Froissart credits with "preventing a number of evil deeds and rescued many a pretty townswoman and many a nun from rape" (1968, p. 75). Chivalric deeds were reserved for the nobility; peasants were simultaneously expected to uphold of laws of war and chivalry but were also not seen as constitutionally capable of the type of self-control a noble would possess. They were not generally expected to follow the rules and received little more from their leadership than head shaking and finger wagging when they committed atrocities before or after battle. Similar slaughter occurs at the crossing of the ford of *Blanchetaque* after the French have broken (Froissart, 1968, p. 78), then at Crécy, and most major engagements. Such slaughter in the Hundred Years War was not limited to Edward III's 1946–1947 campaign.

Chivalric values were integrated into the warrior class of the age, and Froissart and other period chroniclers lauding scores of brave, holy, and chivalric deeds. For example, when Charles VIII paraded his army through Florence after its capture in November of 1494, the citizenry "grumbled at petty thefts by the soldiery but noted with relief that they refrained from rape" (Durant, 1950, p. 611). After watching a long list of atrocities carried out by his troops, upon reaching Calais and setting his siege, Edward III allowed 1,700 civilians to leave the city unmolested, ordering them fed and provided with two pence each. At the end of the siege, wearied and angry at those losses to his army, he orders the execution of the city's representatives who come in surrender. He is only deterred by the pleadings of his wife (recall de Charni's praise for women who make their husbands better knights). Literarily, Froissart is showing the King's temptation and intemperance leading him astray and his salvation from such a blunder by his wife skillfully manipulating the rules of chivalry against him; as de Charni tells us, a Lord is honored to provide any reasonable request, in his power, made to him by his subjects and especially his wife. Indeed, medieval chronicles like Froissart's (or especially Froissart's) are as much literature as they are history. They let us trace the image and actions of the cultural values underpinning knighthood as much as they tell us about the actual behavior of the figures written about. When nobles act unchivlarically, it is glossed over or used to make a specific moral point. Froissart emphasizes Edward III's anger guiding his meeting with the surrendering parties at Calais, contemporary readers realize the unchivalric nature of the deeds and of the motives. Chivalry manuals are clear that knights are to keep level heads and even tempers, Kings more so than anyone. It is his wife's mercy and tenderness that moves Edward's III head and heart in a more chivalric manner and leads him to spare them messengers. He orders the nobles taken prisoner or paroled on their word and allows everyone else to leave the city.

The tenants of chivalry hold a tensioned place between norms and law. They were a set a values, clearly influenced by the Church's teachings and especially the *Pax* and *Treuga*; nobles were exposed to Chivalry's demands, and tropes, almost constantly. Literature, sermons, instruction of pages and squires, and professional manuals ensured that Knights, and those of higher rank, were aware of their duties and obligations within the medieval social contract. Yet, these constant reminders suggest that more than a handful of knights were less than fully faithful in their adherence to chivalric norms. These demands were more than informal social norms, they were codified, though not in the same manner as law. They were part of the recognized laws of war as defined in the period. They also form the foundation of Peter von Hagenbach's trial, an event often referred to as the first international criminal tribunal, a discussion of which will close this chapter. As a system of social and military organization, feudal chivalry does not survive the fourteenth century, but some of the core ideals of behavior highlighted by medieval chroniclers are at the heart of the laws of war and IHL today.

While the culture of chivalry permeated early and late medieval military culture, as discussed, its codification was more literary than legal. The later tradition of issuing articles of battle or ordinances which are composed of the army's rules for campaigning and the punishments for violations does not seem to have been in place in the earlier portions of the period. If such orders were issued they were either not written down or a documentary version did not survive. One exception to this is Richard I's charter issued to govern the behavior those traveling to the Levant on crusade. The rules only covered ship-board behavior, not behavior once they reached their destination. The focus was keeping the peace on the voyage. The ordonnance prohibits murder, punishing it ship-board by tying the killer to the body of his victim and tossing them both overboard. If the murder happens on land, the killer is tied to the deceased and buried alive. Attacking another with a knife and drawing blood would cost a solider his hand; if he only punched someone else, he would "be thrice du[n]cked in the sea" (p. 63). If one were to "reproach, abuse, or curse" a fellow soldier, they were required to pay the victim silver. A thief was to be tarred and feathered and left at the next port.

Why the lack of ordinances once they reached their destination? They could have been issued verbally or a written copy might not have survived. More likely, there were not specific, holistic rules set out. All three Peoples of the Book make it explicit in scripture that their laws and other behavioral expectations only apply to people of their own faith – nonbelievers are not subject to the protections or constraints of the laws.[12] It was perfectly acceptable in Christian morality to deliver any abuses they wished on non-Christians, which Crusaders did with frequency and relish. The additional religious-cultural motives here create a social distance between peoples that heightened the probability of atrocity violence in the Holy Land. Of which it saw plenty. Thus, in this specific context, written rules were not deemed necessary to generate constraint among the troops: carnage was a primary goal of the crusades from the European approach.[13]

Socio-Economic Transformations and the Rise of Mercantilism

The rise of the middle classes and shifts in political and economic power did not totally eclipse the power of the landed nobility, but it changed the landscape of power sources and relations. The nobility long depended on land and land ownership as the pillar of their power and influence; land is the capital in an agrarian society and control of the land and its produce (be it flora, fauna, or human). En-fifing practices were the basis of the political structure, creating chains of obligation to provide economic and military support. The rise of profitable commerce, especially that tied to the important of products from elsewhere, gave the newly emerging capitalist class an engine of wealth creation that rivaled, and surpassed, the wealth generated by land. This is seen in their ability to influence law-making processes. As Chambliss (1964) discusses in his article on historical changes in English vagrancy laws in the fourteenth, sixteenth, and eighteenth centuries. The target, and punishment, of these laws evolved over the period to address new concerns. The first major revisions of these laws,

[12]Jews, Christians, Moslems.

[13]This will also be seen in colonial wars.

originally written to take some of the obligation off of the church for the destitute, refocused on ensuring adequate labor. In the wake of the Black Death, the numbers of rural peasants was reduced by about a third, creating a huge labor shortage on estates. Many of those peasants who survived the plague, immigrated to the cities to take advantage of new economic opportunities and growing wages arising there. So, the vagrancy laws were changed to force people back to work in the fields.

Clearly, this was not a change pushed by the emergent trade classes, as it reduced the number of people available to work in their business endeavors. With the population rebounded from plague losses, vagrancy laws were repurposed in the sixteenth century, this time to squarely serve the interests of the merchant class. Vagrancy became redefined as being unattached to a place or work or fixed residence. Sentences become more severe with branding and execution being the designated penalties. In essence, vagrancy is being punished like the more serious crimes of robbery or burglary. This is not accidental. The law was designed not to get the idle peasant back on a farm, but was used to prosecute highway robbery, an increasing threat as more and more trade goods moved along the roads of England. Instead of needing to catch robbers with clearly marked property or *in media res*, all law enforcers had to do was find a camp of men with no visible means of economic support. This is critical as while nobles did benefit from trade, their wealth was still tied to the land and its produce; the mercantile classes had the most to gain and to lose. This is an early and clear instance of their growing influence on governance, at least in the English Isles. As the late middle ages wore on, the selling of titles and estates became uncommon, providing a narrow path of upward mobility for those few who has benefitted the most from nascent global trade. This further weakened an always creaky system of social organization, as it was now not based solely on birth or battle honors.

While Feudalism failed to survive as a socio-political system, the core notions within chivalry did not disappear from the laws of war or of those concerned with making war more humane. The next chapter focuses the late Middle Ages and the first surviving articles of battle – codification of specific rules and punishments for soldiers in a given army to follow on and off the battlefield. These articles represent the first truly legalistic attempt to constrain soldiers on the field of battle, as they specify: prohibited actions, punishments, adjudication processes, and jurisdiction – everything one would expect of law. As we will see, these articles borrow a lot from the *Pax* and *Truega*, but also address concerns that evolved during the medieval era and concerns specific to given conflicts. They are short, with a scant few articles compared with modern military codes, but they represent a significant shift in the way leaders are thinking of battle and their troops. They also show that armies are growing larger and bureaucratizing their structures; formal rules are an adjunct to this form of social organization.

Chapter 5

The Late Medieval World

By the thirteenth and fourteenth centuries, western armies were growing larger, with more specialized subunits. By the end of the Hundred Years War, the English, the French, their allies, and mercenary Free Companies had to a degree abandoned seasonal musters and campaigns for longer terms of service. With garrisons being permanently armed, sieges lasting beyond the beginning of harvest, and the expectation of pay in wages over loot, militaries begin the keeping of rolls and tying pay to showing up at seasonal musters whether an active campaign was planned or not (Newhall, 1940). Conflicts were increasingly drawn-out affairs, not over after a couple of pitched battles in midsummer. The organizational infrastructure required to assemble and maintain large, semi-standing armies that were begun to be built in the late Middle Ages. Structures of command and control, logistics, and pay became increasingly important. Not surprising, such proto-bureaucratic structures required codified rules to function.

Chivalry and the international brotherhood of knights were still a set of ideas given a lot of lip-service in literary sources and the period continues to see the publication of chivalric manuals, keeping chivalry a key theme in the literature of the period. Chivalric values and virtues are held paramount, but their utility as behavioral controls weakened. In part, this is the difference between literary aspiration and reality. Few knights lived up to the chivalric ideal, a major theme of courtly literature. Yet few knights were held responsible for their behavior under the code of chivalry (see below for the discussion of an exception with van Hagenbach's trial). Chivalry and its tenants *could be* used to try and punish knights who engaged in bad behavior on or off the battlefield, during peace or war. Those found guilty were publicly stripped of the symbols and rights of their office as a knight, an act designed to humiliate the offender and deter others. Doing it publicly also reinforces a king's commitment to justice in the eyes of the citizenry, gaining legitimacy for their rule. The process as described by Froissart and other chroniclers reverse mirrors the ceremony by which knighthood is granted (Froissart, 1968; McVitty, 2014). His sword is taken from him and broken, his spurs removed, as was his clothing. Often, the ignominies did not end there, as many faced execution as traitors as violating their chivalric oath is tantamount to violating their oath to their King. If favored by the King or courts, the knight faced a quick beheading. If not, the death of a traitor awaited.

A Socio-Legal History of the Laws of War, 75–94

Published under exclusive licence by Emerald Publishing Limited
doi:10.1108/978-1-78769-857-420231005

English law in the twelfth and thirteenth centuries required a series of brutalities be committed on one convicted of treason, especially if that individual was of noble birth and thus bearing more responsibility for their actions as the values of chivalry itself were seen not only as central to their sociopolitical position but as being within their very blood (McVitty, 2014). It is under Edward I that the punishment for treason is shifted "from fines and imprisonment to public spectacles that incorporated the much grimmer exemplary punishments of drawing, hanging, beheading, disemboweling, and quartering" (McVitty, 2014, p. 458). Such a grisly end was deemed necessary due to the weight of the crime of treason. Being "drawn" referrers to being drug by a horse to the gallows or execution site. The condemned could be on a sledge or walking behind. Upon reaching the gallows, the traitor was hung but typically not until death. While hung, the man was often eviscerated, with his entails sometimes burnt. At this point, the prisoner is cut down (though they may not be alive after this treatment). Alive or not, next the ultimate bodily and moral insult is quartering the body – literally dividing it into separate parts. This could be done by cutting the body up, or each limb of the body was tied to a horse who were ushered in opposite directions to tear the corpse apart. Sometimes, each piece was buried separately (if at all).

While grisly in today's mind, these elaborate public spectacles are, as Durkheim (1893/1984) establishes, a ritualized version of punishment seen in most if not all societies designed to serve several functions. It visibly and publicly reinforces the community legitimacy of the law. By carrying out punishment, Durkheim argues society is reestablishing a commitment to that normative order. The act of public punishment is designed not only to deter others but is a collective statement of society's values. As it is always the option not to punish a wrong doer, electing for and carrying the punishment out reinforce social solidarity among the community and the community's commitment to that specific norm. Overtime, failing to punish individuals for an infraction reflects a change in underlying norms that promote legal change.

The principles of chivalry when backed by the royal courts appear to be a functional set of laws like military codes of most contemporary nation-states: laws that apply on or off the battlefield and during war and peace. At the core of chivalry is the ideal bond between King and knight, between sovereign and nobleman. And knights breaking their end of the bargain is the worst offense imaginable under arms: it is a violation of their honor, masculinity, and socioeconomic position. It is also seen as a violation of their fundamental nature; nobility was bestowed by blood, with nobles seen as being placed in their positions by God.

The ability of chivalry and the notion of a brotherhood of chivalry bound by principles that held legal weight would be heavily undermined in England during the late twelfth through early thirteenth century. The Treason Trials during the Merciless Parliament of 1388 drew upon the language and ideologies of chivalry to try and convict Richard II's advisors of treason. The drive was not necessarily the sorts of advice being given or the actions of the King, but the fact that his closest advisors were not from the preexisting circle of Dukes, Knights, and the like but were raised to their positions by the merit Richard perceived in them. Accusations that the King was being misled by bad advisors were made by senior royals blocked from access (Saul, 1997). Playing off the ideology of chivalry and nobility as being based in blood, the rhetoric emphasized the low-birth of some advisors and what was seen as a patent inability to give true advice not being of noble blood themselves. While clearly a power play, and not the only one Richard the II would suffer, such blatantly political use of chivalric ideology undermines its legitimacy. In fact, making false accusations is deemed punishable under chivalry.

Hypocrisy plagued the accusations in the Treason Trials. Their very instigation was a cynical use of law designed to hobble an unpopular king, which could be seen as treasonous itself under chivalric ideals. This extended to the absurdity of hauling advisors before the Court of Chivalry, a court only able to try knights, as commoners are not subject to the laws of war and the dictates of chivalry. Once in court, the accused were denied certain privileges of defense, such as trial by combat. Other cases see a similar twisting of both logic and language. For example, Robert De Vere was charged with treason for displaying the king's colors while opposing Gloucester's Appellants in 1387 at the battle of Radcot Bridge. Indeed, raising the king's banner against him was treasonous, except De Vere was acting in the name of the King at the time and was carrying letters that confirmed as much. Twisting the laws of chivalry to suit one's political ends undermines the legitimacy of chivalry as a set of ideals and law. As the political-economic order that was feudalism was creaking and falling apart with the rise of a mercantile middle class gaining more economic power over the landed gentry, the militarist ideology of chivalry which helped prop up feudalism as a system was losing its power as anything other than a set of literary tropes.

It is this same time period that we see the emergence of written, codified articles of battle or ordinances focused on maintaining military order and propriety become common place. There was no longer, at least among the English, French, Scots, and their neighbors, a sense that the code of chivalry in and of itself was enough to ensure military order. As the armies grew in size, fewer and fewer warriors on the field were nobles who felt obligated to follow the tenants of chivalry or who had access to mechanisms like ransoms. Commoners, which distinctly did not hold themselves to chivalry's standards, formed larger and larger portions of the armies, whether the individual soldiers were serving their King or were mercenaries. This gives us the first hints of what a post-chivalry army will look like and points toward the nearing future where forming units of nobles separate from commoners would be replaced with nobles being officers in command of units of commoners. Not surprisingly, larger armies with a more diverse sourcing of fighters also catalyzed the generation and codification of rules for solider behavior before, during, and after battle. Copies of such Articles of War or Ordinances survive, highlighting what medieval commanders saw as essential behaviors to control. It is to the examination of these article we now turn.

Fourteenth-Century Ordinances

It was not an uncommon practice for a King, or other military leader, to issue a new set of ordinances for governing the army for each campaign. This allowed rules and issues specific to a given campaign be included, while being able to remove rules that did not apply. The opponent and a warlord's tactics mattered as much to the rules laid down as any codified morality or law. While the *Pax* and the *Truega* were huge influences on these codes, and they repeat many things mentioned in the chivalric manuals discussed above, these ordinances are an example in a shift in military practice, at least in the British Isles and Western Europe. Establishing specific rules and punishments shows us a legal-military codification of some of the elements of chivalry and Christian teaching combined with the issues that battlefield commanders must attend to in order to have a successful campaign. Such articles are meaningful in what they show us about the King's concerns are, and reflect past behaviors that have been deemed to be problematic and thus forbidden in the articles. They are also significant in that they parallel later national manuals of military law which states will use to codify their military codes (Cox, 2013).

Ordinances issued by late medieval and early modern kings of England have such a strong degree of similarity to each other that there is discussion among historians of an attempt to find the "Ur document," or original statement of the principles in an article of war (Curry, 2008, 2011; Martinez, 2017). The common articles of these documents, after establishing the supremacy of the reigning king, tend reflect specific aspects of the *Pax* and *Truega* of God: not burning or looting churches, not hurting clergy, not abusing women and children. These Chivalric, or Christian, duties reflect the clerical and literary traditions of the period. One of the earliest surviving articles of war is from Richard II's invasion of Scotland in 1385, which contains 26 discrete articles. The first two establish the authority of the king and the sanctity of his person. The third is a summation of key ideas from the Pax – do not harm clergy or rob churches, do not rob or otherwise abuse women, etc. The fourth delineates protection for Herbergers.

Eleven articles involve issues of order maintenance in the army: respecting captains, keeping one's assigned watch, not stealing from other troops in the army, and no dueling or fighting – all common rules in articles of war. Prohibiting such behavior is necessary to maintain unit and army cohesion. Two articles demand soldiers avoid riot or contention, with contention referring to negative actions taken against the army or its current mission (i.e., bringing soldiers into contention with their captains). Also, one of the earliest enforcements of "uniforms" is contained in the articles, with all troops required to wear a red cross of St. George on a white background as an insignia. The concerns expressed in two articles can be traced back to Roman Republican rules; there were established penalties for calling "havoc" or "*mounté*." The former being a signal to disperse and loot, the latter raising a false alarm (literally "to mount"). Both are problematic. Breaking formation to loot before the enemy is completely broken is the best way to snatch defeat from the jaws of victory, as the dispersal of the rank and file means functional military units are no longer in formation, ready to fight. Encountering enemy units still in formation could be disastrous. The latter cause undue confusion and disorder, leading to unthought-through charges or other hasty troop movements. In the fog of battle, the ability of the King and his officers to bring an army in the field under control in these situations is problematic at best. It is likely that we are seeing certain aspects of the unwritten rules or war becoming temporarily codified in these ordinances as the solutions are similar to those devised by their counterparts in prior epoch. Order is a concern for all militaries, as is dissention in the ranks, whether it is conflicts within the troops or between troops and officers.

Two articles forbid both nobles and commoners from commandeering housing other than that which is assigned to them by the Herberger, highlighting the perceived importance of the concern. It is also a good example of how context shaped these articles. The first mention of quartering is fairly standard language aimed at establishing camp housing and prevention of desertion. The second mentioning, toward the end of the list (the 25th article), states that "none be so hardy as to quarter himself" where he was not assigned to do so. Its place in the overall list, and the order which precedes it provides a contextual understanding of why a few of these articles were framed as they were. The 24th article forbids foraging in advance of the army ("before the lords or others") and uses the same phrasing "no one be so hardy to." Here we should use the Middle English definition of hardy as bold or daring.[1] What about the conflict led Richard to issue orders against foraging or leaving camp? While the latter is common, the former isn't, with foraging a standard practice for armies into the modern era. Richard was preparing to invade Scotland, being co-defended by the French. The army was entering hostile territory and men out alone or in pairs foraging, or not quartering in camp, faced real dangers from enemy scouts as well as aggrieved locals. Articles 24 and 25 are written to protect the soldiers in the field from enemies and civilians. Below we will look at similar articles in a different context with a different aim.

Six articles govern prisoner taking, keeping, and how ownership is determined for ransoms. We saw in Chapter 4 issues of ransom ownership were addressed in chivalry manuals such as de Charni's or legal texts such as Bonét's. The late medieval system of prisoner taking and ransom presented two key problems that had to be addressed during or immediately after battle: securing prisoners to keep them from returning to the field of battle and determining ownership of the ransom. This latter issue was the object of much conflict, with multiple people often claiming the right to the same prisoner, especially those of high value. As this is the primary form of remuneration for taking up arms earlier in the period, and still the major form of profit for knights throughout the period, the number of rules is not surprising. While it does not go into the details found in Bonét's *L'Arbre du Battaile*, numerous specifications are made about how much of a knight's ransom each individual gets. Article XVI instructs soldiers to pay 1/3rd of everything to one's "lord or master": the king. Article XII is the first article to address prisoner ownership in one specific situation: if a prisoner is de-horsed or otherwise downed by one warrior who then continues to advance and is taken prisoner by a second solider, the ransom is to be divided between the two. Article XIX instructs warriors to quickly bring prisoners to their captain, who will then have them taken to the "King, constable or mareschall" [sic] for interrogation.

[1]From the Old French hardir "become bold."

After which, the "owner" of the prisoner must secure the prisoner under guard and is responsible if the prisoner is found wandering camp unguarded, thus potentially spying.

Article XXII, the last of the articles dealing with taking prisoners, adds a level of confirmation of ownership in prisoner taking not seen in other articles. Prior articles establish little than word-of-mouth and/or possession of the prisoner as proof of a claim on a portion of a ransom. It is not hard to imagine a lot of conflicts erupting out of the procedures described above in Article XII. Competing claims about who really de-horsed or felled a knight or who might deserve the half for collecting the prisoner and removing him from the battlefield would be little more than one man's word against another's, with little external evidence to weigh the competing claims. XXII modifies XII, by demanding that a knight not only take the prisoner's "faith," or word, but required taking his bacinet or gauntlet as a sign of his capture and proof of being responsible for said capture. This is the procedure de Charni lays out. If knight is downed, and even gives his "faith" to his opponent that he is the prisoner of other, if the gauntlet or bacinet is not taken and another solider comes after and resubdues and takes the item of armor, then the prisoner belongs to the person who took the gear items and the original warrior who de-horsed or downed the prisoner has no claim on the ransom. Why? The enemy was not removed from battle after the first interaction with his captor. He is still able to fight and is still a threat, thus the language about being "re-subdued." The first knight did not ensure the captive was no longer able to participate in battle, thus the ransom goes to the one who did.

The creation of the article is a clear response to earlier incidents where Article XII was not enough to avoid intra-army conflicts over prisoner ownership. This supports the existence of, at least for the English, a set of Articles of Battle that are modified for each conflict (Curry, 2011; Martinez, 2017; Porter, 1946). While there may be no "Ur" Article of Battle for the English (or at least one which is extant), it is clear that later articles on the list appear to be added in response to failures of problems arising with other articles (i.e., XII and XXII) or are specific to the conflict in question. Here, the two next to last articles dealing with foraging and quartering appear to be the product of the specific situations of the 1385 invasion of Scotland. As mentioned, Richard II was about to enter very hostile territory and soldiers who separated themselves from the protection of the mass of the army on the march faced real and present danger.

Unseen except in the Roman manuals, these articles of battle also specified punishments for the violations listed. This is another distinct step in the codification of these norms into formal law, with both substantive and procedural elements. Capital punishment (typically hanging) is specifically mentioned as a punishment in nine articles, loss of horse and armor if a man-at-arms in 12, arrest in eight, disfigurement (specifically, cutting off one's left ear) in four, being "drawn" and hung, loss of the rights to one's prisoner in one article, and loss of "goods and heritage" in one. The high number of executable offenses is not a surprise in the context or the period. Until the modern era, "felony" typically meant a capital crime; many ordinary crimes were capital crimes, such as burglary or rape. We are still in a cultural milieux where life is cheap, death common, and brutality expected in criminal punishments. None of the punishments listed in the 1385 articles would be considered light or lenient in any sense. At best, a solider loses his left ear or best horse. At worst, his life. Though some nobles of the period might argue that a loss of "goods and heritage" are worse than death, as it not only effects the noble in question, but his family and descendants as well.

Social class and age mattered in the punishments defined for some of the violations. For example Article XI, forbidding crying "*mounté*," specifies that men at arms or mounted archers will be forced to forfeit his best horse to the constable, while an archer on foot or "boy" will have their left ear removed. The class differences in penalties here is fairly straight forward – foot archers will not have mounts to confiscate. Article VII against rioting or creating large disruptions in camp and Article XXIV (and by extension XXV) also specifies boys receive a relatively less severe punishment of losing their left ear, as opposed to death for foraging or quartering against orders. Clearly, most of the boys who traveled with and served the army would not possess anything valuable enough to confiscate as a penalty. Yet, we can infer that they are deemed less responsible for their actions due to their age, thus receive comparatively lighter punishments. This marks one of the earliest surviving indicators of using different punishments for different age groups, tacitly acknowledging the perceived differences in responsibility and self-control of boys versus men.

Ironically, Richard's order to avoid forage was not necessary, as the Scots avoided direct conflict and "melted into the hills, stripping the countryside of food as they did so" (Saul, 1997, p. 145), leaving nothing for the English to forage. Other aspects of the Ordinances were ignored as the campaign unfolded. Due to the lack of food and frustration at the lack of engagement with the main Scottish army, the English troops pillaged and burned four abbeys or churches before reaching Edinburgh (Dryburgh, Melrose, Newbattle, and the church of St. Giles) (Cox, 2013; Saul, 1997). After spending about a week in the Scottish capital, the English army returned home.

Cox (2013) reads the destruction of the abbeys and church as a sign that the prohibitions against violating church property only applied when leaders felt like it or had a good reason to follow it; if it was tactically advantageous, they would ignore custom, and the Articles of Battle, to burn and loot. Thus, Cox suggests such articles of battle aren't law because they are violated. By that logic no criminal code is law as it is constantly violated. The violation of a law doesn't mean it is meaningless. Lack of enforcement in a single instance, or even a score of instances, doesn't invalidate the law. In fact, it reinforces the rationale for having it to begin with. Context is important as well. According to the Westminister Chronicle, the English burned Melrose Abby as "it provided harbor for our enemies" (as quoted in Cox, 2013, p. 1392). This rationale is also mentioned in the Kirkstall Chronicle. Seeking safe harbor in churches was a long-held medieval custom codified in the *Truega*. However, both chronicles agree that the Abbey was destroyed *after* a garrison left behind by Richard was attacked and destroyed. If individuals were claiming the protection of the church, then used it as a base to attack the English troops left behind, then they voluntarily gave up their rights to the protection of the church. Attacking them and the Abbey itself would have been in-line with the customs of the period as the assailants and the Abbey surrendered their protected status when they played an active role in hostilities. This is strongly parallel to current IHL and LoW that insist on protection of civilian locales, like churches schools, and hospitals, *unless* they are being used as a base of military operations, are quartering troops, or storing arms or munitions. If involved in any of these, the location becomes a valid military target regardless of civilian use or presence. Recall, one of the key justifications of the *Pax* and *Trugea's* protection of civilians and clergy is their lack of involvement in the hostilities. Taking part would logically nullify that protection. The 1385 Articles clearly stipulate in Article III that the protections listed only apply to those "not bearing arms."[2] This doesn't explain the other instances of attacking religious houses, though St. Giles was likely burned and looted along with the city of Edinburg itself. The main reasons given by writers then and today for the destruction of Edinburg were a combination of the frustration of the Scottish forces continually withdrawing, with an apparent scorched earth policy, and refusing to engage the English army. Denied forage, loot, and ransoms, many suggest that Richard ordered Edinburgh looted and burnt after finding it empty of enemy forces out of financial need. The campaign was expensive to mount and with a lack of engagement between armies, the usual source of funds in ransoms was not being obtained. The need to recoup financial losses is a strong probable motivator for the looting of Edinbugh, as well as the other three clerical houses. Those abbeys were *returned* to and looted, not looted at their first encounter. This suggests strongly that the primary intention upon issuing the Ordinance was to follow it, but the lack of financial success in the adventure provided sufficient motive to violate church property (Cox, 2013; Saul, 1997).

By the end of the fourteenth century, we have seen an evolution in the laws of war through the middle ages, from a system based on "might makes right" to one that acknowledges the complexities of late medieval and early modern warfare. Specific sanction systems are being codified for each war and modified for each war. It also acknowledges the realities and problems presented by a real medieval battlefield over what is depicted in courtly literature. In a perfect army, with Godly and chivalrous knights and footmen, the ideals of chivalry as laid out in the prose and poetry of the era would be enough to limit the harms of war to those engaged in it and even reduce the harms to those warriors. The realities were different, which catalyzed the Church's initial conferences and declarations that evolved into the chivalric ideal to begin with. The problems and concerns of warfare continued to evolve through the Middle Ages, which is reflected in an evolution of articles of battle. The next section of surviving articles of war were issued by Henry V for his invasion of France.

[2]Cox (2013) notes that the Westminster Chronicle also listed heresy as a reason for burning and pillaging the religious orders, which would be allowed under cannon law. However, this rationale is only provided by the author of the Westminster Chronicle.

Henry V

KING HENRY What men have you lost, Fluellen?

FLUELLEN The perdition of th' athversary hath been very great, reasonable great. Marry, for my part, I think the Duke hath lost never a man but one that is like to be executed for robbing a church, one Bardolph, if your Majesty know the man. His face is all bubukles and whelks and knobs and flames o' fire; and his lips blows at his nose, and it is like a coal of fire, sometimes plue and sometimes red, but his nose is executed, and his fire's out.

KING HENRY We would have all such offenders so cut off; and we give express charge that in our marches through the country there be nothing compelled from the villages, nothing taken but paid for, none of the French upbraided or abused in disdainful language; for when lenity and cruelty play for a kingdom, the gentler gamester is the soonest winner.

William Shakespeare, Henry V Act III Scene Six

Henry V's invasion of France, as partially portrayed in the Shakespeare play that bears his name, also produced surviving Articles of Battle. As seen in the famous scene quoted above, Henry is depicted as the ultimate paragon of Chivalric justice in the play. He is more than willing to order his own soldier hung for stealing from a church.[3] Like Richard II, Henry V issued Articles of Battle for his campaign, though there is debate over precisely when and where they were issued (see Cox, 2013; Curry, 2008; Keen, 1978), I follow Keen (1995) and Curry (2008) and will refer to them as the Mantes Ordinances and assume an issuance date of ~July 1419. These articles contain 10 more articles than Richard II's, 26 to 36. Many are identical or similar, while others are distinct to Henry's declaration. Some occur in the same, or roughly the same, order as Richard's, others have moved up or down on the list quite substantially. Seventeen articles are found in both documents that are exactly the same, similar, or similar enough to be considered a repetition from an earlier document. Ten are new to Henry's proclamations. In Henry's Mantes ordinances, two are directly focused on soldiers keeping their watch, whether in camp or lodgings. The first occurs early in the document, as the fourth article. This is substantially sooner than Richard II's list, where it is the 20th article. This suggests that either the perceived importance

[3]Shakespeare uses Bardolph's hanging to cement that Henry has learned to put the kingdom and law ahead of his personal life. In Henry IV Pts 1 and 2 by Shakespeare, Bardolph is a friend of young Prince Hal's.

of the job or a perception of wide-spread slacking from the job arose between the writing of the two sets of articles. The article is repeated as article17.[4]

Some are a similar or same principle but go into much more depth and detail. For example, Henry V's articles are more specific about prisoner treatment than Richard II's. Richard's 1385 articles mention treatment of prisoners in four of the articles, numbers XII, XIII, XIX, XXII. As discussed above, XII establishes that if one knight "downs" a prisoner yet another knight takes that prisoner's parole (being responsible for him), they shall split the ransom (after the King gets his third). XIII forbids soldiers from threatening to kill, or killing, prisoners in ransom disputes. XIX, one of the longer articles, establishes the rules for turning prisoners over to a prisoner-taker's Captain or master, who then escorts the prisoner to the King for interrogation. Afterward, the prisoner is to be kept under guard. XXII adds the clarified procedure of claiming a prisoner by taking their bacinet or gauntlet as proof of ownership. One does get the sense of articles being added to a master list once specific issues become troublesome enough to require control or constraint. XII could easily lead to essentially unsolvable arguments over ransom ownership, and thus instituting a more specific form of indicating whose prisoner is whose in article XXII was no doubt focused on reducing those intra-army conflicts.

Nine specific articles address prisoners and/or ransoms. The regulations seen in Ricard II's 1385 ordinances are repeated, but in different order and with the content of Richard's Article XII changed. Specifically, there were no provisions for sharing a prisoner outlined in Henry V's articles. Both require prisoners be brought to the capturer's Captain, Marshall, etc.; Henry's ordinances require one's captain's permission before a prisoner could be ransomed. This is a way to ensure that prisoners are removed from the battlefield and safety contained and guarded, it also prevents arguments over ransom ownership, which violated article VII. It also ensured the King got his third of ransoms. Article XXVIIII forbids taking a hostage as your own who is sworn to another; it also forbids taking prisoner anyone of English, Irish, or Welsh descent. The logic being such an individual would be a traitor to the king and thus an executable prisoner. This article, along with XXVIII forbidding fights over national origin, tell us that Henry is having to meld troops from different nations into a single army. It also tells us that this was not necessarily occurring easily and without friction.

While Richard's article VII prohibited theft from the army or other soldiers, Henry V extended the ban on robbery and theft to all merchants, but especially those serving the army – a provision often seen in later articles. Henry's intra-camp theft order also expressly mentions the stealing of meat from other soldiers. Such a specific mentioning in an article that already contains prohibitions against theft suggests this was wider spread problem that required specific singling out. A few articles are dropped. For example, Richard II's second article forbade people to touch the King's person without permission; there are no

[4]These are the sorts of details that lead one to consider the existence of an "Ur document" from which these articles were copied and then added to.

such provisions in Henry's articles. Perhaps Richard II's more fragile political standing encouraged him to insert the article; Henry V had no such concern.

Some Articles in Henry V's represented new concerns, not seen in prior articles of battle. Most of these concern order maintenance on and off the battlefield. Article X prohibits captains from having men in their musters that are not "theirs." This alludes to a problem of keeping companies in the army together as soldiers might drift from company to company during a march, camp, or battle. Article XX prohibits being absent from the host without a pass, an expansion into a separate article and specification of the language found in Richard's Article XX, which was focused on maintaining watches and mentions desertion in that context. Two additional articles have no parallel in prior declarations. Article XV prohibits assaults without the "preference of a man of estate." This behavior seems to be covered under Article X concerning calling "*mounte*"; Henry's repetition of the rule highlights the seriousness and potential prevalence of the problematic behavior. The final new ordinance forbids, upon pain of death, anyone who tries to interfere with or resist the King's justice. Article XXI discusses the treatment of *escryers* (spies) – take them to the King or constable for questioning. Spies in camp are also alluded to in Article XIV, which requires the wearing of the Cross of St. George for all members of the army and prisoners and demands execution for anyone caught not wearing the badge or wearing it falsely.

One article stands out as uniquely specific, Article XXV. Article II prohibits attacks on women, a commonly voiced norm in the chivalric literature and in articles of battle. One would assume this refers to all women in all contexts as no exceptions are mentioned in Article II or elsewhere. Article XXV explicitly prohibits rape or pillage of a "woman lying in *gesom*," or child-bed. This represents the specific protection of the some of the most vulnerable people the army would run across: women having recently given birth and their newborns. If the ideals of chivalry had taken even the slightest hold on the minds of Henry V's troops, such an ordinance would be unnecessary as the protection of women and children is assumed due to the demands of chivalric manuals and courtly literature. That it needed to be separated and specifically condemned outside of the usual prohibitions against harming civilians suggests either the behavior was common enough to cause concern or Henry was being particularly detailed and specific in his orders surrounding non-combatants. Yet we don't see this level of granular detail.

There are differences between these disciplinary ordinances, and these, as Keen (1965) and Martinez (2017) point out, arise from the specific context of the wars themselves. For example, both Richard II and Henry V issued orders forbidding, or severely limiting, the amount of foraging allowed by their troops while on the march. As Martinez (2017) points out, the rationales behind the rules were completely different and the product of the type of war the King expected to wage. Richard II was invading Scotland, expecting to face Scottish and French forces as well as a potentially hostile local population. Martinez (2017) argues his foraging prohibitions were a safety precaution where he did not want small groups of his soldiers attacked by civilians or enemies an eminently reasonable concern. Henry V's stated intent upon invading France was to assert his claim to the French throne; he intended to rule the French as their King when the war was over. Such a motivation behind military action often sees key military leaders stress avoiding the abuse of civilians and wide-scale destruction of agricultural infrastructure: Henry V issued the same injunction against destroying fruit trees as we find in Deuteronomy 20:19 (though it does not repeat the order in 20:20 to cut all other trees to use as fortifications). Orchards are a valuable resource that take time to mature and, literally, bear fruit. Thus, in an effort to reduce animosity among the populace and to protect the landscape and his future revenues, his ordinance emphasizes not foraging in the countryside so as his troops were not molesting the locals or depriving them of needed food.[5]

In addition to foraging, Henry V forbade looting in certain contexts. The XXIInd article forbids pillage once peace has been proclaimed. At this point, when a mayor or Burgher gives his loyalty to King Henry, he, his people, and possessions come under the King's protection, especially from the King's own troops. As just mentioned, Article VI forbids robbing merchants who supply the army, an ordinance issued by Richard as well, but Henry's was applied more broadly to all merchants operating in the area, not just those serving the army. Article XXVIII also protects civilians by warning troops to not molest farmers or laborers. While this specific injunction was absent from Richard's 1385 rules, it is found in almost every chivalric manual published to that date (i.e., DeCharney, Bonét, Caxton, Lull) as well as the *Pax* and *Truega*. For Caxton or DeCharney it is dishonorable to visit harm on civilians for both religious and humanitarian reasons. Here, though, Henry is trying to set boundaries about an army invading a land he intends to rule. Again, his rule would be stabilized with support from the peasants and local nobles which is more likely if families and villages were not harmed in the process of the conflict. This concern is mirrored by articles XXXI and XXXV, which prohibit "brenne" (burning or arson) without the King's orders or loot without the approval of one's captain respectively. The Shakespeare scene quoted at the start of this section shows Henry ordering the hanging of solider Bardolph, who stole from a church outside Harfleur. The King orders him hung as a symbol to the entire army that theft from churches will not be tolerated. While clearly dramatized, it was based on a true incident of a solider hung for stealing from a church in Harfleur (Saccio, 2000, p. 82). Enforcement of the rules were real, not just later literary inventions.

Henry V's army that campaigned in France in 1415 appears to be the most rule-bound of the period and before. We know the king insisted on application of the rules during campaign. Yet, at the battle of Agincourt on 25 October 1415, many of the army's guiding ordinances were forgotten or expressly violated, as Keegan (1976, p. 78) points out, "It [Agincourt] is also a story of slaughter-yard behavior and outright atrocity." By mid-October 1415, the English army was low on provisions and tired from marching for 12 days and 200 plus miles. Just as Henry had decided to rest his army, on 20 October, the challenge to battle, which the French had been avoiding since Henry's landing, came. 4 days later, late in the

---

[5]This is a clear difference from The Black Prince's campaign, where he ordered numerous *chevauchées* during sieges. Yet, the future Edward III intended to rule the lands as well.

day, both armies deployed into battles, ready to fight. Nightfall prevented conflict that day, but on the 25th battle would be joined. The field of battle was a clearing on the road to Calais, bounded by forest on both flanks. Henry deployed his troops in a single line, intermixing companies of dismounted men-at-arms with archers. The French deployed in three battles, two lines of dismounted men-at-arms, and a third line of cavalry which wrapped around the French flanks. Arrayed as such, the armies faced each other for 4 hours. Henry ordered his line to advance to approximately 300 yards from the French line – what was considered extreme longbow range. Henry then reset his line and ordered the archers to begin firing volleys of arrows at the French line. This had the desired effect of provoking a French charge by the cavalry on the wings, followed by the men on foot.

The English line held, with the help of the archer's constant rain of arrows. The French cavalry's retreat disrupted the advancing line of infantry. Instead of regrouping, the French pushed forward. Despite taking losses from the continuing fire of the English archers, the French infantry focused their attack on the men-at-arms and engaged the line in melee. At this point, the archers dropped their longbows and attacked with whatever melee weapon they had (i.e., daggers, mallets, swords). With the first line failing, the second French line joined the melee, which was quickly becoming a slaughter of the French. Some French managed to retreat from the melee and rejoin what was left of the French deployment, which consisted of the third line of Mounted Knights. Henry maintained his line in place, knowing the remaining French cavalry constituted a serious threat to his outnumbered force. The English collected surviving combatants worth ransoming and, following Henry's articles, brought them back to the King and Marshall. While waiting for the French line to mount another charge, a group of armed French commoners led by a few knights raided the English baggage camp. This led to Henry's most infamous order of the campaign: he ordered, against the protests of his own men over lost ransoms, that the French prisoners be killed. While the most valuable survived, most of the captives did not. Why would Henry issue an order that violated a basic principle of chivalry, his own articles of battle, and also cost him and his men a large amount of ransom money?

The English army was outnumbered from the beginning, and in Henry's mind the third line of French cavalry was an existential threat to his army. He lacked the manpower to guard a large number of prisoners and have a line in place strong enough to resist another French charge. Afraid of fighting the French in the front and the back, he chose to murder. Keegan (1976) suggests that the lack of repudiation by Henry's peers and the Church indicates the battlefield itself is a legal void, a "legal *dies non*" (109, emphasis in original). This is a dubious interpretation as it would negate the entire purpose of having articles of battle which detail civilian-army interactions or prisoner treatment. It is also an interpretation belied by his own men-at-arms who refused to carry out the order. In part, soldiers were protecting their winnings and their personal honor. The case also presented the classic conundrum armies in the field face – if they treat POWs poorly, they can expect the same treatment if captured. Henry's men-at-arms did not want to set a precedent of prisoner slaughter. Henry's orders were neither approved of nor deemed proper by large part of his host.

To get the order fulfilled, Henry had to task his archers to do the job. As low-born individuals, archers did not fit neatly (or at all) into the calculus of chivalry. Per the Chivalry manuals, they were not placed by God in the ranks of the nobility with the divine-given duty to protect the people and land. As those not of noble birth, their innate constitutional ability to follow the precepts of chivalry was questioned by their Noble peers. These were not men in a socio-cultural position where they would be deemed of even being concerned with concepts such as dishonor; the laws of war – still hung on the skeleton of chivalry and feudalism – didn't apply to them. As we will see below with the trial of Sir Peter von Hagenbach, chivalry was conceived of by its adherents as an international brotherhood of warriors. Knight were bound across nations and states by their social position and obligations. A large number of soldiers of low-birth would be one reason for the issuance of articles of battle. The men at arms would be, supposedly, governed by the laws of war as enshrined in chivalric literature and enforced by each other or a divinity. The commoners were bound by the ordinances and articles enforced by the king and his agents. It may be coincidence that the first extant English Articles of Battle come down to us from a time when the longbow man was an increasingly large part of any force the English fielded. More and more soldiers fighting for England under the banner of St. George were commoners, and the bows of those commoners were winning key battles.

200 archers were assigned to kill an uncounted number of French prisoners. Accounts of the battle indicate the archers had been roaming the no-mans-land between the lines during lulls in fighting to loot the bodies and kill those not worth taking captive. This is not the only incidence of this being recorded in the Hundred Years War. Clearly, at least some of the archers in the English army did not see the killing of a captive or wounded enemy as problematic. It isn't clear how many people were killed. Keegan (1976, p. 111) tells us Henry returned to England with between 1000 and 2000 prisoners. He then raises the astute observation that 200 archers will mechanically have trouble carrying out an execution of such a size, especially with those to be killed still fully armored (save for their gauntlet being surrendered at capture). The slaughter of the prisoners ceased once the third French line abandoned a battle formation and retired from the field. This reinforces Henry's motive as securing a military position, and not wanton murder or revenge for the raid on his own camp.

This is a remarkable event for a number of reasons. The order to slaughter prisoners went directly against the existing normative rules of battle and ransom, as well as directly violating King Henry's own ordinances. If the King is the source of secular law, as was held at the time, he can change those laws at his will His orders on the field overrode those in the articles and thus no "laws" were broken by the killing as Henry's order changed the laws. By using his archers, he evaded the normative expectations of chivalry. Not being of noble birth, archers were not bound by the laws of war as understood by the brotherhood of chivalry in the eyes of Henry and his knights; archers had no honor to lose. Henry's order was also, supposedly, given in response to the violation of the laws of war by the French when they raided the English baggage camp. It is not uncommon behavior in the history of battle for one side to ignore or cast aside protective norms once their enemy has done so.[6] It is possible Henry issued the order to goad the French into quitting the battlefield, as they did. Yet there is nothing recorded to suggest that this would have been anything other than a guess on Henry's part. It could easily have had the opposite effect and triggered the charge of the third French line, which would have put Henry exactly where he didn't want to be: between two large groups of armored French men at arms, even if one group was temporarily unarmed.

The archers at Agencourt, as well as other major defeats of the French in the Hundred Years War, were often portrayed by contemporary chroniclers as either ignorant of the laws of war or we of too base of a nature to follow them. Much of what the archers are maligned for, by both their contemporaries and ours, wasn't a violation of the articles of battle under which they fought, but their innovative use by the English. To begin with, Chivalric honor would define the longbow and crossbow as a dishonorable weapon as using it did not represent true combat – which was properly carried out between two or more men using physical force in hand-to-hand combat to subdue to or kill their enemy. Killing someone at a distance and negating their chance to prove themselves as a warrior was seen as cowardly and unwarrior-like.[7] Archers were so despised that if captured they were either killed or released after having their index and pointer fingers removed from their hands (the fingers which primarily held the bow string as the bow is drawn). This class-based derision led to constant accusations of unchivalric behavior by the archers in multiple English campaigns. However, most of their recorded actions fall well within the orders they were fighting under and the more general norms of war that prevailed at the time.

Apart from the fact that archers were demeaned by men at arms for simply being archers, there were two other main foci of attacks on the base character of archers: their behavior during lulls in combat and after combat, and their use of flanking attacks. Archers, and other common soldiers such as billmen, etc., were well known especially during and after major victories, to roam the battlefield, looting bodies and killing the wounded unworthy of ransoming. At the time, there were no quasi-legal or normative prohibitions against this behavior. It was standard practice for the victors. The French didn't like it as it was a dishonor to the knight and his family to be killed by a low-born archer and left in the mud. But the English or Welsh longbow man was simply doing what was expected. The condemnation of flank attacks is also spurious and more a rationalization of a battle lost than a true assertion of normative or legal principles. Since antiquity, rolling the enemy's flank has always been a primary tactical objective of battle. A key responsibility of a

[6]As a case-in-point, compare the Eastern versus Western theaters of World War II. While all parties violated both the laws of war and growing IHL, the war in the East was waged as "total war" with no concessions or "rules." In the West, there were numerous grave breeches of the laws of war, but they were the exception and not the rule.

[7]This is not a necessary outcome of an honor-based warrior culture. A similar culture of honor, bushido, governed Japanese samurai. It could be argued that in Japan dishonor carried a greater cultural weight, especially as a man's dishonor applied to his whole family. For centuries, the longbow was the favored weapon of the samauri, with the famous kantana only being used if the enemy wasn't routed from a distance.

General when deploying forces is to protect his flanks. Still, at Agincourt, and other major English victories of the war, once the men at arms were engaged in melee and the archers had to be concerned about friendly fire, the archers dropped their bows and swarmed the French flanks. The French men at arms were packed together so tightly, they couldn't easily readjust their formation to defend against the flank attacks. Slaughtering people unable to adequately defend themselves due to their units formation may have smacked of unfairness and cowardice by the French nobility, but it violated no codified or uncodified rules of war. Ironically, it was the arrogance of the nobility, especially pronounced in the French of this period, that excluded the common warrior from the behavioral expectations of chivalry and allowing such behavior. It was the same arrogance that led the French to dismiss the power of the longbow, even though that had repeatedly lost battles to it.

Being unconstrained by the normative matrix of Chivalry, common soldiers were free to do what their captains allowed, without the concerns of courtly honor and prestige. This is another structural impetus to create codified articles of battle to constrain the common foot soldier, while still assuming the laws of chivalry will govern the knights and men at arms. When armies grew and began to incorporate large numbers of commoners who were not as deeply exposed to and were less likely to have internalized the norms of chivalry, other tools were needed to maintain order and direction. Late medieval ordinances or articles of battle arose to fill this social control gap. The context-specific rules also emphasize issuing these types of ordinances was becoming more common and tailored to specific situations, unlike the chivalry manuals which largely ignored socioeconomic or geographic contexts, assuming the rules to be Universally biding on all knighted men.

Salisbury Ordinances

Directly after Henry V's ordinances for the French campaigning, Grose (1786) prints another set of articles, issued by the Earl of Salisbury. The exact date and context of the orders issuance is not clear, but they were issued in the context of army in hostile territory actively claiming geography as it advanced. Some of the articles address concerns we have seen before when armies enter hostile territory. Troops are ordered to keep to their assigned lodgings and to not forage alone. Similar to Henry V's, there are clear concerns here about not abusing the local population. If foraging, soldiers are ordered to only take small amounts of grain for bread, hay for horses, or a "small bestial" [calf/cow]. They were prohibited from stealing and killing the cows, oxen, and other livestock the peasants needed to survive. They were also ordered to not cut down fruit trees. When looting, soldiers were to stay in groups of 5 to 7, with 2 or 3 left behind to guard the unit colors.[8] The order to avoid churches when looting was repeated. There are a few

[8]This is the first mentioning of protecting or guarding a units "colors," or flags with specific identifying insignia and marking. As we will see in the next chapter, capturing and keeping enemies' colors and protecting one's own begins to take on strong symbolic value as military units become more permanent and begin to take on characteristics of more permanent groups.

new ordinances here and those seem to relate specifically to tactical concerns. All archers are ordered to carry a stake, for planting in front of the archer's line to discourage horse charges; this was a common practice among the English army, but earlier surviving ordinances do not spell it out as a requirement. Every two archers were to make pauses of board, head-to-toe shields to protect archers or crossbow men while loading and firing. All men were to cut down a 13 foot tree trunk and strip it of leaves and branches so it could be used to build palisades or other defenses. Every seven men were to have a ladder between them, in anticipation of scaling city walls. These are clearly rules for an army on the offensive expecting to besiege walled towns.

Salisbury's articles also include some of the basic order-maintenance rules typical to such documents. We mentioned the requirement to stay where billeted, troops were warned not to take prisoner a "bulleted man" or child, meaning one who wore the pass/badge of another signifying them to be that person's prisoner. Further, there is an implication in the last article that women of various sorts in camp are disruptive. The troops were ordered to use the bordello established by the army, which was removed from the camp itself. Any soldier found with a woman in camp lost a month's pay and both the soldier and woman will have taken from them all money on their person. Lastly, the woman was run out of camp and had her left arm broken. The issue of female camp followers will be returned to repeatedly as the laws of war evolve. They become a normative element of camp life in this period but pose a number of security issues which must be balanced against the domestic, sexual, and emotional labor they provide. The inclusion of this specific article suggests a strong concern for spies among the female camp followers or prostitutes. The best way to keep a woman from learning key details about the army and then telling the enemy is to ensure she never get into the camp, hence the establishment of a brothel near the camp.

All three of these sets of ordinances highlight the growth of the army as an institution during the medieval era. As armies get larger, more specialized, and more ethnically and operationally diverse, more rules are required to coordinate and control the behavior of individuals within the army. By the twelfth and thirteenth centuries, these are issues that face all nations and their militaries. While chivalry as a normative system and a set of literary tropes is well known, especially by the nobles at the top of the army, the realities of war show that a cultural emphasis on personal honor and a set of scriptural precepts were not enough to maintain order and discipline. In part because armies were increasingly composed of commoners who did not internalize chivalry as a value system and were in fact seen by nobility as unable to follow these rules due to the low nature of their birth. Keeping these men in good order led to the issuance and enforcement of articles of battle. Due to a lack of records, we cannot say how generally successful these rules were at reducing pillage and the abuse of civilians. But we do see, at least among the English, movement toward the codification of rules that apply to the entire army, not just the nobility within it. The Hundred Years War with its multiple, large military mobilizations and deployments provide the impetus for increasing the size of one's army and the need to build and maintain garrisons – either in France or near the English coast. This transforms the army from one based on feudal obligations with service length determined by established rules, into an army that, while not yet a standing army, keeps standing guarded garrisons throughout the territory held. Contracts for terms of service are required, soldiers begin to collect pay for their service, and muster and pay rolls have to be kept. Armies are becoming incipient bureaucracies at this point in western European history. Bureaucracies are by their nature rule bound organizations designed to coordinate and control behavior of the individuals within them (Blau & Meyer, 1987; Perrow, 1984, 1996). The codification of the laws/norms of war into ordinances and articles is part and parcel of incipient bureaucratization due to increasing the size of forces fielded.

By the fifteenth century, there is a recognizable and known set of rules for the behavior of noble and low-born soldiers on and off the field of battle. These norms cut across national and ethnic lines of the time. Yet, we do not have a fully internationalized law, nor do we even have a fully codified and developed code of military law by the end of this period. Articles of War, at least those which survive, ended with the war they were written for (Porter, 1946). There is little to no procedural law discussed in them (as justice was at the discretion of the King or his agents) and no sense of courts martial being used in the field. Curry (2011) argues Richard II's 1385 ordinance represents an internationalized set of laws of war, as the Scottish and French fought under similar articles as the English. While the incestual nature of western European ideas and nobility is well established, it is likely rather than representing a consciously-shared set of semi-codified norms the similarities are the result of a mixture of shared cultural traditions within the noble families of Western Europe and facing the common problems of military organization dealt with by military organization of size. There was a cross-state and cross-nation set of shared norms about waging war in the region and period, and a notion of the Brotherhood of Chivalry superseding national loyalties.

The late medieval ordinances again remind us that war is not a rule-less anarchy of violence and carnage. War is directed violence; normative and human infrastructure is necessary to wage war and guide that violence. It is not surprising as both government, inter-governmental interactions, trade, and the size of militaries increase, we see more conduct codes being written and codified, if only temporarily. It is also not a surprise to see commonalities among these ordinances; the kings issuing them shared a common religious-ideological foundation influenced by the *Pax* and *Truega*. They ruled over similar political economies and faced the same military problems. These codes are a mixture of cultural diffusion and parallel evolution responding to similar forces.

The First International War Crimes Trial (?)

Toward the end of the era, and in many ways exemplary of the core evolution in issues surrounding the laws of war in the period, Sir Peter von Hagenbach is tried for war crimes, an event often seen as the first international war crimes trial in history. When compared with the clearly symbolic show trials discussed in the

Greek era, Hagebach's trial was more "legalistic" drawing on extant procedural and substantive law. The label of "war crimes trial" is not uncontested – most of Hagenbach's crimes were committed during peace time, directed toward civilians, and not committed on the battlefield. In today's terms, these acts would be Crimes Against Humanity under the Rome Statute. Regardless of the name used, that Hagenbach's trial occurred at all and his acts are framed a violation of the international laws of chivalry during the trial, it is notable. Those who sat in judgment were a multinational group; their own position as knights made this more of a military tribunal, than a secular court trial. That they were judging his behavior against the law of chivalry does not necessarily mean he had to commit his actions during wartime. To be pedantic, it wasn't the first war crimes trial, but it was probably the first international military tribunal.

Two distinct historical portraits emerge of Sir Peter, one, which Gordon (2013, pp. 26–27) characterizes as presenting "him as a tyrannical, sexual deviate, bloodthirsty monster," known for levying exorbitant taxes, killing men on a whim, and a sexual licentiousness that went as far as the rape of cloistered nuns. Later writers suggest such a depiction was an unfair portrait presented by his enemies in the wake of the trial. Countering the image of lustful, bloody tyrant, writers such as Vaughan (2002) point out that he was an outsider brought in to govern an unstable border region: Alsace. He was able to secure the peace of the roads and enacted sweeping reforms to reduce local corruption – which did not engender him to all of the local population. But he did so with a heavier hand than his contemporaries. While maybe not the bloodthirsty monster of contemporary depictions, Hagenbach's murders, rapes, and exploitative taxation is unquestioned. On Easter 1474, Hagenbach's garrison mutinied and placed him under house arrest. He was later moved to the local prison. He was repeatedly tortured during his interrogations, eventually confessing to many crimes, including a plot to remove and eradicate the citizens of Breisach, a town on the Rhine opposite Alsace. He was charged with murder, perjury, conspiracy to commit murder, and multiple counts of rape. He was convicted by his peers, other members of the brotherhood of chivlary, and executed.

While this might not have been the first truly international war crimes trial in Europe, it does show a remarkable shift toward the use of law and courts to resolve the problems caused by men such as Sir Peter Hagenbach.[9] In some ways, pre-saged by the tenth-century *Pax and Treuga*, by the end of the medieval period notions of law, both what we would think of as domestic and international laws, have become a tool to control the worst behaviors exhibited by militaries and their leadership. Hagenbach is an exception in the period due to his "heavy-handedness" being put on trial and his facing formal justice proceedings. This is part of a broader movement toward the codification of law and the empowerment of law as the key form of dispute resolution – as political power begins to coalesce

[9]Some question the international nature of the trial, as most participants were subjects of the Holy Roman Empire (HRE). Yet, that was not a national identity, such as being English, Saxon, Frankish, or Flemish. The HRE was a state composed of a plurality of nations.

into nations (if not states), governments (as separate from the a singular head of state) emerge as protectors of local social order. This formalization of social control mirrors other political and economic consolidation occurring in the period. Kings used law to extend their domestic power. Henry II and his heirs mounted a massive project to codify a "common law of the land" in the UK; this is a direct insertion of the Crown into the daily affairs of its subjects. This consolidation of power is the product of, and a key contributor to, a process of violence monopolization that will cumulate in the modern era with nation-states claiming total monopolies on legitimate and legal violence. Thus is should not seem surprising that attempts to curtail war-related violence strongly emerge here. Hagenbach's trial exhibits a broader attempt to bring these behaviors under control and under control in a *legal* resolution process, not a battlefield process. It is a recognition that a military wrong can be resolved in a legal venue and not a military one.[10] It is also highlighted the movement of power from canon to secular courts, which dispense punishments on the living and not the dead. Peter Hagenbach was hung for his crimes, not merely excommunicated for them. The Church is the originator of much of the anti-atrocity law efforts in the period, and Catholic ideology still rests at the core of both canon and secular laws of the age. Hagenbach's trial marks the secularization of the laws of war and their enforcement. It exhibits the extant patterns of leaving the judgment of the wrongdoing of soldiers to other soldiers, of favoring military tribunals over ordinary courts to try these crimes. This is grounded in the belief that only those who know war can judge others actions within it, an extension of the logic which will create the peer-jury. This is a pattern that holds until the second half of the twentieth century and the United Nation's creation of the ad hoc tribunals for the former Yugoslavia and Rwanda. Those trials represent a concerted international effort to bring military and other atrocity crimes into civilian not military courts.

By the end of the late medieval period, we see the beginning of nation-states coalescing, increasing the power and resources controlled by states and increasing the number and severity of wars. The early modern period in Europe was incredibly bloody and violence-wrought. Protestantism's birth gave rise to Europe religious wars whose savagery was at times unparalleled. Trade and global contentions continued to expand, leading to the "discovery" of the western hemisphere and the on-set of colonialism in the Americas. This intensified competition among European powers to collect the resources of the New World, competition that led to war on land and at sea. At the same time, Enlightenment ideologies develop highlighting the innate value and worth of individuals and individual perception and knowing, which will catalyze both scientific advancement of weaponry and nurture ideologies of democracy, which will produce its own series of wars in the forms of major revolutions in the United States, Hatti, and France. These contexts and circumstances will shape the laws of war over the next centuries.

[10]Even if those procedural laws allowed for trial by combat and the like.

Chapter 6

Early Modern Wars and the Birth of the Law of Nations

The Age of Reason saw a rationalization and refinement of the idea of law binding the behavior of nation states, including during armed conflict. Earlier notions of Natural Law are dismissed in favor of rationally deduced principles based upon careful analysis of current actions and behaviors, an early version of *realpolitik*, often referred to as Positive Law. Not only does this period see the development of a new outlook vis-á-vis law and law formation, it also brings the behavior of nation-states under the rule of law, and also attempts to do so with inter-state violence. This is the era of the earliest framing of "laws" of war in the writings of Grotius (1625/1971), as well as the work of Hobbes (1651/1985). War is disentangled from justice and an individualized conception, in favor of a framework that defines war as a condition existing between states, not individuals. Limitations of the means of war also begin to surface, though were not always accepted or practiced in the field (Neff, 2005, p. 150). Many key concerns of contemporary International Humanitarian Law emerge as law is rationalized, as is the state. Law, including the laws of war, become folded into a new positivist world view with an empirical and scientific drive during the seventeenth and eighteenth centuries which reaches its apex in the nineteenth century. While a framework for governing the war-making behavior of states develops in this period, the ideal of sovereignty work against the development of a "community" of nations, with rules binding them to acts. Rather, following the laws of war is voluntary and any sanctions for violating them are at best informal and at the whim of other nation-states. Yet, as seen in numerous conflicts, such whims are often backed by military force, reflecting the penultimate belief of the period: might makes right.

This period sees the formalization of the Articles of War approach to military regulation. These are legal decrees that dictate acceptable and unacceptable behavior for the troops during the course of a military campaign, and appropriate punishments for violators.[1] By the fourteenth century, as we saw in the prior chapter, Articles of War were written for a specific war and were only in effect for that specific war, ending as soon as the conflict did (Porter, 1946; Rodgers, 2004). Later in the period, such

[1]Some were written to apply in peace time as well, but most were not.

A Socio-Legal History of the Laws of War, 95–129

doi:10.1108/978-1-78769-857-420231006

articles will become standing sets of rules and regulations that received infrequent updating, often at the onset of a new conflict.

So what separates Articles of War from law? In some definitions of law, nothing. When Richard II or Henry V issued their ordinances, they carried the weight of any other English law. The same would apply to any other monarchical state whose sovereign issued such orders. Academically, the articles would be considered a legal code like any other as it specifies both substantive and procedural elements, it is codified, and it attached to mechanisms of enforcement. As states evolve and become more bureaucratic, intra-military orders for battlefield behavior are typically developed within the military – this is the root of the contemporary "laws of war" approach discussed in Chapter 1. They function as organizational rules; they are not applied to those unconnected with the armed forces. They are adjudicated and punished internally.

The Early Modern period sees the development of what we think of as modern nation-states, but also the adoption of, or increase in size of, standing armies. Often filled with foreign mercenaries, criminals, and the like early on, these were not the professional standing armies that we think of today. They weren't filled with patriotic volunteers willing to fight for a nation or a people, or professionals trained and committed to a specific ideal, but those in lower socioeconomic classes that either lack other opportunities or were particularly attracted to soldering or violence. The need for discipline was seen as strong, whether in garrison or the field (Rodgers 2004).

New views of law emerge during and after the Enlightenment. For centuries prior, law was made and proclaimed by a King or similar sovereign leader. While some nations had political representative bodies in this period, i.e., England's Parliament, they are much weaker at the start then the end of the era. Toward the end of this period, we see the first true modern republics take shape: the United States and the French Republic. Keegan (1976) argues that by the 1600s, the general Enlightenment focus on classicism captured the military minded as well. Their neoclassicism brought renewed attention to the Roman army, making dominant in the minds of soldiers "Roman military practices—drill, discipline, uniformity of dress—and Roman military ideas—of intellectual leadership, automatic valor, unquestioning obedience, self-abnegation, loyalty to unit" (p. 63). Disciplinary practices borrowed were from the old Roman military manuals, such as flogging as a frequent punishment for a variety of offenses. Keegan points out that even the symbols of Rome were borrowed, i.e., the French army adopting the Eagles of the Caesars as a symbol on both uniforms and standards.

The nature of warfare and army composition continues on the arc of change we see during the late Middle Ages. Armies are getting larger, more bureaucratically organized, have longer service commitments, and are provided (semi) regular pay.[2] France was the first European nation to have a full-time professional

---

[2]I realize using this term to describe social organizations of the period may strike some as anachronistic, but it is applicable. Armies are becoming budding bureaucracies, a trend that will become standardized by Fredrick of Prussia.

standing army; its 1445 *compagnies d'ordonnance* established year-round service with full pay for this group of elite troops (Rogers, 2004). The Genoa Ordinances of 1536 created the Spanish *tercios* system, which lasted until the early 1900s (Gonazález de Lèon, 2004). Through the 1500s and 1600s, the rest of Europe followed. This is a substantial shift from mustering a force based on feudal obligations, where pay was not necessarily expected as one served out of feudal duty. Armies are growing with population size increases, but their size increase is more driven by Kings' desires to raise larger forces. Larger armies require more control and coordination, thus more rules and incipient bureaucracy (i.e., hierarchical offices, top-down control, role specialization, etc.).

Weaponry also changes significantly in this period, specifically the use of black powder weapons. The late medieval period saw the development of early artillery, these bombards were very large cannons which had to be dug into the ground to set up to fire. They had a very slow fire rate, as little as four or five shots per day. This was the combined result of needing to reset the gun in position, wait for it to cool so it could be reloaded, the time it took to load both powder and shot, and a fear of bursting a weapon from overuse (an all too common happening in the early use of artillery). Typically, these cannons fired smoothed rocks (cast iron shot later) and were used to weaken fortifications. They also had a psychological effect on defenders: they were loud, created large reverberations upon shooting and the shot impact, and were the only threat to a city wall or gate. Their successes were less than expected and use was infrequent due to cost of manufacture and transportation. Overall, they had little impact on warfare in the late medieval period but served as a foundation on which innovation would produce different armaments using black powder projectiles. Artillery gets smaller and more mobile, allowing it to be used outside of a siege situation and on the battlefield proper. Individual black powder weapons are developed.

We also see the earliest handguns at the end of the late medieval/start of the early modern period, followed by the earliest muskets in the fifteenth century. Initially, these too are slow firing weapons prone to misfires or explosions. Generals tended to use them in a similar manner as bows and crossbows at first, but they were neither reliable nor accurate. A second doctrinal innovation would reshape the way in which handguns were used. The English Longbowmen and Men at Arms on foot during the Hundred Years War showed the limitations of the heavy cavalry charge. On the continent, another weapon was looked to for defense against cavalry particularly: the pike. Even if one could get a horse to charge into a wall of pikes, the effect is almost predetermined. While the heavy cavalry charge persisted in warfare until World War II, gun powder weapons, with the help of pikes early on, will make traditional uses of cavalry irrelevant.[3] Blocks of pikemen either interspersed with archers and hand gunners or positioned on their flanks became a dominant formation in the early modern period

[3]The Poles used heavy cavalry charges against German tanks. The heavy cavalry charge fell out of favor after the Napoleonic conflicts, though the Crimean war was the last of their wide-spread use (Parker, 2020).

and was seen fully utilized in the War of the Roses. As guns get better (quicker to fire, more accurate, and less likely to explode in the firer's face), the number of longbow men used in English armies declines until they are completely replaced by gunners. The pike and shot doctrine is adopted across Europe in this period. Cavalry is still used; Dragoons, light cavalry often armed with pistols, saw wide use. Heavy cavalry remained but did not have the impact on the battlefield it did in the middle ages. Facing a hail of shot until a company of horsemen charges into a wall of pikes did not produce the best results militarily.

A third significant change which begins in this time, and continues through World War II, is the change in the function nobles played on the battlefield. They no longer made-up mass blocks of heavy cavalry or heavy infantry. While the gun made the mounted, heavily armored knight a thing of the past, it gave nobles a different role to play: as officers. Instead of being grouped into battalions and used as shock cavalry, nobles were scattered across units of foot and horse in leadership roles as officers. There is still a cultural belief in the innate superiority of their superior leadership abilities in this period. There is still a predominance of nobility among cavalry men, though they no longer have the monopoly they did previously.

As Wilson (2004, p. 152) points out that these new forces were "characterized by hierarchical control…[p]ersonnel were subject to greater discipline as their behavior was intended to harmonize relations with civilians and to improve combat effectiveness." This new discipline is often codified in articles of war or other legal proclamations or statutes that contain substantive and procedural legal elements. These laws mark a formalization of military rules, a distinct shift from relying on informal social controls such as the literary concept of chivalry or the basic humanitarianism at the root of Christianity. Controls are being shifted from internal to external. As Reckless' (1961a, 1961b) containment theory explores, individuals are subject to both internal and external social controls. Internal controls are those internalized norms which we use to guide our behavior in various contexts. While they originate from the outside culture, they are brought in and made one's own – a process called internalization. Once a set of norms are internalized, then the social actor draws upon them in determining what is or is not allowable under their own values. Violation of these values tends to produce cognitive dissonance and other negative emotionality, which can serve to deter an individual from breaking such rules. External social controls come from outside the individual; they are imposed by an external social institution and social actors. These can be informal norms and informal control mechanisms, like family, friends, or co-workers, or they can be agents or agencies of government or other formalized institutions. Formal social control, such as law or articles of war. This brings with it the necessity of a centralized power, typically the state (even if embodied in one man or woman – a king or queen), to establish the rules, or issue the articles of war and that has the resources and authority to enforce the regulations. The natural hierarchy of armed forces, which as noted is intensifying in this period, provides the power structure needed to establish structures to identify and adjudicate violations of the articles. That said, there is much here still at the discretion of the captains on the ground or the General or King in bringing charges and in determining punishment. This chapter examines the continued evolution of articles of war by closely examining two sets of war articles issued in the early modern period which strongly reflect the social and military changes occurring. First, I will examine Tudor Articles of War, then discuss the code issued by the Swedish King Gustav Adolphus I.

Tudor Articles of War

On or around 6 June 1487, Henry VII, issued an order that was a combination of concerns for public and military order. The occasion was the last major push of the War of the Roses, with a Yorkist army landing on the 4th of June and picking up Yorkist loyalists as it marched inland.[4] The short decree mirrors earlier and later ordinances. It begins with the common injunction against causing any harm to the church, its peoples or its properties. It follows with orders prohibiting intra-camp quarrels and fighting (which appears much earlier here than in prior articles), then those against harming civilians (both their persons and property). The third paragraph repeats the now typical commands to lodge where your harbinger puts you and to stay with one's battle. Then curiously, the proclamation repeats the content of the second order again but extends it to all quarrels, not just intra-army ones. As this is the end of a long, bloody civil war it is not surprising to see the orders twice tell men not to quarrel based on their backgrounds. In trying to build a singular English army, especially in the wake of a civil war, Henry VII is facing some of the same ethnic and regional tensions as Richard II and Henry V's armies did, yet likely intensified in the immediate political-military context. The order then protects those bringing food to camp.

Unlike earlier articles which punished solders for crying "havoc" or for getting others to mount and move out or charge a position without permission, Henry VII words his orders to provide a set of highly specific commands for mount preparation: saddle your mount at the first trumpet sounding, bridle it at the second, and mount and await orders at the third. Failing to do so warrants imprisonment. The orders also prohibit shouts and horn blowing in camp after the watch has been set. Further, and also new, the orders attempt to curtail the size of the camp followers by prohibiting vagabonds and "common women" from following the army.[5] The final command is to obey the King and his lieutenants when ordered to charge (with the reverse implication, don't charge without orders, a common rule in earlier English articles of war).

What is missing are the, until now, often multiple and complex rules surrounding prisoner taking and ransoming. One could assume that such norms were so deeply built into the army's practices by this time it was unnecessary to state them. Though the repetition of other common articles undermines this claim. Another reasonable assumption is that prisoners were not expected to be taken and ransomed. The

[4]This is two years after the Battle of Bosworth, which cemented Edward VII's control of the throne and paved the way for his marriage to Elizabeth of York.

[5]A frequent euphemism used for prostitute.

Yorkist holdouts were traitors and, by the logic of the era, so were all who fought for them. They faced prison or death, not ransom and not the treatment of equals that ransom implies. The concerns for civilians also take on greater emphasis here as any civilians, or clergy, encountered would be English subjects. Similar to Henry V, Henry VII is fighting on what he considered his territory. Ensuring the proper behavior of the army toward the civilians they will encounter would be a paramount concern. Especially in the waning days of a rebellion.

The next complex war ordinance is issued in London on or around May 15, 1513 in advance of Henry VIII's invasion of France. For the Gascon expedition of 1512, Henry VIII framed his war rationale not on his claims to the French throne or lands (though recovery of the Plantagenet lands was a major aim), but a defense of the Church against the numerous offenses of Louis XII. In 1512, trying to raise monies for the Gascon campaign, Henry VIII had a letter by Pope Julius II read to Parliament which outlined the French King's offenses against the Church and Christianity.[6] He had a doctor of cannon law compose legal commentary justifying the right to war (Cruickshank, 1969; Murphy, 2015), thus establishing, at least in the eyes of Henry VIII, that God favored his side. Henry's use of "defending the church" as a war rationale presages what is to come in Europe once the Protestant Reformation begins (ironically, with Henry's first divorce).

Though promised provisions by Ferdinand once in Spain, after receiving supplies at Bermio, the English were not resupplied later in the campaign. Despite orders against injuring the Spanish, the army was reduced to plundering Spanish goods, which were vigorously defended by the locals (Murphy, 2015). Further, the army lacked appropriate shelter in the field. It also spent great deal of time idle as Ferdinand conducted his Navarre campaign. As the situation worsened so did English treatment of both Spanish and French civilians. Morale bottomed out to the point of outright mutiny in July. Though suppressed, morale didn't improve and, in part, led to the return of the army to England without attacking their main target. The campaign was a military failure and a public relations disaster. A campaign meant to introduce Henry VIII's military might to the world degraded into pillage and in-fighting. This behavior was not unnoticed and "the shameful behavior of the English soldiers was reported at courts across Europe" (Murphy, 2015, p. 54). The results of the campaign led Henry to plan another invasion for the following year; the behavior of his troops in the Gascon campaign clearly influenced his issuance of detailed Articles of Battle for the 1513 campaign.

Said articles were issued in London on or about May 15, 1513. It is recorded that these orders were read aloud to the middle-ward upon its arrival in Calais (Cruickshank, 1969, p. 26).[7] It is likely that the other wards at some point before

[6]This was early in his reign, when he was considered by the Papacy to be one of the strongest defenders of Christendom in Europe.

[7]As with prior English armies, the invasion force of 1513 was divided in three: the fore-ward, the middle-ward, and the rear-ward. Each was transported to France separately and departed Calais separately. In a large part, this is a matter of logistics; if all three wards arrived at once, the number of people would overwhelm the city.

or after their crossing of the channel had the articles read to them as well. The articles start with material not yet seen in preserved English battle orders: the reasons for the war itself are given in the first two paragraphs. The first rule-article is clear and unambiguous: obey the King and his lieutenants or be hung then drawn and quartered. While prior, and later, articles make it clear that death is the penalty for violating much of the King's orders, this is the first time it is clearly stated at the start. Henry VIII was clearly unhappy with his army's performance in Spain. He took steps to avoid some of the problems which led to bad behavior among his troops, for example basing his invasion out of Calais to help solidify his supply lines.[8] Issuing a rather extensive set of orders for troop behavior was another step; Henry clearly did not want this campaign to devolve into what was experienced the year before.

Most of the standard rules we have become familiar with in articles of battle for the English army in this period. Don't stray ahead of your battle, stay where the quartermaster puts you in camp, keep your watch, don't leave without permission, keep good order, no unlawful assemblies or attempts to draw troops out of the host, no pillage without orders, no crying havoc, don't mess with the locals, use the cross of St. George as an insignia, etc. These have become standard fare of the laws of war in Europe, entrenched survivals of the *Pax* and *Truega.*

Many of the rules are familiar, having appeared in previous articles, but sometimes with slightly new twists. For example, there are the standard prohibitions against attacking the church and its property. But, Henry VIII added the condition: unless they support the French King. Then they are legitimate targets of violence and pillage. Since Louis has been excommunicated by Rome, his entire nation has been excommunicated and any clergy still loyal to the French King are deemed heretics and not worthy of protection. This is one of many examples of young Henry VIII's strong support of the Catholic Church, even being named "Defender of the Faith" by Pope Leo X in 1521. In another instance, the typical rule about avoiding fights concerning place of origin is codified here. While earlier expeditionary forces were ethnically diverse (i.e., English, Welsh, Normans, etc.), this force also contained German mercenaries to fill out the ranks, increasing the possibility of intra-army ethnic conflict. Rules about keeping order in camp have added to them prohibitions against dice, cards, or other such games which could easily generate disagreement and thus conflict, as well as rules for maintaining quiet after dark. Through the sixteenth to eighteenth centuries armies were composed increasingly of mercenaries, enhancing ethnic diversity within the ranks but also increasing the likelihood of long-standing interpersonal disputes. An English company may find itself next to a company of Germans in the line; one they might have previously fought against.

As with Henry V, Henry VIII ordered his soldiers to not loot and pillage the countryside, but the later Henry included the stipulation "after peace is declared." Once there was peace and a region's leader had sworn his loyalty to the English

---

[8]Though the victual train would become a target of French forces as the army marched out of Calais.

King, the people were considered English subjects and thus had the king's protection. Until then, they were heretics worthy of abuse.

New, or significantly revised, articles tend to address one of three main issues: camp sanitation, camp followers, and army organization-soldier pay (including ransom). For the first time, we see rules on keep a camp free of human and animal waste. By this time, people understand the connection between sewage and disease to a degree. Thus, the King orders his troops to dig latrines for the burial of their waste if they are going to be in the same camp for more than 3 days. Even on single night stops, the troops were expected to bury their (and their livestock's) excrement away from the immediate camp area. Dysentery (the flux), cholera, and other diseases passed by human waste were a common peril of troops both in camp on campaign and in camp on siege. Since the innovation of mass armies, more soldiers die from disease and accident than from combat. Here we see an early attempt to codify sanitary practices in military camps.

Camp followers were a facet of military life through much of history, a motley assemblage of commoners who trailed after the army for a variety of reasons. This mass of civilians included wives of enlisted men, merchants hoping to sell to the soldiers, women offering domestic or sexual labor to the troops, as well as vagabonds, thieves, and others with no better social or economic prospects. Camp followers were an order problem. They represented a mass of semi-dependents to the army's leaders. They also tended to introduce conflicts and disease, including venereal diseases. The article of battle discussed here attempt to eliminate women from camp followers. One article prohibits common men from bringing their women from home with them on campaign. Another prohibits "common women" from coming within three miles of the camp upon pain of being branded on the cheek.[9] Such women were seen as problematic for several reasons: venereal disease, causing conflicts between men, and being potential spies for French interests.

A number of new rules emerge from the organization demands of providing soldiers with regular pay for service. While at the time England was still relying on the older system of feudal allegiances to muster troops (Cruickshank, 1969; Murphy, 2015), it had instituted regular pay for military service. While expensive, it was hoped that regular pay would cure soldiers of many of the problems most commonly faced on the battlefield, mainly desertion or unauthorized looting. Organizing a pay system for thousands of men is a complex process and Henry VIII added several rules dealing with pay. Captains were responsible for distributing pay to the troops and had 6 days to do so once he received the funds from the paymaster. The muster roles for those under any given Captain were both records of service and pay records. Captains had to report the loss of any battle members within 10 days to the King's men, whether the loss was due to desertion, discharge, or death. This allowed the king to have a reasonably accurate accounting of the number of men in service as the campaign progressed; it also kept the payrolls clean as such individuals were removed. Individual soldiers were required to join the muster relevant to their home. If a man joined a

[9]A euphemism for prostitutes.

muster, he wasn't part of, both he and the muster's Captain would be punished. The solider for being where he ought not be (and unknown for pay purposes) and the captain for not realizing he had an extra man. There was also the common trick of Captain's loaning each other troops to make their own muster quotas (and the salary of a ghost soldier). Captains were also ordered not to take more men into their personal retinue than absolutely necessary, essentially no more than needed to fix the captain's tent (Cruickshank, 1969, p. 34). Violating this would cost a Captain a month's pay and the "extra" soldiers would be imprisoned.

The articles establish, once one entered the army as an archer, one remained an archer unless one had direct permission from the King to take up different arms. This concern is repeated later as well, stating "No one take upon him to bear no new arms other than he is born to blood" unless told to do so by royal order. The articles themselves suggest that this is to reduce tensions between the socio-economic classes, as class was tied to one's role on the battlefield. Recall, chivalric manuals tied the world's order, in which Chivalry was central, to divine will and grace. One was born in the social segment which God intended, the emic logic went, thus to bear arms above one's "blood" was an offense to both military and social order. Men at arms, mounted or on foot, were to be of royal blood, while archers and billmen were commoners. Knights shunned the bow as a peasant's hunting tool (Bartlett, 1995; Gies, 1984) and saw its use as dishonorable. A knight using commoner weapons would face no end of shame and ridicule from his peers. They are also not very useful in the type of formation the knight would be fighting in. Commoners using the arms and armor of a knight were reaching above their station and violating the divine order by pretending to be something they are not. They also would have lacked human capital gained by the year's long apprenticeships knights undertook as squires and pages.

Henry VIII also made changes to the rules surrounding prisoner taking and ransoms. While a token of surrender is still required, it need not be a gauntlet or bassinet, it can be any object. Some rules about prisoner taking and ownership reverted back to the procedures Richard II proscribed. Specifically, the notion of men splitting a ransom is reintroduced for cases where a knight is taken down by one warrior, and surrenders to him, but, later surrenders again to another soldier. Under Henry V's articles, the later solider got the whole ransom. Additional rules were added ensuring the thirds system was maintained (one third of a ransom goes to the king, one-third to the taker's commander, and one-third to the taker of the prisoner). Captains were required to present prisoners to the treasurer of wars, allowing accurate record to be kept, and ensuring the King got his take. Rules were also added for plunder. For common soldiers, they are to give one third of all loot they find to their Captains. The captain pays one third of the total of his receipts to the King. That this process was codified in war articles would suggest that getting an accurate accounting of ransoms and loot to ensure the King received his share was difficult at best. The procedures outlined in the articles are a step toward stricter monitoring of wealth taken in battle. Additionally, codifying the rules also codifies punishment for violation of said rules.

Cruickshank (1969) claims that "[D]iscipline on the 1513 expedition was. . .exceptionally good throughout" (p. 94), especially compared with earlier and later English armies. He attributes this to the popularity of the King, good recruiting practices, and a lack of "war weariness" among the English troops and populace. Noting the small number of offenses recorded, he opts to read this as a lack of problems over a lack of records or lack of enforcement.[10]

After leaving Calais, the first major target was Thérouanne; the Fore-ward stopped about a mile outside of the city and began to set up camp while the middle- and after-ward arrived. On 4 August 1513, Henry had to have additional orders issued by Lord Salisbury to keep order in the camp. Three main concerns are addressed. First, sanitation is reemphasized with the reissuance of the order to bury waste in latrines. The second repeated the injunctions about not fighting among your fellow soldiers, especially over place of origin. The Almains (Germans) are specifically mentioned here, suggesting a level of tension between the English troops and German mercenaries. English troops are also exhorted to turn bad behaving Germans over to their captains. The third was plea to simply obey the laws as set down and to report violations of the law, or any other grievance, to the Lord Marshall on Mondays, Wednesdays, or Fridays. Clearly, life in the camp was more disordered than desired, and critical conduct rules had to be re-issued. Even so, they were not always followed, with a major disturbance occurring on 15 August that pitted English solider against German solider, climaxing in a standoff in the middle-ward between English Archers and German pikemen protecting their countrymen who had commandeered the ward's guns.

At this point in the history of warfare, the importance of ransoms was wanning as is the centrality of plunder as pay for soldiers. By instituting regular pay, for both those mustered for summer service or those serving year-round in garrisons, morale should improve and the desire to steal, from either other soldiers or civilians, would be strongly reduced. Additionally, the forms battles began to take in the period changed and made prisoner taking less relevant. Seeing the effectiveness of ranged weapons at Crécy, Agincourt, and Poitiers demonstrated the proof of concept, if you will, for ranged warfare. This grows as handguns become more available and affordable. Battles are no longer large blocks of men crashing into each other, then entering into man-on-man fights. Primacy is given to bows and guns, protected by billmen or pikes. Neither mass-ranged attacks nor the "crash of pikes" was conducive to taking prisoners or being able to figure out who was responsible for any given man's fall. Henry VIII's 1513 expedition proved quite profitable, but it is one of the last times we see major profits made in war through ransoms. The technology of warfare is changing, the rules of war will change as well. By the fifteenth and sixteenth century, "political elites throughout Western Europe recognized that armies needed to be better controlled" (Parker, 2020, p. 165). It was also clear that the state was the only tool available to do so. Thus, we will begin see a proliferation of Articles of Battle being used until states create permanent laws to control standing armies.

---

[10]Though he acknowledges the possibility that crimes were not recorded or punished.

The Thirty Years War

The Thirty Years War is central to this story for several reasons. The wars of religion saw a militarization of Europe not before seen. While mostly fought in what is now modern Germany, the conflict was both an internal conflict with the Holy Roman Empire (HRE) and an international war. There had been conflict between Catholics and Protestants in the Holy Roman Empire since the Reformation, ranging from riots to warfare. When Archduke Frederick demanded all Catholic lands taken since 1555 at the 1608 Imperial Diet, protestant towns began to fortify and prepare armed forces for conflict. These earliest conflicts were internal to the HRE. However, as the war progressed, most nations in Europe joined in the fighting at some time, making it an international affair (Parker, 2020). Numerous political and social forces catalyzed the war and its growth. Mortimer (2004, pp. 101–102) explains that three key developments in the period facilitated the war. The first was the military contracting system that facilitated the hiring of large numbers of mercenary fighters in a relatively short period of time. The second was the rise of credit and numerous available sources thereof for princes and kings to take advantage of in hiring the large mercenary armies. Often, armies would be fielded with the sovereign paying little more than a down-payment on the mercenary service, with more being paid out as the war went along. This is attractive as the armies can be mustered and put in the field at a fraction of the eventual cost, with the sovereign hoping that pillage or war indemnities would be available to pay off the rest. It was also finically useful to break pay into smaller allotments; as soldiers were killed in battle, payroll was reduced. The third facilitator was extracting monies from occupied territories to continue to fund the army. This was not accomplished by pillage or looting, but by taxation. It is clear by this time that any sort of feudal obligations of service have been fully replaced with a pay-for-service model. This makes war more expensive monetarily for nations and rulers. It also can incite orders for plunder as the main goal of the military conflict may be being driven by religious conflicts but it still costs money to keep an army in the field. Armies have grown too large to support themselves via foraging on the march without leaving a wasteland behind them (Mortimer, 2004). While this may be less of a concern if one does not seek to govern the people of the land the army passed through (or care about good relationships with neighbors), it is increasingly seen as a problematic behavior. While armies in the field will forage down to the current day, this is a shift away from making pillage *the* way to fund and pay an army. At first the concern is about foraging in their home country on the march out to war. A sovereign, like Adolphus Gustavus I of Sweden, will easily realize the disruption – economic, social, and political – of an army preying on its own people. Later, he will be fighting in the territory of allies, thus presenting a similar concern about restraint. His response is the creation of an extensive set of articles of battle to constrain the worst impulses of his troops (we discuss Adophus' articles extensively below).

This approach is also in contrast to that taken by Frederick and the HRE armies, who were well known for infamous sackings of cities. For example, HRE commander Count Tilly sacked Magdeburg in 1631 "in a three-day orgy of killing" which Protestants saw as one of the most serious atrocity events in their recent history but was "justified by Catholics as the chastening of unbelievers enjoined in the Old Testament" (Parker, 2020, p. 162). The war created a rush of diplomacy, with those who shared a faith seeking allies against those who did not. While co-religionist leanings were not always the best political or military choices for allies, the religious divided in Europe was too wide to cross with diplomacy.

With the advancements in firearms and artillery, combat was more lethal than ever and it was growing easier to unintentionally impinge upon civilians and civilian space in the fighting of battles. While civilians are always affected by wars (see Hartigan, 1982), now they are imperiled not only during the sack of a city or an unfortunate meeting with a group of soldiers out foraging, but in their daily lives if they are living near a combat zone. The potential, and real, damage to civilians and civilian property during the wars will drive not only internal military regulations to reduce the impact of military operations on civilians but will also catalyze the stirrings of the civilian movement to reduce the damages of war which will eventually become Internal Humanitarian Law. Europe's wars of religion produced more than their fair share of atrocity events. With something so central to one's identity as religion being the primary driver of warfare, it is easier than usual to otherize an enemy that has historically been a neighbor. The war itself and other conflicts of the era and the way it played out was an impetus for rethinking and revising military laws. The resolution of the war in the Treaty of Westphalia also created a new framework for international relations that makes the idea of real international law a possibility, be it governing military or trade. The treaty doesn't quite create a community of nations, as is envisioned later after each world war, but establishes basic principles of inter-state interactions.

King Gustave Adolphus I and the Swedish Intervention

One central, but later entering, player in the Thirty Years War was the Swedish King Gustave Adolphus. The King was well known as a key innovator of military tactics in the period, Cooper (1981, p. 130) suggesting he is responsible for the first use of combined arms teams. For our purposes, what is of interest is Gustave's 150-point 1621 Articles of War issued and read before his men both before and after leaving their homeland for the continent.[11] This represents that longest, most comprehensive, extant set of war articles we have seen to date. They include most of the same prohibitions as earlier war articles, 17 articles are distinctly religious is nature, 33 address order and internal military organization, 52 address offenses committed by troops against the army or other soldiers in the army, eight address

[11]There two extant printings of these articles. Roe and Watts (1632) and Winthrop (1920). Roe and Watts print the 1621 and 1631 Articles separately. Winthrop prints them all together and the order of presentation differs in places. There are also slight differences in translations, though the content and meaning does not substantially change. Here, I work from Roe and Watts (1632) as it provides the full provenance of the articles where Winthrop (1920) does not.

interactions with the enemy, seven focus on civilians, and 33 focus on procedural law.[12] While there are many articles here, we have seen before, many traceable directly to the *Pax* and *Truega*, there are also quite a number of new articles, and new concerns being expressed.

The extensive focus on procedural issues, while not new, provides a much more systematic discussion of court martial procedures that we have seen to date. It outlines a highly legalistic set of procedures for the administration of justice in his army. Many historians and contemporary commentators noted the high level of discipline among the Swedish troops and the general lack of bad behavior, especially early in the war (Cooper, 1981; Macmunn, 1920). Macmunn (1920, p. 130) states that in contrast to the armies of the Holy Roman Empire, "The ribaldry and license which so often marred the appearance and morale of the troops were entirely absent from even the youngest corps" of Swedish troops. He also links the better discipline to adoption of a definite uniform for officers and enlisted, suggesting the uniformity of appearance increased morale and solidarity in the ranks and intimidated their opponents. Uniforms will become increasingly important and elaborate in the following years, becoming a symbol of the state's strength and national pride.

The first notable aspect of Gustavus' articles of war is that the first 16 articles, and article 119, are religious in nature. This is not surprising as the Thirty Years War was essentially a war of religion. Many long-standing secular disputes and conflicts played out before and during the war, but the main drive of Augustus and his allies was the protection of Protestant nations on the continent from the Catholic Holy Roman Empire who sought to eradicate Protestantism as another heresy. Articles 2–16 set up a number of piety rules: no blaspheming, no taking God's name in vein, do not deride God's words or sacraments, etc. There were also rules of attendance for twice-daily prayers, as well as rules that essentially forbade any other activity in camp during prayer time. Victualers had to close during prayer time, no drinking or eating was allowed, and soldiers were required to attend services or face admonishment by their Captain and eventually imprisonment for the third service missed. Contemporaries and historians have long noted Gustav's strong protestant faith (Macmunn, 1920). If Gustavus' army was visibly more pious in their behavior and comportment than their opposition, it would be a signal of God's favor and the correctness of the Protestants in their struggle. Internalized religiosity should reduce the misbehavior of the troops in camp and the field. Several commentators bear this out as true until later in the war (Macmunn, 1920; Ögren, 1996; Roe & Watts, 1632), which would justify a reissuance of articles in 1631 – troops and commanders needed a reminder of the fundamental rules they were operating under.

As to be expected, the majority of the rules focus on internal organization and order maintenance within the army, whether on the march, in camp, or in battle. While more specific, and enumerating more specific actions, most of these articles

[12]Some articles address concerns more than one area and are counted in each area, thus totals are not 150.

cover familiar territory: rules for laying out camp, for keeping company's together on the march, appropriate chains of command in specific situations, keeping order in the camp, and the like. One major expansion of rules here focus on controlling dueling and fights between troops. Unlike Henry V, Aldophus I did not list rules about soldiers avoiding reigniting prior quarrels or those based on national origin, but it is clear from the number of articles which address the problem that, like other armies, the Swedish force was potentially as prone to infighting, quarrels, and mutinies as other armies of the period. The lion's share of these articles focus on intra-army discipline – offenses against officers or other soldiers (i.e., assaults or theft) or offenses against the army and it's discipline, such as sleeping or being drunk on watch.

These articles also address problems that arise when armies evolve from being grounded on feudal obligations of military service to being based on pay for service. During the feudal era, commanders had to ensure that those who owed military service due to feudal obligations showed up, with the appropriate gear, and in shape to fight. While records would be kept of who turned out for service, they were of little importance once the army was assembled. Earlier war articles emphasized staying with one's battle and in one's assigned rank and file, a concern of military regulations since the Roman republic. The problem was keeping a functional army together. Once regular pay is given to soldiers, the muster roles become critical to regiment operation as they become pay roles. Reflecting this increased importance, a number of articles here address not just obeying the call to join a muster but remaining with one's Regiment during the campaign. One keyway to ensure men stay in the regiments they muster into is making Captains the regiment's paymaster.

As under earlier articles, Captains received their men's pay from the army and they were expected to deliver it to their men. Not being in the proper regiment meant not getting paid. Captains were also given specific muster targets to achieve. Not wanting to miss his targets, a practice developed of "loaning" men to another Captain so their muster count hit the required target. Later the soldiers would return to their original regiment. Article 104 directly address this practice, prohibiting it and punishing the guilty by being proclaimed a traitor and being put out of camp, a rare punishment for an officer and more intense than prescribed in earlier articles. The specificity of this rule suggests it was not an uncommon shenanigan pulled by Captains. The severity of the punishment, especially when considering the man's rank, indicates how serious the matter was viewed by the King and Generals. While forces "on paper" rarely match those in the field even in modern wars, the loaning of men inflated the number of troops the King and his generals thought they had with potentially disastrous consequences if tactical decisions were made assuming full regiments. Using under strength regiments requires more care and thought as the unit will have fewer men and less firepower. It also fraudulently represents the unit size to the pay maser.

Ögren (1996) points out that only 6 of the articles are "humanitarian" in nature, meaning they are concerned about the interaction of the army with civilians and not intra-army order and discipline. These six are fairly typical of prior Articles issued since the twelfth century. Article 88 forbids rape and 89 forbids prostitutes in camp. One is allowed to bring one's wife or, if he takes up with an unmarried woman, she is allowed in camp if the couple marry, otherwise she is to be removed. We have seen articles forbidding rape since the initial tenth century *Pax*, and the attempt to control prostitutes/spies/common women in camp goes back to the thirteenth century at least. Articles 90, 91, and 100 prohibit arson – no burning of towns at home or abroad and no burning of churches, hospitals, schools, or mills. Article 99 forbids the pillage of churches, again a command as old as the original *Pax*, and hospitals. The last four articles, however, are given a single, and quite expected, exception: "except hee bee commanded" [sic] (Ögren, 1996; Roe & Watts, 1692). This tells us that even in the attempt to bring his army under a religious-humanitarian order, Gustav Aldophus I believed that, at times, the norms had to be laid aside for strategic or tactical goals to be accomplished. It is also a potential social control mechanism in that it communicates to the leaders of towns in the region that those who cooperate will be treated with Christian charity, while those who do not can face the full force an army unleashed. The generally good behavior of the Swedish army early in the campaigns provided ample evidence that the army would not pillage every city it came across or who surrendered to them. By showing restraint early on, Burgo-masters, mayors, and other civilian leaders we presented with evidence they could trust the King and his commanders to keep their word. Seeing as the war itself is fought on the main continent in the lands of allied protestant nations, such rules constrain the old norms of war by prohibiting troops from looting and pillaging the lands of their supposedly friendly neighbors and co-religionists.

Aldoplhus' articles also contain the first records of rules concerned with the legality of orders given and the consequences for following them, a crucial aspect of current international criminal and humanitarian law. Article 48 states that if one is "commanded upon a service which is to our [the King's] prejudice" the order should be disobeyed and the solider is to report the officer who gave the orders. This injunction is in almost every military code of conduct for modern nations and forces. A legacy of Nuremberg, "following orders" is not an accepted affirmative defense against war crimes charges. While it took until the twentieth century to codify this principle in International law, Sweden's King was aware of the issue in the seventeenth century and took steps to address it within his forces. To follow 48, Article 49 instructs officers against giving unlawful orders.

These articles are also of interest in that they provide for a more complex procedural law in case adjudication. While prior articles and military manuals do address some aspects of procedural laws, Gustavus Aldophus I included 33 procedure-specific articles. This shows that these articles are becoming more and more legalistic both in content, tone, and implementation. The 1621 articles dwell at length on the composition of the lower and higher courts, down to seating arrangements during trials. The articles give quite a bit of discretion to the High and Lower courts to determine punishments; often instead of prescribing a specific punishment, the documents say that the soldier or officer will have to "face the court" with nothing more specific given. A High Court is established with jurisdiction over the entire army; per the articles, its main purpose was to hear appeals from the Lower courts or to serve as a court of origin for crimes by officers of all ranks (including, as stipulated in article 139, the King himself). Each regiment was required to have a lower court to hear cases involving soldiers attached to the regiment. Those who are found guilty are sentenced by the army general. There are also provisions for trying individuals *in abstenia*. This is the first codification of an appeals process for those charged and convicting of violations of the laws of war.

We also see a wider range of punishments proscribed in these articles. As with other Articles of War, a common punishment is execution. In some cases, there is no formal adjudication called for, rather, depending on the specific ordinance, any fellow solider or any officer that witnesses the act can immediately shoot and kill the perpetrator. For example, Article 64 specifies that the first man of a line that flees can be shot by others with no penalty. If he is caught and brought to his regimental lower court, to be declared a traitor and dismissed from out of camp. In addition, if that man is later hurt or killed by a member of the army, he shall have no recourse to law. Article 97 allows officers to kill soldiers who start looting before commanded. This is a refraction of the old Roman rules concerning breaking the battleline to loot or flee. Anyone who sees the infraction can apply the sanction. This is clearly perceived as urgent in generating both general deterrence and order in the line.

These articles also revive the Roman practice of decimation – killing every tenth man in a unit. This is likely a product of the neo-classicism associated with the early modern period. Through the medieval and early modern periods, translations of Roman military manuals were very popular and their practices often incorporated into the practices of armies. The first context where decimation is a possible punishment is described across articles 61–63. Article 61 criminalized charging the enemy but retreating before they "come to the dint of sword." One would assume this refers to a charge that breaks and retreats under fire before coming in contact with the enemy. Officers will be publicly disgraced and cashiered from the army. Soldiers are decimated, with every tenth man hung and the rest of the unit assigned to "carry filth" out of the camp until they redeem themselves on the battlefield – a dirty, degrading duty that is used as punishment in other articles as well.[13] Article 70 prescribes decimation for soldiers who enter into treaty or agreement with the enemy, which is ironically a humane policy as treason tends to lead to hanging for all involved. Here, 90% of a unit guilty of treason is allowed to live. Ironically, the return of decimation is justified as a form of Christian charity.

In addition to executions in situ or after trails, a number of other punishments are listed. Loss of pay is used, as is imprisonment, placement in irons, and reduction of rations to bread and water (or some combination of these). Officers faced being cashiered and either removed from the army or demoted to the rank and file – a particularly harsh social insult for the noble born officer. A common

[13]Latrine duty is a common punishment in many militaries down to today, due to its perception as dirty, demeaning work.

punishment is being turned out of camp. This leaves the man in a dangerous position. He is (likely) a foreigner in a hostile territory during an active war, with only the clothes on his back. In addition, his former fellows are free to abuse him as they see fit if they encounter him outside of the camp, with no repercussions. This isn't quite a death sentence, but that a likely eventual outcome. In addition to being removed from the camp, some crimes demanded the convicted run the "Gate-lope" before being put out. This involved the man's regiment splitting itself in half, leaving an aisle down the middle. The troops were equipped with whips, cudgels, and other sundry items used to flail and beat the man and he ran between the two lines of his soon-to-be former comrades in arms. As with the Roman use of collective punishment, such punishments are not only designed to generate general deterrence among the troops (especially among the regiment involved) but it is also an attempt to generate informal social control within the regiment. Most soldiers would find participating in the "Gate-lope" as punishers uncomfortable at best.[14] The desire to avoid having to be a part of a "Gate-lope" would encourage soldiers to police their own. There is a similar logic behind decimation, though there the pressure to internally police would be stronger as who constitutes the tenth is determined randomly. There is also a substantial difference in severity between having to strike a former colleague as he runs past you (or at least pretend to, one would not be punished for missing) and being hung simply for belonging to the offender's regiment.

Under the new regimental army organization, regiments were identified on the field, march, and parade ground by their colors – unique flags and pinions specific to the regiment. Regiments would add to their colors as they experienced success on the battlefield, embroidering the names of major victories and campaigns on their flag, and adopting other meaningful icons. The use of such markers is not new; the Roman legions used standard bearers in each legion, carrying the legion's Eagle. A symbol that would be appropriated by the French post-revolution. In the medieval era, nobles flew their own banners that identified their battalions or their men within a battalion. Kings had their unique heraldic flags indicating their presence on the battlefield. The medieval French used the infamous *Oriflame*, a bright orange flag that signified the army would not be giving quarter or taking prisoners (save the most valuable). Organizationally, the various types of banner serve several tactically useful purposes in allowing a commander or solider to identify where each part of the army was in the battleline. They were also used to mark a regiment's space in camp and in a marching column. In addition to heraldic and aesthetic purposes, the colors became a symbol of the regiment itself, as individual solders came and went.[15] Protecting

[14]This is not to say there were not sadists among the ranks who took inordinate pleasure in participation, nor is it denying that some soldiers would see the convicted crime's and punishment as reflecting poorly on the unit and derive some measure of satisfaction from participating in his punishment.

[15]This is the period where nation-states begin to focus on keeping their armies uniformed. Uniforms themselves will become elaborate symbols with nations competing to outdo their peers in various aesthetic aspects of their military uniforms.

one's regimental colors was seen as a task of utmost importance; taking an enemy's colors was a highly regarded battle honor for the regiment taking the colors and a disgrace for the unit which lost its colors.

Signifying the importance that regimental colors have gained in army culture of the period, Aldophus Gustavus I included several articles specifically about colors. Articles 55, 56, 58, and 60 all directly reference colors. 55 and 56 reference them as mustering points when called to fall out for battle or march (assemble at your colors and follow your colors on the march). 58 and 60 both tell soldiers not to flee their colors, listing the punishment as death. Article 58 demands a solider "defend them [colors] to the uttermost of his power." While articles 55 and 56 indicate a specific functionality of colors, and article 60 is one of many articles the proscribes death for flight from battle, article 58 illustrates the strong meaning that has been attached to these emblems. The specific legal demand to protect the colors with your life (or lose your life) goes beyond order maintenance on the battlefield and into a level of symbolic identity. Being willing to risk one's life to protect their unit's flag shows how deeply soldiers identified with their regiment, at times over the army itself, or their nation.

As discussed earlier in the chapter, the Swedish troops seemed to keep to the articles for the most part. There were two notable cities sacked by the Swedes on this campaign: Frankfurt der Oder in 1631 and Gőttingen in 1632. Ögren (1996) attributes this to a disruption in the soldier's pay. While he understood that his articles would be broken on occasion, he did not express or show a level of tolerance seen previously by other commanders in the field. When asked what to do with officers who had broken the laws laid down, Gustavus responded: "Has my brother-in-law no gallows in his country, or is he short of timber?" Clearly, he felt his rules applied across the ranks and was insistent on their application. But he was merciful to enemies guilty of similar or worse offenses. For example, Macmunn (1920, p. 188) discusses an incident where Gustavus is brought before Holy Roman Empire prisoners, who up to their capture had been charged with taking small Swedish or allied garrisons and putting all within to the sword. As he approached, they supposedly threw themselves at his feet, begging for mercy. The King is reported to have told them to "Get up. . .I am no God to fall before. You are all brigands, but I spare your lives." The exact motivation of his mercy is not given. Many of these men may have been offered enrollment in the Swedish ranks, as "there are better uses to put men to than hanging" (Macmunn, 1920, p. 188).

The sacking of Frankfurt der Oder likely catalyzed the issuance of Gustavus' 1631 set of 20 war articles. This second set of articles, while much briefer, does not eclipse the 1621 articles, but highlights issues that have proven problematic over the prior decade of warfare. Only one of these articles is specifically religious, and it is the standard order we have seen since the ninth century to not attack the church or its people and properties (including schools, hospitals, and colleges). Six focus on issues of army internal organization, four address intra-army discipline, nine address civilian treatment, and one focuses on procedural law. Many of the articles are rephrased regurgitations of items in the 1621 articles. There are minor changes that reflect the different circumstances of 1631. The second article spells out that local political officials will be the ones to assign quarters, not the quartermaster, and article eight reminds men of one's obligation to obey and keep those quarters. This applies to officers as well. Similarly, officer's servants are expected to lodge with them and not use the town's housing. Additionally, article three reminds the troops that cities are not obligated to provide the army anything not ordered by the King (here: lodging, firewood, candles, vinegar, and salt). At this stage of the war, the army is spending more time in German towns between engagements, thus the basic rules of quarter assignment and comportment are tweaked to reflect this. These are allied towns whom the Swedish army has come to defend from the armies of the Holy Roman Empire. Troops are ordered to not steal from the citizenry, but only to acquire items when given a warrant by the King or general and that the items be paid for with a fair price.

Other provisions ensure safe passage for civilians, require nobles to use their own troops for personal protection, not the general army, and prohibit soldiers from collecting tolls or custom duties. These rules are significant as the army is camped in cities in a highly riverine environment, with several key bridges being essential for travel through the region. The armies sought to control these cities and bridges. The Swedish forces, their allies and mercenaries are being forbidden from taking advantage of this position for their personal gain. Another rule that emerges out of this context concerns garrison horses. Being spread out, the army used couriers (called posts in period documents), to carry messages from commander to commander in different cities. Routes were carefully staged out and posts were expected to change horses at each of these stations or garrisons. The idea being to not overwork the horse due to the critical role horses serve in the army. Speed of delivery was important, but so is proper use and preservation of army equipment, including livestock.

Gustavus Aldophus is killed at the Battle of Lutzen (1632) and while the war will drag on until 1648, the Swedes would be essentially done with their participation by 1634 and their defeat at Nordlingen (Beaulac, 2004; Macmunn, 1920), but the war would carry on for 14 more years, primarily fought between the French and the Hapsburgs on German soil. As Beaulac (2004) points out, at the end of the Thirty Years War, Europe had no over-arching political structure. With the Holy Roman Empire and the Papacy reduced in power and influence due to the spread of Protestantism and the war itself, a power vacuum emerges. The old order, the order that produced trail of Peter Hagenbach, that saw the primary political and international connections held between noble families and reinforced by a Catholic ideology crumbled. Bringing an end to the war, or rather wars that composed the Thirty Years War, after 4 years of negotiations left no clear victor. Thus these agreements were not imposed by one nation on another after military defeat; they were negotiated by several parties none of which were clear "winners" or "losers" in the war. Religion and incipient nationalism drove the wars and would be reflected in the peace.

Gustavus' Sweden was central in the military out comes of the Thirty Years War, but the articles of battle were quickly adopted by other, allied powers. For example, in 1639, the Lords which composed the Scottish National Covenant, issued articles of war in their conflict versus Charles I's England. Referred to as the Bishops Wars, they were an attempt by Scotland and the Scottish Presbyterian church to prevent Charles I from replacing their religion with Anglicanism (Episcopalianism). It is an abbreviated version, with only 25 listed articles, but for all intents and purposes it replicates the majority of the rules laid down for the Swedish Army. The Edinburgh Articles of 1639 begin with a justification of jurisdiction to enact articles of war; it essentially argues that "the word of God and the rules and order of Discipline used in the Kirke [church] of Scotland" (p. 3) during peace have just as much power and relevance in war. While it also contains requirements for worship, it is very explicit that there is no tolerance for religious freedom and all worship and ecclesiastical authority will come from the Church of Scotland. As this is at its core a religious war, the use of the church as legitimation emphasizes the nature of the struggle. In another change from the Swedish articles, here are few outright sentences of death listed in the articles, replaced with the court's judgment for punishment.

Intentionally or not, the articles distinguish between what we now call ordinary crimes and violations of the articles of war. Article II establishes that after the court's sentence is made public, "No superior officer, Colonel, Captain, shall solicit for any man that is lawfully convicted by the court either for any crime *or for not observing the article of war* (emphasis added)." This clearly indicates that the two are seen as separate sets of rules and the language used suggests that violations of the articles are not view as criminal violations but disciplinary violations. Not only does this acknowledge two separate systems of justice depending on whether one was at war or not, but that both systems simultaneously applied to armed forces (else why insert the phrase, "either for any crime or").

Westphalia and the Creation of a "Law of Nations"

There is too much ink spilled over whether or not the Treaty of Westphalia (1648) is the beginning of international law as we know it or not (see Beaulac, 2004; Croxton, 1999). As we have discussed throughout this volume, much of the rules regarding warfare and interstate interaction were informal norms held among groups of like-minded and similarly socially-positioned individuals. Today, common practice and tradition form a large (uncodified) portion of international law and international relations. As we saw with the trial of Hagenbach, the notion of a transnational brotherhood of knights and arms existed through the medieval period and representatives could be brought together when needs be to compose and carry out a tribunal. But these ideas are only codified in literature of the period, whether chivalric manual or medieval romance. It was their specific empowerment by the French King in this case that gave them the authority to try Sir Peter, not an established treaty or international organization. The Treaty of Westphalia is the first codification of many principles of international interactions that are directly important to the evolution of the laws of war.

Most of the treaty, as to be expected of a treaty ending multiple conflicts, the majority of the treaty is devoted to hashing out who controls what and whose hereditary rights are acknowledged over time. Yet, both as a whole and in specific articles, the Treaty attempts to establish a framework for future European State interactions. It resolves some of the more typical problems that remain in the wake of a conflict. Article XLI specifies that convictions for ordinary crimes during the war, even if convicted by an occupying power, stand unless evidence to the contrary is prevented. Ensuing articles grant amnesties to the belligerent's armies for atrocities done in the wars. Article CX requires the return of all prisoners, be they "gown or sword." Article XXXIX allows those who experienced "violent extortion" of their property or the like during the war to seek renumeration for their loss. Yet, the "debtors" as the treaty names them, have 2 years to provide proof they made appropriate payment at the time. By the wording, this would cover any damages civilians experienced from pillage or foraging armies. However, it is likely limited in scope of thought to those whose had items "requisitioned" from them as per articles of war, which promised payment for all horses, food, or the like taken. This article specifies a statute of limitations for claims being brought and specifies a generous amount of time for the "debtor" to respond. While on the surface, this article seems to restore wealth lost by citizens due to the war, it provides a legalistic cover for war crimes as it requires a civilian to bring a specific claim in court against a specific solider, likely a foreigner, well entrenched in their home country by this point. It is unlikely that a civilian will know the exact identity of their victimizer; with the international composition of forces on both sides, they might not even know which state the solider serves.

The major legal and socio-political legacy of Westphalia are evident in Articles LXXVI and LXXXIX. Each respectively gives sovereignty to France and the Holy Roman Empire, using the river Rhine as the border between the two. Each also comes with the promise of non-interference in the activities of the other and the other's allies. This is the central reordering of Europe – moving from a social space where might made right and was retroactively legitimated after a conflict to a space where the expectation is a lack of hostile or violent interactions between states. No matter their size or relative power. Small states need no longer be in fear of being gobbled up by larger states as a part of a broader struggle for continental dominance between the major powers. In theory at least.

Westphalia creates a social space. It establishes a sphere of inter-state interaction of a real social realm, with rules, sanctions, and structures for dispute resolution. In creates a socio-cultural space for diplomacy over warfare as a way to resolve disagreements. In constructing a social arena where states more deliberately and consciously interacted with each other, "international relations" for the lack of a better term, creates a rationalized space between states to normalize interactions of peace, diplomacy, and commerce. Westphalia deliberately and specifically sees war as the aberrant state that the mutual agreement of the entreating parties *ends* and whose future cooperation eliminates or suppresses, especially with its injunctions to go to court or third parties before resorting to arms. This is the first secular attempt to create mechanisms between nations to resolve conflicts before they escalate to military action. This same drive will be behind the creation of the League of Nations, the United Nations, and the International Criminal Court as supranational organizations designed to oversee and keep transnational space peaceful and orderly. While the Treaty of Westphalia is not the be all and end all of international law, it is the first clear multilateral treaty that acknowledges that nations exist *within a community* and that the community is one driven by rules and one central idea: national sovereignty.

What this community will look like is addressed by later articles in the treaty. In article CXVIII, it is agreed the only defensive armies will be kept by any party to the treaty. Article CXXII introduces the crime of "infringing of public peace," meaning a violation the treaty. This will be developed by later jurisprudence into the crime of aggression, which will play a prominent role in the International Military Tribunal and Nuremberg Military Tribunal after the World War II. All parties are bound by the treaty's articles; if the treaty is broken or states parties have arguments concerning the meaning of the treaty or how actions might be interpreted, they are required to submit themselves to a court or third party for arbitration. Article CXXIV states that if the dispute is unresolved within three years, all signatories are obligated to unite in military force against the party not abiding by the treaty.

The Treaty of Westphalia creates a new social arena for interactions between states. One where they are equals in so far as all had the rights to expect non-interference in their affairs by their neighbors. New spaces require new norms or the recreation, reassertion, or reformulation of existing or older norms. Such changes were possible due to Westphalia. This new social sphere is not automatically the locale of new behaviors and mandates. Change vis-á-vis military law and behavior happens incrementally and slowly, in one nation at a time. Articles of war will become more restrictive and holistic, though order in the army takes precedence over humanitarian concerns. Better nations will do their best to limit humanitarian damage, but it will be the late twentieth and early twenty-first centuries before we see anything approaching a war where at least one side holds fast to its rules of engagement. Westphalia opens up the ideas that you can have an external, binding, law of armed conflict. Much of the second half of the nineteenth and all of the twentieth century will be focused on what that law should and will look like. Both substantively and procedurally.

In terms of military law, the only direct relevance Westphalia has is that it serves as the first international, multilateral treaty that begins to frame the idea of the crime of aggression – waging an offensive war without a legal reason to do so, typically some wrong that needed correcting (i.e., taking of territory, illegally capturing ships, interfering with commerce). The new international order established on national sovereignty highlights a state's right to self-defense. Larger countries cannot invade and consume other smaller countries just because they can. This is an essential concern of smaller powers in the negotiating of the treaty. The Thirty Years War, and other conflicts, while focused on religious differences was also a war of larger powers (i.e., Spain, England) fighting for control over smaller nations (i.e., the Netherlands, Flanders, and the rest of the low countries). The idea of a crime of aggression is not fully set out and realized here. But a foundation is established upon which it can be built. We see concerns about the crime of aggression going back to the earliest writing. Much of the Greek and

Roman laws about what was and was not a legal war revolved around the issue of aggression or other wrongs committed that needed addressing. Medieval writings on legality of war have the same base concern: just wars are those that are wages to right a wrong. As discussed in earlier chapters, in the medieval consciousness war was simply an extension of the King's duty to bring justice to his people. Localized criminal justice is handled by the King's courts; international justice is provided by the King's armies. Lawful war in this period required specific harms or injuries done to one state by another; dynastic wars being the exception, being driven by claims to rightful sovereignty over geography and people (i.e., The Hundred Years War, the Wars of Spanish Succession, etc.).

As we move into the early modern period, national and military leaders are not necessarily using military force to right perceived wrongs in the same understanding of injustice as their medieval counterparts, but rather, as Grotius (1625/1972) observed, they use war as just another political tool to obtain state objectives. Grotius publishes his famous *The Law of War and Peace* in 1625, in the heart of the Thirty Years War. The work has become a central piece in the literature on the laws of war. Much of Grotius' book draws upon classical sources, Greek and Roman primarily, and does not centralize humanitarian concerns. In places it outright contradicts many of the humanitarian concerns addressed in the *Pax* and *Truega* that became part of medieval military law. He is supportive of pillage, killing prisoners, and "the slaughter even of infants and of women is made with impunity and this is included in the laws of war" (p. 34). Grotius then cites the Old Testament and Homer to support his claims, especially about harming women and children. When discussing the law of nations, those laws made by men, compared with natural or divine law, Grotius offers different guidelines and norms for interacting with the enemy and the citizens of the hostile nation. Here, he is more liberal in terms of constraining soldiers than the articles of war by Gustave Augustus I. Much of what Gustave tried to prevent, Grotius tacitly approves of. He presents a picture of legitimate war that includes the sorts atrocities chastised by the Church and other military law makers. Yet, while noting that killing of all captives is allowed, keeping them in slavery is seen as a better option as this allows the belligerent to "willingly refrain from recourse to the utmost degree of severity" (p. 67) in treatment of the captured and defeated.

In Chapter 10, Grotius shifts his focus and positionality, saying what he had written up to that point was considered legal as there were customs or laws made specifically regulating these actions and making them legal *as long the war being fought is just/legal.* If the war is unjust, than none of the provisions of pillage, capture, or killing apply. Chapter 11 addresses the legal right to engage in certain behaviors during war, and here Grotius begins to insert rules to reduce harm to enemy soldiers and civilians. He discusses ancient cases where mercy was shown and war limited, especially in terms of how a defeated foe is treated. He draws upon may of the same stipulations we have seen throughout this volume where caution is urged to avoid harshness toward the soldiers and civilians of the defeated. The chapter also makes an important distinction separating the culpability of leaders of unjust wars and those who follow them, giving more responsibility and thus harsher punishments, to top leadership and not the rank and file.

This is a thread that IHL and ICL will follow into the current times. The ICC's focus on "Those Most Responsible" is a direct reflection of the principle of command responsibility, putting the legal responsibility more on the commander than the solider. From here, Grotius' work draws heavily on church pronouncements and previously examined articles of war (and the culture in general that produced both). While not presented as *requirements*, humanitarian treatment of others by the army is highly suggested in a wealth of contexts. He urges no captives be killed, especially those which surrender voluntarily. Chapter XII recasts the lawfulness of pillage by placing contexts around lawful destruction of alien property. Grotius gives three reasons that would allow destruction to visited on enemy property: if it is a necessity, if it is restoring a debt, if the owners have committed some sort of evil that needs punishment. Then, Grotius says out loud what was only said in the heads or chambers of Generals and Kings since the Chariot Wars era: "Devastation should be refrained from *if* the area is profitable for us and out of power of the enemy" (p. 95, XII.II). He then goes on to list the numerous restrictions about destroying fruit trees, crops, and the like discussed earlier which would reduce the economic value of a territory. Protection of sacred or other culturally important property is specifically mentioned as something to preserve if possible. These are two key issues which both the laws of war and IHL will address as each evolves.

The rest of Grotius is devoted to moderation in the destructive acts of war. He recognizes that violence and destruction is a central aspect of warfare, and spends the first half of his work providing legal support for not-quite total war, but definitely a war where winners have all the rights and the defeated few, if any. His mid-point shift toward moderation brings him in line with much of the thought and norms we have been exploring so far. The second half of his book embraces humanitarian concerns as long as the overall aim of warfare is not forgotten. His focus on moderation is a step away from the total war of his age. Yet, winning the military conflict is the primary goal and concern of an army. Humanitarian concerns laid out here are secondary. They are also presented as recommendations. As he establishes at the start, much of the worst things done during war are legal if the cause is just. His humanitarian limitations are presented as "*shoulds*" not "*musts*." They are a philosophical discussion of what should be appropriate actions in wartime, not the legal boundaries surrounding warfare. Grotius makes clear that he sees the laws of nations and the laws of war as allowing just about anything as long as the cause is just. However, the second half of the volume is an attempt to shift those norms and laws, to acknowledge and support some of the humanitarian concerns that have surrounded warfare for centuries. But these are in many ways aspirational – they are the *should*s not the *musts*. Commanders are advised by Grotius to follow his guidelines when practicable. Throughout the volume, Grotius cherry picks examples from antiquity to support his points, he avoids recent or contemporary examples or conflicts, or even medieval conflicts. While he adds few truly new humanitarian restrictions to warfare, his work becomes highly influential on both sides of the Atlantic in the middle nineteenth century for those creating early IHL. His writings, among others, will lead to a peace movement on the European continent one of whose goals is the creation of an international law of armed conflict applicable to all that is focused on humanitarian issues and seek to constrain the increasingly deadly military technologies being developed.

The Thirty Years War was not the only major continental war during the period. Wars were fought over religion, economics, control of the "New World," and dynastic succession. The rules and laws that guided them remained essentially stable, with the expected local variations. Voluntary adoption of articles of war that constrained troop behavior along traditional lines were the major innovation and evolution from the fifteenth through eighteenth centuries. Building and maintaining standing armies, even if portions were foreign mercenaries, increasingly became standard. This establishment and support of a standing army strengthened the development of the state as it monopolized political power and violence (see Weber, 1919/2015). The requisite bureaucratic elements of organizing a large army mirror those of maintaining a state embodied in a government. The co-evolution of the two will create a synergy that strengthens state rule at home and provides it with the ability to either protect itself or exert its influence on others via force or threat thereof. With the passing of the fourteenth century and fifteenth century free companies and the integration of these sorts of mercenary groups into state armies, centers of military power that were not state based became essentially non-existent. Hierarchy and specialized divisions of labor shape the growth of both states and standing militaries. In many nation-states these two institutions will become fused and inseparable. The military becomes an arm, or a tool, of the state. As Grotius acknowledged.

The Age of Revolutions

The end of the eighteenth and start of the nineteenth centuries saw numerous attempts to overthrow dynastic powers and establish citizen-run governments.[16] Rebellions were seen in the North American British colonies, France, Haiti, Ireland, Serbia, Greece, and throughout Latin America. Obviously, revolts and the like are not new. All of the civilizations we have talked about in this book had to endure internal insurrections, or worse, at certain points in their history. And in these cases a state's (or Sovereign's) military was used to quell the revolts. As discussed earlier in the book, fighting a group of people one expects to govern adds a layer of concern to the conflict, unless one plans to govern heavily and harshly (i.e., the Khmer Rouge of Cambodia in the mid-to-late 1970s). If wise and seeking to reduce the amount of discord during the repatriation of rebels, a leader will not use the military in a heavy-handed way against the citizenry. We see this in both Henry V, Henry VIII, and Adolphus Gustavus I's articles of war. They

[16]While many scholars will refer to this as a period of the expansion of democracy, what is seen is the expansion of republics with democratic ways of selecting representatives. It won't be until the twentieth century that these nations extend sufferance and a political voice to their whole adult populations. Women and minority groups will find various barriers to participation in these new political systems until the systems have matured and a culture of civil rights develops in the twentieth century.

specifically call for decent treatment of civilians and their property. While there is a Christian/Humanitarian influence here, there is also a practicality as one hopes the citizenry will accept their new political masters quickly and peacefully. The worse they are treated by the army, the less likely that is to occur without additional application of coercive force – both physical and economic. This political dimension of post-war life was well understood at the time, at least by some leaders. When presented with an internal conflict or revolt, the state (and its armed forces) are put in a difficult and highly delicate situation. Force will be required to maintain the integrity of the state, but too much force or wanton uses of force will enhance motivation for the insurrectionists and potential draw new people to the struggle.

Wars, and the killing that takes center stage in them, is only possible with high degrees of cultural otherization of the enemy. As discussed in Chapter 1, humans while highly capable of violence seem to spend more time and energy devoted to peaceful coexistence and the generation of social solidarity to maintain a society (Durkheim, 1893/1984). Social bonds, what Roth (2009) calls "fellow feeling," reduce individual proclivity toward violence (Hirschi, 1969) and promote positive interpersonal interactions. Insurrectionists typically have a spate of grievances against the state they are rising against, a set of grievances that have likely produced the social distance required for the insurgents to otherize their government. Bonding over shared grievances, and the other natural affinities that bind people together, strengthen and motivate insurgent groups (see McCauley & Moskalenko, 2008; 2017). In the process the state and those who run it are otherized – they are the group enacting the behavior triggering the insurgents. If the state is seen as the other and the enemy, so are the agents of the state. The armed forces used to quell such uprisings have a fine line to walk between doing their jobs, removing a threat to state stability and security, and causing grave harm to their fellow citizens. This will lead to otherization of the citizenry (at least that portion in revolt, a group notoriously hard to identify individually or collectively); this poses risks for overuse of violence and atrocity events as the soldiers battling the insurgency are fighting not just for the legitimacy of their nation-state but of their own armed forces.

Historically, we have seen revolts harshly suppressed. It is a direct attack on a King's sovereignty which, until more recent eras, was also interpreted, at least by the sovereign, as an attack on the god who put them in their place of rulership. In the age of reason, such wanton brutality was not seen as an acceptable solution to civil disturbances. At least normatively. As the idea of innate human rights becomes articulated culturally during the enlightenment by the likes of Rousseau (1762), at least as applied to certain segments of the population, it becomes the philosophical and political basis on which to ground grievance against a government or its leaders. With the growth of a mercantile and professional middle class, a social segment gaining large amounts of economic and social capital which they sought to translate into political capital and power. While these cultural norms are not defining "humanity" very broadly – in this context it is typically limited to whites of European ancestry (wherever in the world the communities are) – it is the beginning of a conversation about natural rights and liberties that will upend European politics for a century. Simultaneously, much of this conversation and political action will be held during a period of European colonial power and domination where states are using their armies in brutal, atrocity creating, ways. At this point in time, discussions about liberty are discussions about liberty for the middle classes, at least the men. And in racially heterogeneous societies, these discussions were also limited to those of Caucasian ancestry.

At this juncture, the story of the norms and laws of war becomes two different tales: one of Europe and it's descendant nations slowly but steadily building IHL and ICL, the other clearly showing that when in the colonies or in wars of colonial domination, the rules were utterly different. Most of the indigenous inhabitants of colonized geographies were denied inclusion in the ranks of humanity, the laws we have been exploring of did not apply. Not due to any codified legal exception of jurisdiction, but due to European racism and belief in the inferiority of non-Europeans.

The US Colonial rebellion of the late eighteenth century against George III's policies is the first successful establishment of a representative democracy. There is much in the way of lore and falsehoods that characterize the view of this conflict, especially in the eyes of US citizens. The first is the belief of constant and extreme brutality by the British visited on the colonists. Often portrayed in US-based historical fiction as treacherous, lascivious, pillagers, the atrocities committed by the British forces are strongly overstated, especially when compared with King Philip's War or other conflicts on the continents. For example, the US television show Turn: Washington's Spies, took excessive liberties with historical reality in its telling the story of the Culper Spy Ring during the revolution. While the changes and exaggerations are many, one key example is the portrayal of Captain John Simcoe. The show makes Simcoe the primary villain of the series, portrayed as a merciless British officer with a sadistic streak who seemed to have nothing better to do during the revolution than harass the Woodhull family (the son is the show's key protagonist). This is often motivated by little more than Simcoe's lust or meanness. In real life, Captain Simcoe had a long, distinguished, and prosperous career, returning to England after his service in the Americas, served as an MP, then was appointed Lieutenant Governor of Upper Canada. While he and his unit engaged in military behavior that would be considered problematic today, at the time he was far from one of the more brutal British officers, especially in relationships toward civilians (though see Stewart, 1985 for a less flattering portrayal).

The second major myth of the American Revolution is that the colonists "fought like Indians," i.e., adopting skirmishing tactics over line formations. While at times this was true, it is a better description of how conflicts against indigenous peoples were fought in the colonial areas. The Continental Army modeled itself on European forces of the time, especially the British, which is understandable as many of those who formed and joined the Continental Army had experience in King Philips War or other conflicts serving in the British Army. The militia member, the iconic citizen solider, is too often lauded as the backbone of the army. General Washington and the Continental Congress sought to create and field an army that looked and acted like their British foes tactically and organizationally. The Continental Congress on 30 June 1775 passed articles of war to govern the continental army during the conflict. It did so as that was what European nations did, a community which the break-away colonies aspire to join. The colonial army was often derided early in the war as nothing more than militia and backwoods farmers. Establishing articles of war placed the Continental Congress on the same level as other governments, providing it legitimacy. It also established a set of disciplinary ordinances that would organize and oversee the army in the field (Journals of the Continental Congress, 1775/1905).

The 1775 articles are very similar to those we have been examining the past couple of chapters. There are minor wording changes, removing statements about King's duties and the like, as would be appropriate for the incipient nation. Yet there is little difference in the rules themselves and even the order in which they are presented. For example, the second article establishes the centrality of religious services. Like prior articles, it punishes those who act inappropriately during the service – behaving in ways that could disrupt the service. But, instead of attendance being mandatory, and punished if avoided, the Colonial articles of 1775 "earnestly recommend" attendance. This is produced by the lack of a state religion among the colonies (one of the colonials' grievances against George III). New England has also suffered significant religious conflict in the decades leading up to the revolution. (Erikson, 1996). Requiring attendance at services could lead to tension and disruption in camp. Articles against being absent without a pass, sleeping or being drunk on watch or duty, striking officers, causing disruptions after retreat is sounded, and the like are all present. Changes in substantive laws are few and specific: details of using passwords, letting an officer of any unit intervene in a dispute between any soldiers in camp, and the like including holdovers from the middle ages such as court marshalling those who surrender their entrenchments or forts. One significant change comes to the rules about plunder. Article XXIX states that all plundered enemy stores belong to the United Colonies, not soldiers, unit, or specific leaders. 23 of the articles are procedural law, establishing the proper manner to conduct courts martial. There are three articles that establish the jurisdiction of the articles: Article I, all officers and soldiers of the army are covered; Article XXXII extends the articles to "suttlers and retailers in camp" (p. 117), and Article XLVIII extends the articles to "All officers, conductors, gunners, matrosses,[17] drivers, or any other persons whosoever, receiving pay or hire in the service of the continental artillery" (p. 119). Nine articles cover the rules for mustering and pay; three articles cover suttlers in camp. The last articles cover filling in gaps in the chain of command due to death and injury, new to codified articles and potentially a reflection of the Continental Army not having an organizational history and tradition of how this was to be addressed.

The Continental Congress adopted a second set of articles on September 20, 1776 (Journals of the Continental Congress, 1776). While largely the same as the

[17]Gunners assistants responsible for sponging, loading, and firing artillery.

prior years, it is clear in the ensuing year of the army being in the field, issues arose that the congress felt necessary to address. Many of the added articles focus on behaviors addressed in Henry VIIIs or Gustavus I articles and read similarly if not exactly as their predecessors. This can be chalked up to experience; the colonial army had no experiences fighting outside of those who fought in the various "Indian" wars of the period, which were conducted under different rules of engagement. After a year in the field, many of the more minor and fine distinctions between types of crimes and exact punishments or procedures are expanded upon. For example, a section of five new article all address theft, sales, or other misuse of army material. Organizationally, it separates articles pertaining to officers from those pertaining to the enlisted. This reflects the fuller establishment of an officer core in contemporary armies and initiates the still-current system of military regulations that treat officers and enlisted differently. Showing that the colonists were continuing continental discipline practices, flogging is mentioned as an allowable practice, if limited to no more than 100 strokes. The two articles in Section X are new. The first provides that "any officer or solider shall be accused of a capital crime, or of having used violence or committed any offense against" people of the US face court martial. Any officer that knows of such a crime but does not report it or do everything reasonable to assist in the suspect's apprehension, is to be cashiered from service. Congress makes it clear that depredations on civilians by the army would not be tolerated. The second article in the section strikes the author as uniquely situated for a US army: it prevents officers from protecting their men from debt collectors. Congress makes is very clear that even the hardships suffered in the army, which often included long stretches without pay, are no excuse for not paying one's debts. The coldness of hyper-capitalism was at the roots of US politics and culture since before there was a US. The results of this article were the loss of farms and other family property which in the soldiers absence and the absence of the soldier's pay could not be financially supported.

In 1779, Congress established a new set of regulations for the army. These are not specific articles of war with jurisdiction limited to a single conflict, they are universal rules for the armed services. Developed by Friedrich von Steuben, and adopted by Congress in March of that year, *Regulations for the Order and Discipline of the Troops of the United States* (1779/1786/2019), also known as the "Blue Book," governed the army through the War of 1812; many sections remain in today's US Code of Military Conduct. This work is part rule book, part procedure manual, but the bulk of it is a drill manual and rules/orders for regiments on the march. Some of the rules highlight officers keeping a closer watch on their men, a function of the evolution of the US army as an institution. For example, by this point the army is to call the muster roll twice daily – at reveille and noon. Further, NCOs were to count heads again after taps was sounded. This was in addition to a morning equipment check, where soldiers faced fines for missing or broken kit. Solders were also subject to a monthly general inspection that examined the personal property of the troops, looking for theft or gear abandonment.

One innovation that arises in these regulations is a strong concern with the health of one's soldiers. The manual states: "There is nothing which gains an officer the love of his soldiers more than his care of them under distress and sickness" (p. 113). Thus, officers are instructed to give ill soldiers "every comfort necessary" which typically involved sending them to the camp or base hospital. Once there, it is ordered the solider be given no duties until the surgeon considers him healthy enough to serve again. This is the first time that a military manual gives such direct attention to solider health and well-being. Camp health has been a matter of central importance since classical times, often being the one thing which limits a besieging power's ability to stay in the field. Even today, armies tend to lose more men and women to illness and accidents than combat itself. The proportions grow as we go back in history. Yet here is a more rationalized approach to health care and the treatment of the sick in the field and in camps. Separation from the rest of the body of troops and focusing on healing are both rational approaches to illness, preventing its spread and hastening the return of the solider to duty. Principles of humaneness also arise, as the soldiers are to be given all needed to heal and heal quickly.

The Blue Book does not contain articles of war. There are no rules about prisoners. Civilians are only mentioned in the rules establishing where suttlers must set up within camp and they must close up shop during church services. It was written with the regimental commander in mind, as that is the organizational unit of focus in the manual. It was written by von Steuben to provide the US army with a professionalized European model of soldering. As Chandler (2022) points out, the soldiers of the Continental Army saw themselves "first and foremost as military professionals and members of 'Military Europe'"(p. 324). Counter to some European views of the time, and later myths the US will build about itself, the Army that fought the British in the American Revolution was organized and governed along the lines of other European Armies. Some assistance was provided by foreign advisors, like von Steuben, but the core of the continental army's officers and enlisted saw themselves as part of the broader tradition and culture of European warfare, what Chandler (2022) calls "Military Europe." The implication is they would act in the same professional manner as continental forces, drawing on the same rules and understandings of warfare.

As it came into being, Washington's army looked little different from King George III's or other European forces in organization and in culture. Officers were mostly drawn from the upper social classes, while the rank and file from the agrarian or laboring classes. Officers were held to a higher moral standard, often grounded in cultural norms. Formations, drill, and basic orders were the same. Unlike it's European counterparts, what would become the US Army was built during the enlightenment and strongly influenced by the rationalistic and humanistic approaches to warfare building currency at the time. Being born during this period allowed the military to develop by aspiring to contemporary European ideals, instead of medieval and early modern Europe's aspirational neoclassicism which worked against making warfare more humane. While early US generals studied classical authors, they never showed the cultural bond and aspirational emulation of Rome that their continental counterparts did. Thus the norms adopted are the same that we have been tracing the development of in this volume. The US doesn't have a deep history of ties to classical culture and warfare. What becomes the foundation of US military values are those current and developing in the early modern period, post-enlightenment, and renaissance. It never undergoes the processes examined earlier in this chapter and the prior one; it doesn't shift from a system of feudalized military service through the heavy use of mercenaries to the emergence of a more "modern" army. Its history begins at the end of this period and is shaped by the European developments of the time and less governed by the past. Through the middle twentieth century, the US will often find itself at the forefront of the development of International Humanitarian Law and, though less so, International Criminal Law. It won't be until the cold war of the later twentieth century that the US will begin to work directly against an international legal order designed to constrain the carnage of combat for both solider and civilian.

Conclusion

Throughout the early modern period, we see military norms taking on a more legalistic form. As more nations begin to utilize articles of war, codification of these norms continues. The similarities of articles of battle across nations and across wars is itself proof of a broadly held set of international military norms. Military Europe evolved a specific set of shared norms and practices to guide their armed conflicts. As we have seen, while even the earliest societies had rules about warfare, the nature and context of these rules change through time. There are two main lines of this evolution: content and justiciability.

Content-wise, norms of all periods examined here attempt to reduce the overall harm caused by warfare. Greece's highly ritualized form of war declarations and their practice of having their armies clash on flat plains away from cities if possible were ways of reducing the harms of war. Classical Greek generals often sought one decisive battle and were willing to see the issue as settled. This was another normative limitation that kept warfare confined to its liminal social space. Rome's attempt to professionalize its Legions and bind the men tightly under the Legion protocols is reflective of their realization of the effects of unrestrained warfare. Carthage aside, Roman sought to destroy few civilizations. Rome sought to rule the lands their legions conquered. And thus abided by many of the laws we see established in the chariot wars period about not destroying a people, but more particularly about not destroying the land and its flora (Bédoyére, 2020; Hoyos, 2019). Rome's strongest military legacy is the military manuals which made their way as often utilized sources down into the medieval and early modern periods. The Roman rules that survive the longest are those that deal with punishments and camp life.

Many of the camp rules are fairly straight forward in purpose and are applicable to armies across historical periods. Rules about quartering, watches, camp followers, and the like are solutions to common problems all armies have. While death is an oft proscribed sentence for military offenders, fines and other bodily punishments are more often used. Unless the crime is deemed severe, armies saw it better to punish a soldier's coin purse or his body in a non-lethal manner. Such punishments would keep soldiers able to march and fight, and hopefully catalyze specific deterrence against future infractions. Flogging in particular will be reintroduced in late-medieval/early modern armies as a preferred form of non-lethal punishment. It will be seen simultaneously as a positive and negative practice. Those who favored flogging saw it as a severe, but non-lethal way to keep order. While brutal, when done in public it was believed by officers to serve as an effective deterrent to other soldiers. It's brutality and its connection with slavery led to demands to cease the practice (Singha, 2016; Underwood, Pfaff, & Hechter, 2018), which didn't fully occur until the twentieth century. Under the rules of both the British and American armies, soldiers were allowed more lashes in punishment than US laws allowed to be given to slaves as punishment. Sailors, especially in the British Navy had it even worse (Underwood et al., 2018). Officers tended to have low opinions of their troops, with Wellington even "lamenting that many [soldiers] joined up primarily for the drink ration" (Callister & Whitbread, 2022, p. 11) and little else. Hence officer justifications of their often-animalistic treatment of the rank and file. To neutralize the guilt associated with such brutality, officers of the period draw upon a denial of victim rhetoric (see Sykes & Matza, 1957): by denying the men's humanity, brutal punishments were more likely to be accepted, at least by the officer class. If soldiers were perceived by their officers as coming from the lowest social ranks, they would be guided by the core values of their day, which suggested that such men were innately inferior, less capable of reasoned thought, and naturally inclined toward laziness and petty crime. This belief constellation led to two distinct views being commonly held by officers: tough, physical punishment was the only way to teach someone of such social origins and they were easily led astray, often by each other, making the prevention of looting and the like difficult to impossible. Which in turn would led to fewer men being punished for doing so, which reinforces the behavior among the rank and file to loot when given an opportunity.

Even those armies with the most thorough rules and a strong desire by the leaders to see them enforced will engage in atrocity behavior on occasion, though it seems to occur much less frequently. The Swedish Army of Gustav Adolphus operated under the most comprehensive and strict set of articles of battle of their time, yet still engaged in a couple of atrocious city sackings (Cooper, 1981; Macmunn, 1920; Ögren, 1996). The opportunity to violate military laws is ever present in a theater of operations; warfare and initial occupation are chaotic affairs. This chaos allows men to slip out of their units to pillage; it can separate officers from their charges creating the absence of a critical restraint when it might be needed the most. The chaos of battle and after can also create a Durkheimian sense of anomie (Durkheim –division of labor), pervading the liminal space of battle. In the conflict-produced anomie, as Merton (1938) suggests, most troops will simply do their jobs. Just as the majority of people in the civilian world don't engage in crime even when confronted with strong social anomie. Yet some, an unidentifiable portion that is no doubt variable depending on the circumstances, will violate their army's norms as a response to European anomie (Durkheim, Messer and R, Merton). Even when a military's rules gain wide purchase across the force, inevitably some will deviate from acceptable behavior (Durk again).

Their exact motivations have been poorly studied by historians and criminologists, as there is often little surviving evidence of what soldiers thought or believed through much of the time periods covered in this book. Most of the rank and file, from Sumer to the Thirty Years War and beyond, would be illiterate, thus not leaving a historical record of their perceptions and experiences. In the late eighteenth and early nineteenth centuries, we see memoirs and other accounts of battle from the eyes of the regular troops. More were literate and letters home were often preserved. Also, some of the men wrote retrospective accounts after their service. By the American and French revolutions, we begin to see more records generated and more records surviving to the present. This trend will only intensify through nineteenth and twentieth centuries. A scholar wanting to understand the daily life of a US Federal army solider in the civil war has a wealth of materials to draw upon. Trying to understand the daily internal life of a Greek Hoplite or Saxon Fyrd-man is much more problematic.

There are those who assume soldering and soldiers are pretty much the same everywhere and every when; this is clearly not the case. Armies, their laws and rules, and the behavior of their soldiers is a direct product of the sociocultural milieux which produced a given army. There are commonalities across armies across periods; they are all organizations with similar goals facing similar. There are only so many ways to organize a regiment, prepare a march column, set watch on a camp, or engage the enemy in pitched battle. There are also some nearly universally desirable traits for soldiers: bravery, obedience, strength, mental fortitude, and situational awareness to name just a few. There are also a handful of nigh universal opportunities or temptations soldiers in the field face: looting and pillaging, assaulting civilians (sexually or not), animus manifest as cruelty or aggression toward prisoners, and laxness toward camp rules. This book has examined how leaders and commanders have addressed these issues in different times and places. Some problems may be universal, but solutions are not. As nascent, and later full-on, bureaucracies, military forces required rules to coordinate and control the behavior of their members at all levels. Such is the nature of complex organizations. These rules will emerge from the needs and goals of the organization, (Blau & Meyer, 1987; Morgan, 1997; Weber, 1919/2015), but also from other existing social norms and beliefs (Callister & Whitbread, 2020).

The Greek's highly ritualized war declarations spring from their religious beliefs, believing divine figures required formal declarations of onset and of ending. As discussed in chapter one, this is the liminal nature of war, requiring it to be given its own social space, separate from daily life and the rules that govern it. What helps you in peace time is a hazard is war and vice versa. What is and isn't acceptable in war versus peace can also be diametrically opposed. Ritualized declarations of war make it clear that the battle is being fought in a different social space by different social rules than commerce and other inter-city state activities.

Early and late medieval theologians would argue about the precise nature of just and unjust wars, looking for clear definitions in scripture, the writings of philosophers, and their own debates (Aquinis, Augustine, etc.). Here a precise declaration of war and specifically the articulation of it as a just war are central to the cultural precepts of the age and critical for those engaged in the fighting. Starting an unjust war is a cardinal sin. The penitential manuals also make it clear that fighting in war is too. Fighting in a just war is still a sin, but as examined earlier, one with a specific (and minor) penance. Cause was important as from it would be gleaned God's favor or disfavor. In the ninth through eleventh centuries Common Era, bishops and other church leaders pushed European nobility to accept the Church's attempt to impose order on the chaos of war through the *Pax* and *Truega*. Drawing on Christian principles of mercy and hoping to prevent continuous sackings of their monasteries and churches, a distinct set of principles to follow when waging war was developed. While it was never codified into state-based law, it was transformed into a literary tradition which would influence nobles, and others, for centuries. The Chivalric tradition, be it in romance form or military manual form, blended Christian and military values into a semi-consistent whole. This literature had a profound impact on the Middle Ages view of warfare and warriors. It has also been continuously reinterpreted through the centuries, massaged to fit a given eras values while simultaneously harkening back to a glorified past of noble-led warfare and the noble warrior. It is partially through this literature and its continued popularity through the ages that the term "noble" itself takes on a meaning concerning someone's behavior and inner personality, and not referring to a facet of their birth.

With the introduction of articles of war in the later Middle Ages and the early Modern Era, we take a step closer to having codified military laws. The jurisdiction of such articles is very limited. They are conflict specific and are decidedly not international – they only apply to the soldiers of the army issuing the articles. But they are codified rules and have articles addressing procedural law aspects as well. They are justiciable via courts martial, most even have some sort of appeals process. Officers handle justice's administration. They compose juries, act as prosecutors and judges. The articles do not indicate any formalized defense actor, soldiers were expected to speak in their own defense. Some articles allow accused to call supporting witnesses. It should be noted at this time, there is no legal system that promises the accused a right to representation in a civilian trial at this time. Thus, a lack of representation for military defendants here is not surprising.

By this point in the evolution of military norms and law, we have reached cultural artifacts and practices that are easily classify as law: codified, justiciable rules with clearly articulated punishments and rules for adjudication. It is military law, not humanitarian law. The primary focus is the maintenance of order in the military. Many of the semi-humanitarian rules we see in these articles as much about order maintenance as they are treating people in a humane fashion despite being in a military conflict. The prohibitions against robbing suttlers and victulers are a direct attempt to ensure the army has access to these commercial services. Prohibitions affecting camp followers help provide security and prevent numerous types of disorder (e.g., generally loud reveries, soldiers fighting over female camp followers, limiting the amount of venereal disease in the army). Early rules about protecting the church and its property were more political than religious or humanitarian in nature, especially as the Church itself became a major power. Even the rules against abusing citizens had other than humanitarian purpose, as discussed throughout. They are political issues, designed to help leave a population governable after the conflict, not driven by a concern about the innate rights of people or populations to security.

Absent in this discussion, and in the historical records, are the actual applications of these articles. Systematic, or even partial, lists of courts martial cases are almost nonexistent. A plea roll from Edward I's 1269 Scottish campaign survives (Neville, 1990). Most are minor property crimes that results in acquittals, pardons, or minor fines. It is not until the US Federal army during the US civil war that we see systematically kept records of courts martial.

By the end of the eighteenth century, at least for many European armed forces, soldiers were governed by framework of rules that controlled how they acted in camp, in battle, and in garrison. Most of the principles within the articles are highly similar if not the same, showing that as an institution, armies are responding to social and cultural rationalization by rationalizing, systematizing, and codifying their disciplinary codes and practices. While law is present in all of the societies discussed through this study, military law, or the laws of war as we have been calling them, are very slowly codified over time. That there is a shared sense of military culture across the region across time is undoubtable. Different, and hostile, armies adopt almost exact articles of battle, highlighting this shared understanding of the rules that are to guide the fighting and the aftermath.

Appendix: Articles of Battle

In much of the later half of the book, specific articles of battle were examined closely. Where possible, I have included the full text of key articles of battle. Where it isn't possible to provide here, the reader is provided with links to electronic versions of the articles. The following articles of war reproduced in full here are: Richard II's Scottish invasion, Henry versus invasion of France, Scottish articles issued in 1639 and the incipient United State's 1775 articles for fighting the British. I have preserved the spelling in the originals (including type-setting elements such as "f"s for "s"s). I have provided links to sources if readers care to explore Henry VIII's French invasion ordenances and Gustav Adolphus' 1621 Articles.

Ordinances of Richard II.[1]

I. FIRSTY. That all manner of perfons, of what nation, ftate, or condition they may be, ihall be obedient to our lord the king, to his confiable and marefchall, under penalty of every thing they can forfeit in body and goods.

II. that none be fo hardy as to touch the body of our lord, nor the veifel in which it is contained, under pain of being drawn, hanged, and beheaded.

III. that none be fo hardy as to rob and pillage the church, nor to defiroy any man belonging to holy church, religious or otherwife, nor any woman, nor to take them prifoners, if not bearing arms; nor to force any woman, upon pain of being hanged.

IV. that no one be fo hardy to go before, or otherwife than in the battail to which he belongs, under the banner or pennon of his lord or mafter, except the herbergers, whofe names shall be given in by their lords or mailers to our confiable and marefchall, upon pain of lofing their horfes.

V. that no one take quarters, otherwife than by the affignment of the confiable and marefchall and the herbergers; and that, after the quarters are affigned and delivered, let no one be fo hardy as to remove himfelf, or quit his quarters, on any account whatfo-ever,

[1]Taken from Grose, F. (1786, 1788) The Antiquities of England and Wales. S. Hooper publisher.

under pain of forfeiture of horfe and armour, and his body to be in arreft, and at the king's will.

VI. that every one be obedient to his captain, and perform watch and ward, forrage, and all other things belonging to his duty, under penalty of lofing his horfe and armour, and his body being in arrefi to the inarefchall, till he !hall have made his peace with his lord or mafier, according to the award of the court.

VII. that no one be fo hardy as to rob or pillage another of money, victuals, provifions, forage, or any other thing, on pain of lofing his head; nor ihall any one take any victuals, merchandife, or any other thing whatfoever, brought for the refreiliment of the army, under the fame penalty; and any one who ·ihall give the names of fuch robbers and pillagers to the confiable and marefchall, !hall have twenty nobles for his labour.

VIII. no one ihall make a riot or contention in the army for debate of arms, prifoners, lodgings, or any other thing whatfo-ever, nor caufe any party or aifembly of perfons, under pain (the principals as well as the parties) of lofing their horfes and armour, and having their bodies in arreft at the king's will, and if it be a boy or page he !hall lofe his left ear. Any perfon conceiving himfelf aggrieved !hall make known his grievance to the confiable and mare-fcha11, and right fh.all be done him.

IX. that no one be fo hardy as to make a contention or de-bate in the army on account of ariy grudge refpecl:ing time pafi, or for any thing to come; if in fuch contefi or debate any one lliall be flain, thofe who were the occafion fl1all be hanged; and if any one fhall proclaim his own name, or that of his lord or mafier, fo as to caufe a rifing of the people, whereby an affray might happen in the army, he who made the proclamation ilrnll be drawn and hanged.

X. that no one be fo hardy as to cry "havok," under pain of lofing his head, and that he or they that fhall be the beginners of the faid cry fhall likewife be beheaded, and their bodies afterwards be hanged up by the arms.

XI. that no one make the cry called mounte, or any other whatfoever in the army, on account of the great danger that may thereby happen to the whole army; which God forbid! and that on pain, if he be a man at arms, or archer on horfeback, of lofing his befi horfe; and if he be an archer on foot or boy, he fhall have his left ear cut off.

XII. if in any engagement whatfoever an enemy shall be beat down to the earth, and he who fliall have thus thrown him down shall go forwards in the purfuit, and any other fhall come afterwards, and fhall take the faith or parole of the faid enemy, he fhall have half of the faid prifoner, and he who "overthrew him the other half; but he who receiv; d his parole Chall have the keeping of him, giving fecurity to his partner.

XIII. if any one takes a prifoner, and another fhall join him, demanding a part, threatening that otherwife he will kill him (the prifoner), he fhall have no part, although the fhare be granted to him; and if he kills the faid prifoner, he fhall be in arrefi: to the marefc all, without being delivered till he has fatisfied the party, and his horfes and armour fhall be forfeited to the confiable.

XIV. that no man go out on an expedition by night or by day, unlefs with the knowledge and by the permiffion of the chief-tain of the battail in which he is, fo that they may be able to fuccour him fhould occafion require it, on pa.in of lofing horfe and armour.·

XV. that for no news or affray whatfoever that may happen in the army, any one fhall put himfelf in difarray in his battail, whe-ther on. an excurfion or in quarters, unlefs by affignment of his chief-tain, m1der pain of lofing horfe and armour.

XVI. that every one pay to his lord or mafi:er the third of all manner of gains of arms; herein are included thofe who do not receive pay, but only have the benefit of quarters, under the banner or pennon of arms of a captain.

XVII. that no one be fo hardy as to raife a banner or pennon of St. George, or any other, to draw together the people out of the army, to go to any place whatfoever, under pain, that thofe who thus make them-felves captains fhall be drawn and hanged, and thofe who follow them be beheaded, and all their goods and heritages forfeited to the king.

XVIII. that every man, of what efi:ate, condition, or nation h·e may be, fo that he be of our party, fhall bear a large fign of the arms of St. George before, and another behind, upon peril that if he be hurt or fiain in default thereof, he who fhall hurt or flay him fhall fuffer no penalty for it: and that no enemy fhall bear the faid fign of St. George, unlefs he be a prifoner, upon pain of death.

XIX. if any one fhall.take a prifoner, as foon as he comes to the army, he fhall bring him to his captain or mail.er,. on pain of lofing his part to his faid captain or mafter ·; and that his faid captain or mafier fliall bring him to our lord th. e king, confi:able, or mare-fchall, as foon as he well can, without taking him elfewhere, in order that they may examine him concerning news and intelligence of the enemy, under pain of lofing his third to him who may firfi make it lmown to the confiable or marefchall; and that every one ihall guard, or caufe to be guarded by his foldiers, his faid prifoner, that he may not ride about at large in the army, nor fhall fuffer him to be at large in his quarters, without having a guard over him, left he efpy the fecrets of the army, under pain of lofing his faid prifoner; referving to his faid lord the third of the whole, if there is not a part-ner in the offence; -and the fecond part to him that fuall firfi take him; and the third part to the confiable. On the like pain, and alfo of his body being in arrefi} and at the king's will, he fhall not fuffer his faid prifoner to go out of the army for his ranfome, nor for any other caufe, without leave of the king, confiable, and marefchall, or the commander of the battalion in, vhich he is.

XX. that every one fhall well and duly perform his watch in the army, and with the number of men at arms and archers as is affigned him, and that he fhall remain the full limited term, unlefs by the order or permiffion of him before whom the watch is made, on pain of having his head cut off.

XXI. that ho ohe Chall give paffports or fafe conduct to a prifoner nor any other, nor leave to aily enemy to come into the army, on pain of forfeiture of all his goods to the king, and his body in arrefi and at his will; except our lord the King, Monfieur de Lancafier, fenefchall, the confiable, and marfhall: and that none be fo hardy as to violate the fafe conduit of our lord the king, upon payne of being drawn and hanged, and his goods and heritage for-
.feited to the king; nor to infringe the fafe-condu& of our faid lord of Lancafier, fenefchall, confiable, and marefchall, upon pain of being beheaded.

XXII. if any one take a prifoner, he fhall take his faith,
and alfo his bacinet, or gauntlet, to be a pledge and in fign that he is fo taken, or he fhall leave him under the guatd of fome of his fol-diers; under pain; that if he takes him, and does not do as is here directed, and another *comes* afterwards, and takes him from him (if not under a guard) as 1s faid, his bacinet or rjght gauntelet in pledge, he shall· have the prifoner, though the first had taken his faith.

XXIII. that no one be fo hardy to retain the fervant of another, who has covenanted for the expedition, whether foldier, man at arms, archer, page or boy, after he ihall have been challenged by his mafier, under pain that his body !hall be in arrefi: till he ihall have made fatisfacl: ion to the party complaining, by a ward of the court, and his horfes and armour forfeited to the confiable.

XXIV. that no one be so hardy to go for forage before the lords or others, whofoever they may be, who mark out or align the places for the foragers, if it is a man at arms, he shall lofe his horfes and harnefs to the confiable, and his body !hall be arrefi:ed by the marifchal, and if it is a valet or boy, he !hall have his left ear cut off.

XXV. THAT none be fo hardy as to quarter himfelf otherwife than by the affignment of the herbergers, who are authorifed to diftribute quar-ters, under like penalty.

XXVI. that every lord whatfoever caufe to be delivered to the confiable artd marifchal the narnes of their herbergers, under penalty, that if any one goes forward and takes quarters, and his name is not delivered in to the confiable and marefchall, he fhall lofe his horfes and armour.

King Henry V's Calais/Mantu Ordenances[2]

Obeisance

First that·all maner of men of what soever nacion estate or condicion soever he be, be obbeis"unt to our Soveraigne lord the Kinge and to bis Constable and Marshall, upon peyne of as moche as he may forfeite in bodey and in goodes.

For Holy Churche

Also that no man be so hardy, of lesse that be prest, to toucbe the sacrament of Godes bodey, upon payn to be drawen and hangede therfor; nor that no maner man be so hardy to· touche the box or vessell in the whiche the precious sacrement is in, upon the same p1lyne aforsaide.

For Holy Churche

Also that no maner of man be so hardey to robbe, ne to pille Holy Church of no good ne ornament th!lt longeth to the Churche, ne to slee no man of Holy Churche, religious, ne non other, but if he be armed, upon payne of deathe. Nether that no man be so hardey to slee, ne enforce, no woman upon the same payne; And that no man take no woman psoner, man of Holy Church, ne other religious, but if he be armed, upon payne of cnprisona-ment, and his bodey at the Kingea will.

For Herbergage

Also that no man be so· hardey to go to for in the bataill2 undre the baner or penon of his lorde or master, exccptc herber-gers, the names of whome shalbe delyvered and take to the Con-stable and Marishall by their saide lordes and masters, upon this payne, he that otherwise offemleth shalbe put from his hors and h1lrnes bothe unto the warde of the Constable and Marshall unto the tyme that he that offcndeth have made his fyne with the snide Constabell and Marisball, and fonde surties that he shall no more offende.

[2]Taken from Grose, F. (1785–1787) The Antiquities of England and Wales. S. Hooper publisher.

For Herbergage'

Ali; o that no man take non herbergage, but if it be by the assignement of the Constable and Marishall or of the herbergers, and that after tyme that the herbergage is assigned and delyvered, that no man be so hardy him self to remove ne to disaraye for any thinge that maye falle, without comandement of him that bathe power, upon payne of hors· and harnyes to be put in areste of Constable and Marishall to the tyme they have made fyne with theim, and more over his bodey at the Kinges wille.

For Kepinge of Wacche and Warde

Also that every man be obeysaunt to his capitayn to kepe his wacche and warde and forye, and to doe all that longeth a soul-deour to doon, upon payne of his hors and harnes to be put in the warde of the Marishall unto the tyme that he that in this offendeth bathe agreede with his capitayn, after the warde of the courte.

For Takinge of Prisoners

Also be it at Bataille or other dede of a,.-mes wher that presoners be take, he that furst may have his say shall have him for his psoner, and shall not neJe to abide upon him to the ende of the Joumey; and none other shall more take him for presoner but if that it be· that the saide presoner be founde for his defendaunt.

For Robinge of Marchantes Comyng to the Market

Also that no man be so hardy to pille ne robbe non other of vitaile, ne of noe other lyvelode th-e whiche they. have by beinge, upon payne of deathe; and that no man robbe no• vitiller ne mar-chant, ne non other persone comyng unto the marke, vitillers, or other marchandies, for the refresshement of the oste, upon the same payne; ne that no man robe from other horsemen or manes mete, ne non other thinge that is goten of enemyes goodes, upon the payne his body t-o be arested at the Kings-will.

For Barteteurs

Also that no man debate for armes, prisoners, lodging, ne for none other thinge, so that no riott, contek, ne debate be in the oste; ne that no man make him ptye in assembly of people, ne non other wise, and that as well of papall as of other pties, upon payne of lesinge their hors and harnes till they have made fyne with the Constable and Marishall, and their bodies to be arestede at the Kinges will, and if he be grome or page he shall lese his lifte eare therfor, and if any man fynde him greved let him shewe his grevance to the Constable and Marishall, and right shalbe done.

For Debate

Also that no man make no debate nor contek for any hate of tyme past, ne for tyme to come,[6] for the whiche hate if any man be dede for suche contek or debate, he or they that be encheson or pateners of the deathe, shalbe hanged therfor; or if it hape that any man escrye his owne name, or his capitayne, lord, or master, to make a risinge of the people, by the whiche any affraye myght fall in the oste, he that in suche wise asketh shall be drawen and hanged therefore.

For Theim That Crye Havoke

AlsoT no man be so hardey to crye havok upon peyne that he that is founde begynn'? to die therfor, and the reme•unt that don the same, ther hors and harnes to be put in the warde of the Counstable and Marishall unto the tyme they have made fyne with theim, and their bodies in preson at the Kinges will till they have found surties that they shall no more offende.

For Unlawfull Scryes

Also [8] that non escrye, the whiche is called mount, ne non other unresonable escrye be in the oste, upon peyne. that he that is fonde begynner of suche unresonable escrie be put from his hors and harne and his bodie in areste of Counstable and Marishall to the tyme he have made his fyne with theim, and his bodye at the Kinges will and his life; and he that certifiethe whoe is the begyn-ner shall have an Cs for his labor of the Counstable and Marishall.

For Mustres

Also when it liketh the Kinge to take must res of his hoste, that no man be so hardy to have other men at his musters than thoo that be with him self witholde for the same viage, without fraude, upon payne to be holde fals and re.pved, and also to lose his wages and payment that shulde longe to him.

For Prysoners

Also if any man1 dede of Armes be, and if any man be borne to the earthe, he that first so hathe borne him to the earthe shall have him to prysoner; but so be that a nother cometh after, and tnkethe the fey$_T$ of the saide presoner, then the smyther down shall have the one half, and the taker of the feithT the other half; but be that taketh the feith [1] hall have the warde of the presoner, making sufficient suertye to his partyner for the other half.

For Prysoners

AJso if that any man take a prisoner, and any other man come unto him askinge parte, manatyng ells [8] that he wolde slay the saide presoner, he shall have no parte thoughe so bee that }?tie have hen graunted him; and if he slaye the presoner he shalbe arested by the Marishall, and put in warde without delyverance till he have made a fyne after the a warde of [the] Counstable.

For the Paynge of Thyrdes

Also that every man pay his thirdes to his capitayne, lorde, or master, of all maner wynyng by wares, and that aswell thoo that be not in soulde but longynge under the baner or penon of their capitayn, upon payne to lose his parte of his forsaid wynyng to his capitayn, and his body to be in warde of the Marishall unto the tyme he have agreede with his forseidc master.

For theim that maketh themselves Captianes to withdrawe men from the Hoste.

Also that no man be so hardy to rese baner or penon of Sinte George, ne of no other, to drawe together the people, and to with drawe theim out of the oste to goe to eny other partye, upon peyne of theim that in suche wise make theim self Capitaynes to be draw and hanged; and they that him sue or folow to have their hedes smyten of, and all their goodes and haritag forfaited to the Kinge.

A Statute for Theim That Here Not a Bande of Seint George

Also that every man of what estate [or] condicion that he be, of our vtie, beare a bande of Seint George sufficiant large, upon the ville if he be wounded or dede in the fawte therof, he that him wondeth or [sleyeth] shall here no payne for him; and that non enemye here the saide signe of Seint George, but if he be pre-soner and in the warde of his master, upon peyne of deathe therefore.

For Theim That Assaute Without Leve of the Kinge

Also that no man1 assault be made to Castell ne to Strength by Archer ne by non other of the Comons without the psence of a man of astate; and if any assault be and the King, Constable, or Marshall, or any lorde of the office, sende to distourbe the saide as-saulte. that no man be so hardy to assault after; and if any man do it, he shalbe presoned and lose all his other pfett that he bathe wone by the forsaide assault, and his hors and [harness] in the warde of the Counstable and Marishall.

For to Bringe in Prisoners in to the Kings Knowledg, Counstable, and Marishall

Also if any man take any psoner, anon right as he is come into the oste, that he bringe his psoner unto his Capitayne or master, upon pnyne of losinge of his parte to his forsaide Capitayne or master; and then that his saide Capitayne or master bring him within viij dayes to the King, Counstable, or Marshall, or as sone as he may,·so that he be not ladde non other waye upon peyne to lose his parte to him that shall doe furst the Counstable and Marishall havyng witing therof; aud that every man kepe or do keep his prisoner that he ride not, nor goo at large in the oste, ne in lodginges, but if warde be had upon him, upon pcyne of losinge of the same presoner; resvyng to his lorde or master his thyrdes of the hole if he be not ptyc of the defaulte, and the iij pte to him that first shall accuse him, and the iijde pte to the Counstible and Marishall: also more over, his bodye areste to the Kinges wille; also that he suffer not his psoner to go out of the Ol!te for his ransom,. ne for non other cause, without sauf concluyte, npon the peyne aforsaide.

For Kepinge of Wachc

Also that every man kepe duley his wache in the oste that with as many men of armes and archers as to him shalbe assigned, but if he have a cause resonable; and to bide upon his wache and warde the tcrme to him lymytied, nor departing from the wachc no way be it by the assignement or lycence of him by the whiche the saide wache is made, upon payne of smytynge of his head that otherwise departeth.

For the Gyving of Saufcondute or Conges and for to Breke Theim

Also that no man geve no saufcondute to prysoner, ne to non other, nor lycence to non enemye to come nor to go owte of the oste, ne into the oste, upon payne to forfaite all his goodes to the Kinge and his bodye in areste at the Kinges wille, excepte our liege lord the Kinge, Counstable, and Marishall; and that no man be so hardy to breke our liege lorde the Kings saufcondute upon payne to be drawen and hanged, and his goodes and heritages forfayte to the Kinge, nother the Constable and Marishall sauf-condutc upon payne of deathc

For the Withdrawing Mens Servauntes From Ther Masters

Also that no man be so hardey to take no servant of other, the whiche is in covenant with him for the viage, as well souldiour, man of armes, archer, grome, page, after tyme he is kcnde or cha-langed by his master, upon payne his body to be arested to the tyme he have agrede to the vtye complayn•nt after the warde of the courte, and his hors and harneys to the Counstable and Marisha!) till he have made his fyne.

For Departing From the Oste Without Leve

Also that no man departe from the stale without)eve and licence of his lorde or master, upon payne that he that otherwise devteth to be arested and in the warde of [the] Marishall and at the Kinges wille of his life; and also to lose all his wynynge of that day, reserved to his lorde or master the thirdes of his wynynge, and to the lorde of the stale surplus of the same wynyng wone by him that same day, and so from day to day till the ordynance be kepte.

For Scryes Made by the Enemyes in the Oste

Also if any ascrye fall in the oste when they be logged, that every man drawe him to the King or the chiefteyn of the bataill wher he is lodged, levinge his lodging sufficiantly kept, but if the ene-myes fall on that side ther as he is lodged, and in this case the said Capitayn shall abide therin himself and all his men.

For Kepinge of the Countre

And if any Countrey or lordcship be wonne other by fre wille offered unto the Kinges obeysaunce that no man be so hardey to robe or pille therin after that the peas is proclamyed upon payne of deathe; and if any man of what degre soever he be come unto our saide lordes obeisaunce, that no man take him, robe him, nor pille him, upon the same payne, so that he or they that this wille obeye here a token of our soveraigne lorde the King.

For Theim That Raunsom Their Prisoners or Sell Without Leave of Ther Lordes or Capitanes

Also that no man be so hardey to raunsome or sell his presoner without cspecall licence of his capitayn, the whiche indenteth with the King under his letter and seale; and that upon payne that he that doeth the contrarye therof to forfaitte his parte in the psoner unto his capitayn, and he to be undcrareste of the Marishall to the tyrne he have aggred withe his capitayn, and that no man by no suche psoner upon payne to lose the golde and money that he paieth for him, and the presoner to be arested to the Capitayn aforsaide.

A Statute for Children Within the Age of Xiiij Yeres

Also that no man be so hardey to take no childerne within the age of xiiij yere, but if he be a lordes sonne, or els a worshipf ull gentelmans sonne, or a capitayne; and that as sone as he bathe brought him into the oste or in to the gernyson where he is abyding that he brynge him to the lorde, master, or capitnyn, upon payn of losing hors, harneys, and his part of the same childe, re- 'il vyng unto his lorde, master, or capitayn his duety, so that they be not consentant unto the defaulte; also that the saide lorde, master, or capitayn bryng him unto the King or Counstable within viij dayes upon.

For Women That Lye in Gescm

Also that no maner of man be so hardy to goe into no cham-ber or lodging wher that any woman lieth in gesem, her to robbe ne pille of no goodes the whiche longeth unto her refressheing, ne for to make non affray wher through she and her childe myght be in any disease or dispere, upon payn that he that in suche wise offendeth shall losse all his goodes, half unto that acuseth him, and halfe unto the Counstable and Marshall, and himself to dede but if the King geve him his grace.

For the Resisting of Justice

And if any man bejuged to the death by the Kinge, Counsta-ble, Marishall, or any other Juge ordynarye, or any other office lawfull, that no maner man be so hardy to sett hand on the con-dempned to resiste the Kings jugct, upon payn that, and the saide condempned be traytour, he *that* is the chif to have the same death that unto him belongeth; and all those that be }?ticipaot or consenting to have their hedes smeten of; and if it be any other cause criminall, the causer of the resistinge to have the same deathe that the saide jugged shuld have, and the remeoant at the Kinges wille.

For Theim That Fortifie Places Withoui Leave of the Kinge

Also that no man be so hardye to edyfie nor to strcngti no maner of place disappered by the King or his Counseill, without espall comaundement of theim that have power; and also that o man compell the countrey, the whiche is in the obeysaunce or appatysede19 unto our soveraign e Jorde the Kinge, to come unto the donage, re acon, wacche or warde, of the saide place, upon payne of losynge his hors and harneys and to restowr ayen or make satisfaccon unto the countrey wher that he hathe offended the costes and damageF, and mor over his bodey at the Kinges wille.

For Theim That Robbe and Pille Lodginges

Also that no man be so hardy to robbe nor pille non others lodginge after tyme it is assign ed by the harbyngcrs, ne to lodge ther within without leave of him the whiche the lodginge is as-signed to, upon payne of emprysonament after the warde of the Counstable and Marishall.

A Statute for Them That Jette Labourcs and Men Going to Plow

Also that no man er of man be so hardy to take fro no man going to the plough, harowe, or cart, hors, mare, nor oxc, nor non other beste longinge to labour within the Kinges obeysaunce without louing and bcdinge, au <l grede the partye, upon payne of deathe; and also that no man gcve none impedyment unto no man of labour, upon payen of empresonament unto the tymc he have ma < le a fyne after the awarde of the Counstable and Marishall.

For Theim That Geve Men Reprochc

Also that no maner man geve no reproche to non other by cause of the countrey that he is of, that is to saye, be he Frenche, Eng-lisshe, Welshe, or lrisshc, ort > f any other countrey whens that ever he be, that no man saye no vilony to non other, throughe the whiche vilony saynge, rniy falle sodcnly man slaughter, or risinge of people, all suche barvators shall stand at the Kinges wille what death they shall have for ther noys making.

For Theim That Taketh Traytours and Put Thcim to Raunsom

Also if any man take any enemye the whiche bathe ben shornc and had billet, or any man the whiche outhe ligeaunce unto our liege lord the Kinge, that is to witt, Englishe, Welsshe, lrishe, or nny other, that as sone as he is comen in to the oste or elswher that he be brought into the warde of Counstable and Marishall upon payne to have the same death that the saide traytour or enemv sholde have, and he that any suche bryngeth in shall have an C. s. of the Kinge, Counstable, or Marishall, for his travell.

For Theim That Breketh the Kinges Areste

Also that every man obey unto the Kinges sergauntes porters of place, or any other officers made by Counstable, Mari hall, or by any other offices cofiimssede, that no man be so hardy to breke the Kinges areste, upon payne to lose hors and harnes and his body at the Kioges wille, and if he mayne them or hurte to be dedc therefore.

For Bornynge

Also withouten comandement speciall of the Kioge that no man bourne upon payne of death.

For Wache Within Loflgings

Also both daye and nyght that every Capitayn have wache with-in hls lodginge, upon payne his body to be arestede till he. have made f yne and rauosom with the Kinge and at the Kinges wille.

For Theim That Be Wastours of Vitaill

Also if any man finde wyne or any other vitaille, that he take him self therof as muche as him nedes, and that he save the re-meoant to other of the oste, without any discencion, upon payne bis hors and harneys to be areste till he have made fyne with the Counstable and Marishall.

For a Copie to Be Had of the Premysses in the Oste

Also theis articles afor written the whiche that thinketh the Kinge be ncdefull to be cryed in the· oste, he wolde that the copie be geven to every lorde and governor of men in the forsaide oste, so that they may have playne knowlege and enforme ther men of ther forsaide ordenances and articles.

For Makinge Rodes

Also that no man make no rodes by day nor by nyght but by licence and kuowlege of the chefteyns of the warde, so that the chefteyncs may knowe what way they drawe theim that they maye have soucour and helpe, and nede be, upon payne of theim that offeodeth of their hod y and goodes at the Kinges wille.

For Rodes

Also that no Capitayn of no warde graunle no rodes without licence of our sovcraigne lorde the Kinge that no man disaray him in. the Bataile for no scrie that cometh in the Oste Also that for no tydinges, ne for no maner of scrye that may cor:ne in the oste, that no man move him in disaraye oute of the bataille if they ride, but by)eve of the chefteyne of the bataille, upon payne that he that offendethe shalbe put fro his hors & hameys to the warde of the Counstable and Marshall unto the time that he have made his f yne with theym, and founde surtie that he shall no more offende; and more over, his body to stand at the Kinges wille.

OTHER ORDENANCE MADE BY THERLE OF SHREUSBERY AND OF PERCHE LORDE OF MOUNTHERMER, AT 111S SIEGES IN MAYNE AND OTHER PLACES[3]

[3]Immediately follows Henry V's above articles in Grose, F. (1785–1787) The Antiquities of England and Wales. S. Hooper publisher.

First that no maner man of armes, ne archer, ne of what estate, condicon, or nacion, that evE:r he be, that they abide not, nor hold theim under the coloure of oure saide soveraigne lorde therle, but tliat their capitoyn be in this psent assemble and company and they be mustred and mustre at all tymes that they be required; nod also that they lodge theim under the standarde of ther ca-pitayn and in suche lodging as is delyvered theim by the har-bengers, upon payne of losynge hors, and harnes, and ther goodes; more over ther bodies at the Kinges will.

For Forcyinge the Said Countre Appatised

Also that no man foraie in the countre apputised but if it be haye, ottei;, rye, and other necessary vitailles, nor that no man geve unto his hors no wheate, nor to gader non but if it be only to make brede of; anp if the said foraiers take any bestaill for ther sustenance that they take resonably, and to make no waste nor for to devoure nor destroye no vitailles, upon payne of losinge hors, and harness, and goodes, and ther bodies at the Kinges wille; and also that the saide forainours 15 take nor sle no great oxen ne no mylche keene, but smalle bestaill, and that they accorde with the ptie upon the payne aforesaide.

For Theim That Bye or Sellc Pylage in the Saidc Countrey, or Take

Also that no maner of man, souldiour, or marchaunt, using the warre, bye no pilage, nor take non within the grouude appatised, upon payne of deathe; and if so be that any man have any of the enymyes goodes whiche he will selle, that he bringe it in to the comon marchaunt market, and pclaime it by an officer of the mar-chalcey, or els of the market, upon payne the byer to be arested of the Marshall to the tyme he have made a fyne with the Coun-stable and Marshall, and to lose all his mony or golde that he bathe paide for the same pylage, and the seller to lose hors and harnys, and his bodye at the Kinges wille.

For Theim That Destroyeth Vines and Other Tres Beringe Lrute

Also that no maner of man bete downe how singe to borne, ne non apletres, peretres, nottres, ne no other tres beringe frute, nor that no·man put no best into vynes, nor drawe up the stakes of the same vynes, for to destroye theim, upon pnyne to lo:; e their saide beastes and theim self in warde unto the tyme that he have made a fyne withe the Counstable and Marishall for the deflate.

For to Bery Careyn and Other Coropcions in Seging

Also that every Jorde, capitayues, or governor of people, do com-pell thcr servnts and menye, to berye ther careyn and bowelles abowte ther lodginges and within earth, that no stynch be in ther lodginges wher thorough that any pestelence or mortalite myght fall within the oste, upon payne to make a mendes at the Kingcs wille.

For the Taking of Prisoners of Men Bulleted

Also that no man take no presonerof that saide grounde patiscd, nor no man nor childe having bullet, 16 upon payne to lose hors and harnes and ther bodies at the Kinges wille.

For Dryving Awaye the Bestaill Oute of the Oste

Also that no souldiour of what estat soever he be, goo fro the oste with no bestaill, upon payne that he that is founde in defalte shalbe presoned and lose the saide bestaill, notwithstandinge what plac,-e soever he hath taken theim; and he that him taketh or aresteth shall have the half dele of the saide bestial) and the Kinge the other half, but it be so that he have leve of the Coun-&table and Marishall, of the whiche)eve he shall have a billet under the Counstables signet and also that he psent up the nom-ber of the bestes which he dryveth.

For to Make Stakes Ageyns a Bataill or Journey

Also that every Capitayne doe compelle ther yogmen, every man in $11 haste, to make him a good substanciall stake of xj foote of length for certeyne tydinges that lordes have harde, and on payne to be punesshed as therto longeth.

For Making of Fagottes at Siges for Bolewerkes & Diches

Also that every man make him a good substanciall f agott of xiij foote of length without leves ayens day next comynge upon pa yen of losing a mon-ethes wages; and that as welle the mar-chante whiche cometh unto the market, as other souldeours; and also that every capitain doe ley his fagottes aparte to that entent that it may be sene whether he have his nomber of fagotes after the compayne the whiche he ledeth.

For Holy Churche

Also that no man take from no hous of religion, ne non other place having saufgarde, no maner of goodes, ne vitaill, without accordinge and wille of the wardens of the same place, upon peyn to be arestede and at the Kinges wille of his life That no man spek withe theim in the Castell or in the Towne after that they be charged. Also that no maner man be so hardy to speke with theim of the towne or of the castell from hens forthe upon payne to be chastised at my lordes wille.

Ordinaunces for Foraiers in Places Dangerous

Also that no maner man goe for no forage but it be with a stale the whiche shall fowrth twise a weke, that is to witte day and day upon peyne to be chastised at my lords wille.

For Ladders

Also that every vij gentelhnen, or men of armes, ma theim a goode sufficiaunt ladder and a strong of xv rongs, and that it be redey bctweixt this and day upon payne to be chastised at my Lordes wille.

For Pavtses

Also that every ij yomen make them a goode pavise of hordes or of pap, in the best maner they cane best devise, that on may hold it, whiles that other dothe shctc, upun the payne &c.

For Theim That Sault or Renners Ro Make Theim Boty

Also that all men make them boty, vij, or v to gader, that always iij of the vij, or ij of the v, be assigned to wayte, and not to depte from the standers, upon payne to lose all the wynynge that may be wonne by him as that day, or by the feliship of him, half ot the Kinges wille; and that every capitayn geve by day all the names of his men as they be made in their botye, certifying by name whiche be those that shall abide with the standerdes, and whiche shall doe ther avauntage.

For Wemen That Usen Bordell the Whiche Lodge in the Oste

Also that no maner of man have, ne holdem any common woman within his lodging, upon peyne of losing a months wages; and if any man fynde or may finde any common woman lodging, my saide lorde geveth him leve to take from her or theim all the mony that may be founde upon her or theim, and to take a stafe and dryve her oute of the oste and breke her arme.

Articles of War Issued by Henry VIII 15 May 1513.

Contained in Tudor Royal Proclamations. 1964. Vol 1. Ed P. Hughes and J Larkin. Yale University Press.

Available via: https//archive.org/details/tudorroyalprocla0000unse/page/n9/mode/2up.

Articles of War issued by King Gustavus Adolphus II in 1621.

Contained in The Swedish Discipline: Religious, Civile, and Military.1632. Nath: Butter and Nish: Bourne.

Available via: https//www.google.com/books/edition/The_Swedish_Discipline_Religious_Civile/5MUBMwEACAAJ?hl=en.

Scottish Articles of Militarie Discipline. 1639.[4]

I. THAT in everie Regiment under a *Collonell*, there bee an ecclesiasticall Eldership or Kirke Session, consisting of the Minister or Ministers of the Regiment, and of Elders to be chosen to that effect; who shall sit at their appointed times, and judge in all Kirke affaires, according to the word of GOD, and the rules and order of Discipline used in the Kirke of SCOTLAND for censuring of delinquents, as fornicatours, whooremongers, adulterers, swearers, cursers, drunkards, profaners of the Sabbath, and all scandalous persons, that they may be brought to repentance: or being found obstinat and incorrigible, that the extreame censures of the Kirke passe against them. And that all things bee done herein, as in every parosh in the time of peace. Also, that tender care may be had of the poore and needie, and of all such as are not able, or may be disabled to helpe themselves: There bee some Deacons appointed in everie Regiment according to the order used in particular paroshes and that in matter of greatest weight, there be a generall Eldership, or common ecclesiastick judicatorie, made up of all the Ministers of the Camp, and of an Elder direct from every particular Regiment, who shall choose their own Moderatour and Clerk, have power to set down order in matters ecclesiasticall for the whole Armie: that there may bee an uniformitie of worship and of Discipline. To whom appellation may bee made from the inferiour Sessions and elderships.

II. It is ordained also for deciding of all controversies, and that the following articles of war and camp Discipline may be the better observed and obeyed. That there be in the Armie two courts of justice: one higher and another lower court: In every Regiment there shalbe a lower court, where the *Collonell* shal be president, and in his absence his Leive-tenant, with them are two Captains to bee joyned, two Leivetenants, two Ensignes, foure Serjants, and two Quartermasters, that together with the President they may be to the number of thirteene at least.

In the high martiall court shall the generall bee President, and in his absence the field Marschall, his associats shall be the Generall of the ordinance, Sergeant-major Generall, Generall of the horses, Quartermaster Generall, Muster Masters, and all the Collonels, or their Leivetenants in their absence, all these shall sit together every man in his owne place and ranke, whensover there is any matter of great importance in controversie both in the higher Court and lower, there shall be one sworne Secretarie or Clerke appointed, who shall not only make note of the processe and sentences, but

[4]From Articles of Militarie Discipline. 1639. James Bryson.

shall also make diligent record of all notable things that fall out in the armie, whither in any pitched battell, skirmish, leaguer, or any other piece of service whatsoever, with all the circumstances of time, place, or persons; he shall also set his hand to all sentences signed by the Generall, and keep a true register of all interprises, that the Generall with his councel of war, shall give order to be done. It shall be lawfull also in all civill and criminall actions of great importance, to make appellation from the lower to the higher Court: The sentence of the court shall bee publickly read in the hearing of all men, but not put in execution, till the Generall give command. No superiour officer, Collonell, or Captaine, shall solicite for any man, that is lawfully convicted by the Court, either for any cryme, or for not observing the articles of warre, unlesse it bee for his very neare kinsman for whom nature compelleth him to interceed; otherwise, the soliciter shall bee holden as odious as the Delinquent, at least shalbe cashiered from his charge. The foresaid judicatories as wel of the Kirk matters, as of war, shalbe subject to the councel of estate, and generall Assemblies *respectivè*.

III. All the Iudges both of the higher and lower Court shall solemnly swear before GOD this folowing oath:

I N. N. Do here promise before God, that I both will and shall judge uprightly, in all things that shall be presented before the Court, according to the law of God, the laws of the Kingdome of *Scotland*, and the articles of warre agreed upon, so farre as I have knowledge or understanding, neither will I for favour or hatred, for good will or evil will, for fear, for revenge, or for any gift or bribe whatsoever, judge wrongously, but judge him free that ought to •e free and doome him guiltie that I finde guiltie, as the great God the Lord of heaven and earth shall helpe me, and be my judge at the great day.

IV. All the officers and Souldiers that shall be admitted, shal with lifted up hands in all reverence swear this following oath.

I N. N. do here promise and swear, that unto the kingdome of *Scotland* I will be a faithfull servant according to the Covenant, and unto the Generall of the armie I will be a true and faithfull Souldier, everie manner of way doing my best endevours for the good of the Kingdome, and obedience of the Generall: to my power, also, shall I hinder all actions prejudiciall to the Kirk and Kingdome; and if I have tidings of any thing of that kinde I shall give notice thereof to some one or other of the councel of war. Moreover, I will doe my best to observe carefully all the Articles of warre, and points of camp Discipline: I shall behave my selfe manfully in battell, skirmishes, and every piece of service in all times and places, when and where I shall be commanded: I shall keep watch and ward, and do all other dueties willingly, as I shall bee directed: I shall carrie my selfe obediently toward my superiour officers, in all that they command me for the service of the Kirke and Kingdome: In like maner, as I shall answer before God, and every honest man, I shall not flee from my Collours, or token whatsoever that I am commanded to follow, nor absent my self from them at any time, so long as I am able to go after them: I shall bestow my life & goods for advancing of this service of the Kingdome, and to the uttermost of my power endure all distresses, that can possibly fall out in the warres, fighting manfully to the very last, so farre forth as I am able, or that any true souldier ought to doe: Furthermore, if hereafter I be put into any place or charge by the Generall, or called to anie imployment, I shall doe my best endevour, valiantly and honestly to acquite my self according to my place. This oath shall I well and truly keep, as the great God, the Lord of heaven and earth shall helpe me at the last judgement.

V. For doing of service and worship to God Almightie, the Lord of hosts, for whose Covenant this war is under taken, from whom we look for assistance, and on whom the successe of warre depends; it is thought necessary that there be publick prayers, every day morning and evening throughout the whole Leaguer, for which purpose, some token or warning shall bee given by sound of trumpet or drum. That on the Lords day there bee publick preaching, both before and afternoone, and if the time permit, two dayes in the week also. If any Minister shall neglect his time of prayer, or preaching, he shall for every absence forfault an halfe months pay, or as much as may be accounted an halfe months pay, to be taken up by the Deacons, & at the direction of the Eldership to be distributed to the poore. And whatsoever souldier shall neglect the time of prayer or preaching, shall forfault a dayes wage for every absence, and if after admonition by his Captaine he shall bee found guiltie of neglect or contempt, hee shall ly in prison for the space of twentie foure houres, and be further punished, as his fault deserveth.

VI. There shall bee no mercat nor selling of commodities whatsoever, after the warning is given for divine service, till it be closed: and if any shall happen to contraveine, they shall make forfault of all things so sold, whereof the one halfe shall be disposed upon by the Generall, or such as shall be appointed by him, and the other half to be given to the Deacons for the use of the poore. Over and above which the offender shall for one whole day be put in prison.

VII. All Officers and Souldiers shall be obedient unto the Generall and field-marshall with other officers next under them, in whatsoever they shall command upon the paines following. Whosoever behaveth not himself reverently and obediently unto the Generall of the Armie, shall be kept in yrons or prison, till he be brought to answere before a councel of war, where being found guilty, whatsoever his qualitie be, hee shall stand to the order of the councell, to underly what punishment they shall thinke convenient according to his merite.

Whosoever shall offer to discredit these great officers by word of mouth, or otherwise, and be not able by proofe to make it good; and whosoever shall lift up any manner of armes against any of them, whither he doe them hurt or not, shall be punished by death. And if any officer do strick any of them with his hand, whither he hit or misse, he shall losse his right hand.

If it shall hapen that the Generall, or any of the great and generall officers at any occasion shall offer injurie to any noble man, knight, gentleman, or other which standeth not with their honor to put up, Then shall they give in their complaint to the Councel of war, where the offender shall answer, and bee censured according to the qualitie and importance of the fault.

If any Souldier or inferior officer serving on horse or foot, shall offer any injurie by word, or deed, to his Collonell, Leivetenant Collonell, Sergeant majour, Quarter-master, Captain or any of his superiors, or shall refuse any dewty commanded him, he shall be punished according to the importance of his fault, and if it shall happen that any officer shall command any thing which tendeth rather to the prejudice nor to the good of the publick, then shall he who is commanded modestly refuse to obey and presently give notice thereof.

If any inferiour officer shal challenge any common Souldier to be guilty of any dishonest action, he shall answer for it before the court as if he were his equall.

If any Souldier horse or foot, shall offer to strike his officer that commands him any dewty or piece of service, he shal lose his hand and be turned out of the quarter, and if it be done in any fort or beleaguered place after the watch is set, he shal lose his life for it; but if he not only offer but do hurt to any of them, whether in the field, or not he shall be shot to death. Whosoever in the presence of the Generall shall draw his sword to do mischief with it, shall lose his hand: He who shal in anger draw his sword, while his Colloures are fleeing, either in batell or in march, shall be shot to death: He who shall presume to draw his sword in any court of justice, shall lose his life: He that draws his sword in any strength or fort to do mischief therewith after the watch is set, shal lose his life.

VIII. The Provest-marshall-general may apprehend any man by his own authority & keep him in irones or in prison, but by no means may do execution upon him although he be sentenced by the court of war, without first giving notice thereof to the Generall and obtaining warrand for that effect.

The same is to be understood of the Provest-marshals of every regiment and companie: And if anie shall be found to hinder the Provest-marshals when they are to apprehend any man or when they are about to execute any thing that becomes them, they shall not escape unpunished in the martiall court.

IX. Common & ordinarie profainers of the sabbath, swearers and drunkards, especially such as shall be found drinking in time of prayers or divine service, shall not only be punished in their means, but shall also make their publick repentance in the midst of the congregation, and if they cannot be reclaimed, they shall be casheired and discharged as unworthy to do service in any place of the armie.

X. No duell or combate shall be permitted to be foughten; If any man offer wrong to another, it shall bee decided by the officers of the regiment, the challenger shall answer it before the Martiall court. And if any Captaine, Leivtenant or other inferiour officer shall give leave or permission unto any under their command to enter combate, and doth not rather hinder them, he shall be presently casheired from his charge and serve afterward as a common Souldiour: but if any harme be done he shall answer it as deeply as he that did it.

XI. He that forceth any woman and the matter be proved, he shall die for it.

No whoore shall be suffered in the leaguer, but if any will have his own wife with him, he may.

If any man keep an unmaried woman, he shall either marrie her or be constrained to put her away, and make his repentance for his fault.

XII. All Souldiers shall dewly repaire unto the generall musters upon the day and houre appointed, nor shall any Colonell or Captaine of horse or foot keep back his Souldiers from being mustered at the time when the muster masters shall desire to view them, if any refuse, he shall be holden for a mutiner.

No Colonell or Captaine shall lend any of their Souldiers unto another upon the musterdays for the making up of their numbers compleat: he that thus makes a false muster, shal answer it at a martiall court, where being found guilty he shall be proclaimed a deceaver, after which being put out of the quarter his Colours shall flee no more.

If any horsman borrowes either horse, armour, pistols, sadle, sword or harnise to passe the muster withall, so much as is borrowed shal be eschited, and both himself and he that lent it him, shall be turned out of the leaguer, the one half of the armes forfaulted shall go unto the Captaine, and the other half unto the Perforce.

XIII. When any march is to be made, every man that is sworn shal follow his colors, whosoever presumes without leave to stay behinde, shal be punished.

If any upon mutinie be found to do it, be they many or be they few, they shall die for it.

Every man is to keep his own rank and file upon the march, and not to put others from their ordour, nor shall any man cast himself behinde, or set himself upon any wagon or horseback: The offenders to be punished according to the time and place.

XIV. He that after warning is given by sound of Drum or Trumpet for setting of the watch, doth wilfully absent himself without some lawfull excuse, shall be disgraced and be put to bread and water, or some such punishment as the matter is of importance.

He that is taken sleeping upon the watch to the indangering of the armie, shall be shot to death.

In like sort shall he be punished who drinks himself drunk upon his watch or place of sentinell that he cannot do his dewty, or that cometh off his watch where he is commanded to keep his guaird.

XV. Whatsoever regiment shall once charge the enemie, and then retire afterward from them before they come to dint of sword, shall answer it before the high martiall court: and if this be occasioned by any officer, he shall be publickly disgraced, and turned out of the leaguer: If the fault shall be found to be in the Souldiers, then shall every tenth man be hanged and the rest condemned to carry all the filth out of the leaguer, till by some exploit they procure their pardon and recover their reputation; provided alwaies, if at the first any man can by the testimony of sufficient witnesses prove himself not guilty of the couarddice, he shall go free.

If any occasion be to enter any strength or sconce by assault or breach, he who reteires from the place before he hath been at handy blows with the enemy & hath used his sword so far as it is possible for him to do service with it and before he be by maine strength beaten off by the enemy, shall be so punished as the court shall finde him to have deserved.

XVI. Whosoever runs from his Collours and doeth not defend them to the uttermost of his power so long as they be in danger, shall suffer death for it.

When any occasion of service is, he that first runs away, if any man kill him he shall be free, and if at that time he escape and be apprehended afterward, he shal be proclaimed traitour & put out of the quarter.

Whatsoever ensigne-bearer shall flee out of any place of Battrie, sconce or redoubt before he hath indured three assaults and receives no relieif, shall be in like manner punished, providing alwayes the place be defenceable.

If any regiment, troup or companie shall flee out of the field or battell, they shall answer for it before the high court, and if there it can be proved to have broken their oath, they shall be proclaimed traitours.

XVII. Whatsoever regiment, troupor companie shall be found to treat with the enemie or to enter in any conditions with them, without knowledge and leave of the Generall or chief commander in his absence, the officer shall be put to death for it and all his goods confiscated; of the Souldiers every tenth man shall be hanged and the rest punished as is a foresaid.

But if any that then were in companie of such can free themselves from being partakers of the crime and can prove that they did their best to resist it, then shall they be rewarded according to their truth and faithfulnesse.

Whosoever gives advice unto the enemy any manner of way or keeps any discourse with him without leave of the Generall, or giveth unto him any private intelligence by letters or otherwaies or maks any signe unto him for his advantage shall die for it.

XVIII. They that give over any strength to the enemy, unlesse it be for extremity of hunger or want of amunition, the governour with all the officers shal die for it: All the Souldiers be lodged without the quarter and be made to carry all the filth out of the leaguer, till by some new proof of their worth they blot away the former cowardice.

XIX. If any numbers of Souldiers shal without leave of their Captaine assemble together for raking mutinous counsell amongst themselves, so many inferior officers as be in company with them shal suffer death, and the Souldiers be so punished, as they that give up any strength: And whatsoever Captaine shall permit unto his Souldiers to hold any such meetings amongst themselves, shall answer it before the high court of justice.

If any shall fall in quarrelling, and fighting and shal call for help of his friends or familiars with intention to be revenged or to defend himself, he shall suffer death for it, and they that come to help him shall be punished like mutiners.

He also shall be reckned for a mutiner who shall not be content with that quarter or place that shall be assigned him, whither in a town or in the leaguer.

XX. Whosoever casts his arms from him either in the field or other where, shall be scourged through the quarter & disgraced as before, til he redeem his credit.

He that sels or enpawnes his armes or any kinde of amunition, or any spades, shools, picks, & other the like necessary instruments used in the field, shal be for the first and second time beaten through the quarter, and for the third time, punished as for other thift: He also that buyes or taks them upon pawne, be he Souldier or be he victualer, he shall both loose his money and be punished as he that sold them.

He that wilfully breaks any of his armes or instruments aforesaid, shall not only pay for the mending of them, but shall be put to bread and water, and shal be punished otherwise at the discretion of the court.

XXI. No man shal presume to set on fire any town or village in the land or camp, if any doeth he shall be punished according as the judges shall finde the matter important.

XXII. Billets and lodgings in every place must be directed by the quarter-master or quarter-master generally; No commander or common Souldier shall exact or extort any thing besides what is appointed.

All must deal courteously with their hoste and his houshold servants: He that beats any of them, for the first and second fault he shall be put in irones and made to fast with bread and water, but if he do any of them greater hurt he shall be punished at the discretion of the court.

None shall presume to do wrong to any that bring necessaries unto the leaguer, whither by taking their goods or by taking away their horses; which who so doeth shal be severely punished.

They that pillage or steal any thing, whither from them that furnish the leaguer or from uther subjects of the kingdome, whither Covenanters or not Covenanters, they shall be punished as for other thift.

XXIII. If it so please God that we beat the enemy either in the field or in the leaguer, no man shall fall upon the pillage till the enemy be utterly put to the rout; which done, every man may fall upon his own quarter and rest contented with it, without plundering of others: If any man shal fall upon the pillage before the time, and any evill to the armie shall ensue upon their greedinesse after the spoile, then shall all of them suffer death for it, and although no damnage come thereby, yet must they be punished as their fault deserveth.

When any fort or place of strength is taken in, no man shall fall upon the spoile before the enemy be beaten out of all his holds and the quarters be dealt out and assigned.

If any be found drunk in the enemies leaguer before he hath forsaken the same and laid down his armes, he shall be severly punished according to the damnage done by his drunkennesse, and although there be no damnage, yet shal he be punished for his drunkennesse, especially at such a time.

XXIV. No Captaine shall with-hold any off his Souldiers meanes from him, which if he do, he shall be censured in the court of justice; And if any such evil follow thereupon, as that the Souldiers mutine, be sicke, endure hunger, or give up any strength, then shall he be answerable for all these inconveniences.

If any Captaine lend money unto his Souldiers which he will have payed again, let it be repayed in parcels as the Souldier may spare it, that the commō service be no wayes hindered or neglected thereby.

If upon necessity it come to passe, pay be not made at the due time, yet shall every man be forward in his service all having victuals for the present & certaine expectation of the meanes so soon as may be.

No Captaine shall presume to go out of his station to demand his pay without leave of the Generall, providing he be intertained: who so doth shall be casheired from his place.

XXV. No Colonell or Captaine shall give leave to his Souldiers to go home out of the field, without leave of the Generall or chief commander, under the paine of the loose of three Monethes pay, and to answer it before the court.

No Souldier shall desire his passe, whilest there is any present service to be done against the enemie.

If any Souldier desire to be discharged from the wars because he is sick, or maimed, or upon any such reasonable cause, he shall be discharged by warrand from the Generall.

If any Souldier shal run away from his Collours, without a passe of his officers, he shall be apprehended where ever he can be found and punished according to the articles foresaid.

United States Continental Congress – Articles of War, June 30, 1775[5]

[5]Source: *Journals of the Continental Congress* 1774–1779. Vol II Pages 111–123. W. Ford, Ed. Government Printing Office.

Rules and Regulations

Whereas his Majesty's most faithful subjects in these Colonies are reduced to a dangerous and critical situation, by the attempts of the British Ministry, to carry into execution, by force of arms, several unconstitutional and oppressive acts of the British parliament for laying taxes in America, to enforce the collection of these taxes, and for altering and changing the constitution and internal police of some of these Colonies, in violation of the natural and civil rights of the Colonies.

And whereas hostilities have been actually commenced in Massachusetts Bay, by the British troops, under the command of General Gage, and the lives of a number of the inhabitants of that Colony destroyed; the town of Boston not only having been long occupied as a garrisoned town in an enemy's country, but the inhabitants thereof treated with a severity and cruelty not to be justified even towards declared enemies.

And whereas large reinforcements have been ordered, and are soon expected, for the declared purpose of compelling these Colonies to submit to the operation of the said acts, which hath rendered it necessary, and an indispensable duty, for the express purpose of securing and defending these Colonies, and preserving them in safety against all attempts to carry the said acts into execution; that an armed force be raised sufficient to defeat such hostile designs, and preserve and defend the lives, liberties and immunities of the Colonists: for the due regulating and well ordering of which;-

Resolved, That the following Rules and Orders be attended to, and observed by such forces as are or may hereafter be raised for the purposes aforesaid.

Article I. That every officer who shall be retained, and every soldier who shall serve in the Continental Army, shall, at the time of his acceptance of his commission or inlistment, subscribe these rules and regulations. And that the officers and soldiers, already of that army, shall also, as soon as may be, subscribe the same; from the time of which subscription every officer and soldier, shall be bound by those regulations. But if any of the officers or soldiers, now of the said army, do not subscribe these rules and regulations, then they may be retained in the said army, subject to the rules and regulations under which they entered into the service, or be discharged from the service, at the option of the Commander in chief.

Art. II. It is earnestly recommended to all officers and soldiers, diligently to attend Divine Service; and all officers and soldiers who shall behave indecently or irreverently at any place of Divine Worship, shall, if commissioned officers, be brought before a court-martial, there to be publicly and severely reprimanded by the President; if non-commissioned officers or soldiers, every person so offending, shall, for his first offence, forfeit One Sixth of a Dollar, to be deducted out of his next pay; for the second offence, he shall not only forfeit a like sum, but be confined for twenty-four hours, and for every like offence, shall suffer and pay in like manner; which money so forfeited, shall be applied to the use of the sick soldiers of the troop or company to which the offender belongs.

Art. III. Whatsoever non-commissioned officer or soldier shall use any profane oath or execration, shall incur the penalties expressed in the second article; and if a commissioned officer be thus guilty of profane cursing or swearing, he shall forfeit and pay for each and every such offence, the sum of Four Shillings, lawful money.

Art. IV. Any officer or soldier, who shall behave himself with contempt or disrespect towards the General or Generals, or Commanders in chief of the Continental Forces, or shall speak false words, tending to his or their hurt or dishonour, shall be punished according to the nature of his offence, by the judgment of a general court-martial.

Art. V. Any officer or soldier, who shall begin, excite, cause, or join in any mutiny or sedition, in the regiment, troop, or company to which he belongs, or in any other regiment, troop or company of the Continental Forces, either by land or sea, or in any party, post, detachment, or guard, on any presence whatsoever, shall suffer such punishment, as by a general court-martial shall be ordered.

Art. VI. Any officer, non-commissioned officer, or soldier, who being present at any mutiny or sedition, does not use his utmost endeavours to suppress the same, or coming to the knowledge of any mutiny, or intended mutiny, does not, without delay, give information thereof to the commanding officer, shall be punished by order of a general court-martial, according to the nature of his offense.

Art. VII. Any officer or soldier, who shall strike his superior officer, or draw, or offer to draw, or shall lift up any weapon, or offer any violence against him, being in the execution of his office, on any presence whatsoever, or shall disobey any lawful commands of his superior officer, shall suffer such punishment as shall, according to the nature of his offense, be ordered by the sentence of a general court-martial.

Art. VIII. Any non-commissioned officer, or soldier, who shall desert, or without leave of his commanding officer, absent himself from the troop or company to which he belongs, or from any detachment of the same, shall, upon being convicted thereof, be punished according to the nature of his offense, at the discretion of a general court-martial.

Art. IX. Whatsoever Officer, or soldier, shall be convicted of having advised or persuaded any other officer or soldier, to desert, shall suffer such punishment, as shall be ordered by the sentence of a general court-martial.

Art. X. All officers, of what condition soever, shall have power to part and quell all quarrels, frays, and disorders, though the persons concerned, should belong to another regiment, troop, or company; and either order officers to be arrested, or non-commissioned officers, or soldiers, to be confined and imprisoned, till their proper superior officers shall be acquainted therewith:

and whoever shall refuse to obey such officer, (though of an inferior rank) or shall draw his sword upon him, shall be punished at the discretion of a general court-martial.

Art. XI. No officer or soldier shall use any reproachful or provoking speeches or gestures to another, nor shall presume to send a challenge to any person to fight a duel: And whoever shall, knowingly and willingly, suffer any person whatsoever to go forth to fight a duel, or shall second, promote, or carry any challenge, shall be deemed as a principal; and whatsoever officer or soldier shall upbraid another for refusing a challenge, shall also be considered as a challenger; and all such offenders, in any of these or such like cases, shall be punished at the discretion of a general court-martial.

Art. XII. Every officer, commanding in quarters or on a march, shall keep good order, and, to the utmost of his power, redress all such abuses or disorders which may be committed by any officer or soldier under his command: If upon any complaint [being] made to him, of officers or soldiers beating, or otherwise ill-treating any person, or of committing any kind of riot, to the disquieting of the inhabitants of this Continent; he the said commander, who shall refuse or omit to see justice done on the offender or offenders, and reparation made to the party or parties injured, as far as the offender's wages shall enable him or them, shall, upon due proof thereof, be punished as ordered by a general court-martial, in such manner as if he himself had committed the crimes or disorders complained of.

Art. XIII. If any officer should think himself to be wronged by his colonel or the commanding officer of the regiment, and shall, upon due application made to him, be refused to be redressed, he may complain to the General or Commander in chief of the Continental Forces, in order to obtain justice, who is hereby required to examine into said complaint, and see that justice be done.

Art. XIV. If any inferior officer or soldier, shall think himself wronged by his captain or other officer commanding the troop or company to which he belongs, he is to complain thereof to the commanding officer of the regiment, who is hereby required to summon a regimental court-martial, for the doing justice to the complainant; from which regimental court-martial, either party may, if he thinks himself still aggrieved, appeal to a general court-martial; but if, upon a second hearing, the appeal shall appear to be vexatious and groundless, the person so appealing, shall be punished at the discretion of the general court-martial.

Art. XV. Whatsoever non-commissioned officer or soldier, shall be convicted, at a regimental court-martial, of having sold, or designedly, or through neglect, wasted the ammunition, arms, or provisions, or other military stores, delivered out to him, to be employed in the service of this Continent, shall, if an officer, be reduced to a private centinel; and if a private soldier, shall suffer such punishment as shall be ordered by a regimental court-martial.

Art. XVI. All non-commissioned officers and soldiers, who shall be found one mile from the camp, without leave in writing from their commanding officer, shall suffer such punishment as shall be indicted on him or them by the sentence of a regimental court-martial.

Aft. XVII. No officer or soldier shall lie out of his quarters or camp, without leave from the commanding officer of the regiment, upon penalty of being punished according to the nature of his offense, by order of a regimental court-martial.

Art. XVIII. Every non-commissioned officer and soldier shall retire to his quarters, or tent, at the beating of the retreat; in default of which, he shall be punished according to the nature of his offense, by order of the commanding officer.

Art. XIX. No officer, non-commissioned officer or soldier, shall fail of repairing, at the time fixed, to the place of parade or exercise, or other rendezvous appointed by the commanding officer, if not prevented by sickness or some other evident necessity; or shall go from the said place of rendezvous, or from his guard, without leave from his commanding officer, before he shall be regularly dismissed or relieved, on penalty of being punished according to the nature of his oilence, by the sentence of a regimental court-martial.

Art. XX. Whatsoever commissioned officer shall be found drunk on his guard, party, or other duty, under arms, shall be cashiered for it; any non-commissioned officer or soldier so offending, shall suffer such punishment as shall be ordered by the sentence of a regimental court-martial.

Art. XXI. Whatsoever sentinel shall be found sleeping upon his post, or shall leave it before he shall be regularly relieved, shall suffer such punishment as shall be ordered by the sentence of a general court-martial.

Art. XXII. Any person belonging to the Continental army, who, by discharging of fire-arms, heating of drums, or by any other means whatsoever, shall occasion false alarms, in camp or quarters, shall suffer such punishment as shall be ordered by the sentence of a general court-martial.

Art. XXIII. Any officer or soldier, who shall, without urgent necessity, or without leave of his superior officer, quit his platoon or division, shall be punished according to the nature of his offense, by the sentence of a regimental court-martial.

Art. XXIV. No officer or soldier shall do violence, or offer any insult, or abuse, to any person who shall bring provisions, or other necessaries, to the camp or quarters of the Continental army; any officer or soldier so offending, shall, upon complaint being made to the commanding officer, surlier such punishment as shall be ordered by a regimental court-martial.

Art. XXV. Whatsoever officer or soldier shall shamefully abandon any post committed to his charge, or shall speak words inducing others to do the like, in time of an engagement, shall suffer death immediately.

Art. XXVI. Any person belonging to the continental army, who shall make known the watch-word to any person who is not entitled to receive it, according to the rules and discipline of war, or shall presume to give a parole, or watch-word, different from what he received, shall suffer death, or such other punishment as shall be ordered by the sentence of a general court-martial.

Art. XXVII. Whosoever belonging to the continental army, shall relieve the enemy with money, victuals, or ammunition, or shall knowingly harbour or protect an enemy, shall suffer such punishment as by a general court-martial shall be ordered.

Art. XXVIII. Whosoever belonging to the continental army, shall be convicted of holding correspondence with, or of giving intelligence to, the enemy, either directly or indirectly, shall super such punishment as by a general court-martial shall be ordered.

Art. XXIX. All public stores taken in the enemy's camp or magazines, whether of artillery, ammunition, Loathing, or provisions, shall be secured for the use of the United Colonies.

Art. XXX. If any officer or soldier shall leave his post or colours, in time of an engagement, to go in search of plunder, he shall, upon being convicted thereof before a general court-martial, suffer such punishment as by the said court-martial shall be ordered.

Art. XXXI. If any commander of any post, intrenchment, or fortress, shall be compelled, by the officers or soldiers under his command, to give it up to the enemy, or to abandon it, the commissioned officer, non-commissioned officers, or soldiers, who shall be convicted of having so offended, shall suffer death, or such other punishment as may be inflicted upon them by the sentence of a general court-martial.

Art. XXXII. All suttlers and retailers to a camp, and all persons whatsoever, serving with the continental army in the field, though not inlisted soldiers, are to be subject to the articles, rules, and regulations of the continental army.

Art. XXXIII. No general court-martial shall consist of a less number than thirteen, none of which shall be under the degree of a commissioned officer; and the president shall be a field officer: And the president of each and every court-martial, whether general or regimental, shall have power to administer an oath to every witness, in order to the trial of offenders. And the members of all courts-martial shall be duly sworn by the president; and the next in rank on the court-martial, shall administer the oath to tile president.

Art. XXXIV. The members, both of general and regimental courts-martial, shall, when belonging to different corps, take the same rank which they hold in the army; but when courts-martial shall be composed of officers of one corps, they shall take their ranks according to their commissions by which they are mustered in the said corps.

Art. XXXV. All the members of a court-martial, are to behave with calmness, decency, and impartiality; and in giving of their votes, are to begin with the youngest or lowest in commission.

Art. XXXVI. No field officer shall be tried by any person under the degree of a captain; nor shall any proceedings or trials be carried on, excepting between the hours of eight in the morning, and three in the afternoon, except in cases which require an immediate example.

Art. XXXVII. The commissioned officers of every regiment may, by the appointment of their Colonel or commanding officer, hold regimental courts-martial for the enquiring into such disputes or criminal mutters as may come before them, and for the inflicting corporal punishment, for small offences, and shall give judgment by the majority of voices; but no sentence shall be executed till the commanding officer (not being a member of the court-martial) shall have confirmed the same.

Art. XXXVIII. No regimental court-martial shall consist of less than five officers, excepting in cases where that number cannot be conveniently assembled, when three may be sufficient; who are likewise to determine upon the sentence by the majority of voices; which sentence is to be confirmed by the commanding officer, not being a member of the court-martial.

Art. XXXIX. Every officer, commanding in any fort, castle, or barrack, or elsewhere, where the corps under his command consists of detachments from different regiments or of independent companies, may assemble courts-martial for the trial of offenders in the same manner as if they were regimental, whose sentence is not to be executed till it shall be confirmed by the said commanding officer.

Art. XL. No person whatsoever shall use menacing words, signs, or gestures in the presence of a court-martial then sitting, or shall cause any disorder or riot, so as to disturb their proceeding, on the penalty of being punished at the discretion of the said court-martial.

Art. XLI. To the end that offenders may be brought to justice; whenever any officer or soldier shall commit a crime deserving punishment, he shall, by his commanding officer, if an officer, be put in arrest; if a non-commissioned officer or soldier, be imprisoned till he shall be either tried by a court-martial, or shall be lawfully discharged by proper authority.

Art. XLII. No officer or soldier who shall be put in arrest, or imprisonment, shall continue in his confinement more than eight days, or till such time as a court-martial can be conveniently assembled.

Art. XLIII. No officer commanding a guard, or provost-marshal, shall refuse to receive or keep any prisoner committed to his charge, by an officer belonging to the Continental forces; which officer shall at the same time deliver an account in writing, signed by himself, of the crime with which the said prisoner is charged.

Art. XLIV. No officer commanding a guard, or provost-marshal, shall presume to release any prisoner committed to his charge, without proper authority for so doing; nor shall he suffer any prisoner to escape, on the penalty of being punished for it, by the sentence of a general court-martial.

Art. XLV. Every officer or provost-martial, to whose charge prisoners shall be committed, is hereby required, within twenty-four hours after such commitment, or as soon as he shall be relieved from his guard, to give in writing to the Colonel of the regiment to whom the prisoner belongs (where the prisoner is confined upon the guard belonging to the said regiment, and that his offense only relates to the neglect of duty in his own corps) or to the commander in chief, their names, their crimes, and the names of the officers who committed them, on the penalty of being punished for his disobedience or neglect, at the discretion of a general court-martial.

Art. XLVI. And if any officer under arrest shall leave his confinement before he is set at liberty by the officer who confined him, or by a superior power, he shall be cashiered for it.

Art. XLVII. Whatsoever commissioned officer shall be convicted before a general court-martial, of behaving in a scandalous, infamous manner, such as is unbecoming the character of an officer and a gentleman, shall be discharged from the service.

Art. XLVIII. All officers, conductors, gunners, matrosses, drivers, or any other persons whatsoever, receiving pay or hire, in the service of the continental artillery, shall be governed by the aforesaid rules and articles, and shall be subject to be tried by courts-martial, in like manner with the officers and soldiers of the Continental troops.

Art. XLIX. For differences arising amongst themselves, or in matters relating solely to their own corps, the courts-martial may be composed of their own officers; but where a number sufficient of such officers cannot be assembled, or in matters wherein other corps are interested, the officers of artillery shall sit in courts-martial, with the officers of the other corps.

Art. L. All crimes, not capital, and all disorders and neglects, which officers and soldiers may be guilty of, to the prejudice of good order and military discipline, though not mentioned in the articles of war, are to be taken cognizance of by a general or regimental court-martial, according to the nature and degree of the offence, and be punished at their discretion.

Art. LI. That no persons shall be sentenced by a court-martial to super death, except in the cases expressly mentioned in the foregoing articles; nor shall any punishment be inflicted at the discretion of a court-martial, other than degrading, cashiering, drumming out of the army, whipping not exceeding th~rty-n~ne lashes, fine not exceeding two months pay of the offender, imprisonment not exceeding one month.

Art. LII. The field officers of each and every regiment are to appoint some suitable person belonging to such regiment, to receive all such fines as may arise within the same, for any breach of any of the foregoing articles, and shall direct the same to be carefully and properly applied to the relief of such sick, wounded, or necessitous soldiers as belong to such regiment; and such person shall account with such officer for all fines received, and the application thereof.

Art. LIII. All members sitting in courts-martial shall be sworn by the President of said courts, which President shall himself be sworn by the officer in said court next in rank:-The oath to be administered previous to their proceeding to the trial of any offender, in form following, viz.

> Yon A. B. swear that you will well and truly try, and Impartially determine the cause of the prisoner now to be tried, according to the rules for regulating the Continental army. So help you God.

Art. LIV. All persons called to give evidence, in any case, before a court-martial, who shall refuse to give evidence, shall be punished for such refusal at the discretion of such court-martial:-The oath to be administered in the following form, viz.

> Yon swear the evidence you shall give in the case now in hearing, shall be the truth, the whole truth, and nothing but the truth. So help you God.

Art. LV. Every officer commanding a regiment, troop, or company, shall, upon notice given to him by the Commissary of the musters, or from one of his deputies, assemble the regiment, troop, or company under his command, in the next convenient place for their being mustered.

Art. LVI. Every colonel or other field officer, or officer commanding any corps, to which there is no field officer, and actually residing with it, may give furloughs to non-commissioned officers and soldiers, in such numbers, and for so long a time, as he shall judge to be most consistent with the good of the service; but no non-commissioned officer or soldier shall, by leave of his Captain, or inferior officer, commanding the troop or company (his field officer not being present) be absent above twenty days in six months, nor shall more than two private men be absent at the same time from their troop or company, excepting some extraordinary occasion shall require it, of which occasion the field officer present with, and commanding the regiment or independent corps, is to be Judge.

Art. LVII. At every muster the commanding officer of each regiment, troop, or company, then present, shall give to the commissary of musters certificates signed by himself, signifying how long such officers, non-commissioned officers, and soldiers, who shall not appear at the said muster, have been absent, and the reason of their absence; which reasons, and the time of absence, shall be inserted in the muster-rolls, opposite to the respective names of such absentees: The said certificates shall, together with the muster rolls, be by the said Commissary transmitted to the General, and to this or any future Congress of the United Colonies, or Committee appointed thereby, within twenty days next after such muster being taken; on failure whereof, the Commissary so offending shall be discharged from the service.

Art. LVIII. Every officer who shall be convicted before a general court-martial of having signed a false certificate, relating to the absence of either officer, officer, or private soldier, shall be cashiered.

Art. LIX. Every officer, who shall knowingly make a false muster of man or horse, and every officer or Commissary who shall willingly sign, direct, or allow the signing of the muster rolls, wherein such false muster is contained, shall, upon proof made thereof, by two witnesses, before a general court-martial, be cashiered, and moreover forfeit all such pay as may be due to him at the time of conviction for such offense.

Art. LX. Any commissary who shall be convicted of having taken any gift or gratuity on the mustering any regiment, troop or company, or on the signing the muster rolls, shall be displaced from his office, and forfeit his pay, as in the preceding article.

Art. LXI. Any officer who shall presume to muster any person as a soldier, who is at other times accustomed to wear a livery, or who does not actually do his duty as a soldier, shall be deemed guilty of having made a false muster, and shall super accordingly.

Art. LXII. Every officer who shall knowingly make a false return to the Commander in Chief of the American forces, or to any his superior officer, authorized to call for such returns, of the state of the regiment, troop, independent company, or garrison under his command, or of arms, ammunition, cloathing, or other stores thereunto belonging, shall, by a court-martial, be cashiered.

Art. LXIII. The commanding officer of every regiment, troop, independent company, or garrison, in the service aforesaid, shall, in the beginning of every month, remit to the Commander in chief of said forces, an exact return of the state of the regiment, troop, independent company, or garrison under his command, specifying the names of the officers not then residing at their posts, and the reason for, and the time of their absence: whosoever shall be convicted of having, through neglect or design, omitted the sending such returns, shall be punished according to the nature of his crime, by the judgment of a general court-martial.

Art. LXIV. No suttler shall be permitted to sell any kind of liquors or victuals, or to keep their houses or shops open, for the entertainment of soldiers, after nine at night, or before the beating of the reveilles, or upon Sundays, during divine service or sermon, on the penalty of being dismissed from all future settling.

Art. LXV. All officers commanding in the camp, or in any forts, barracks, or garrisons, are hereby required to see that the persons permitted to suttle shall supply the soldiers with good and wholesome provisions at a reasonable price, as they shall be answerable for their neglect.

Art. LXVI. No officers commanding in any camp, garrisons, forts, or barracks, shall either themselves exact exorbitant prices for houses or stalls let out to settlers, or shall connive at the like exactions in others, nor lay any duty or impositions upon, or be interested in the sale of such victuals, liquors, or other necessaries of life, which are brought into the camp, garrison, fort or barracks, for the use of the soldiers, on the penalty of being discharged from the service.

Art. LXVII. That the general, or commander in chief for the time being, shall have full power of pardoning, or mitigating any of the punishments ordered to be inflicted, for any of the offenses mentioned in the foregoing articles; and every offender, convicted as aforesaid, by any regimental court-martial, may be pardoned, or have his punishment mitigated by the Colonel or officer commanding the regiment.

Art. LXVIII. When any commissioned officer shall happen to die, or be killed in the service of the United Colonies, the Major of the regiment, or the officer doing the Major's duty in his absence, shall immediately secure all his effects or equipage, then in camp or quarters; and shall, before the next regimental court-martial, make an inventory thereof, and forthwith transmit the same to the office of the Secretary of the Congress, or assembly of the province in which the corps is stationed or shall happen to be at the time of the death of such officer; to the end that his executors may, after payment of his debts in quarters, and interment, recede the overplus, if any be, to his or their use.

Art. LXIX. When any non-commissioned officer or private soldier, shall happen to die, or be killed in the service of the United (colonies, the then commanding officer of the troop or company, shall, in the presence of two other commissioned officers, take an account of whatever effects he dies possessed of, and transmit the same, as in the ease above provided for, in order that the same may be secured for, and paid to their respective representatives.

Ordered, That Mr. [Silas] Deane, Mr. [Thomas] Cushing and Mr. [Joseph] Hewes, be a Committee to examine the rules and articles of war agreed to by the Congress, and get them printed as soon as possible.

On motion, Resolved, That the Congress will, on Monday next, take into consideration the trade of America.

On motion, Resolved, That the Committee for Indian Affairs, do prepare proper talks to the several tribes of Indians, for engaging the continuance of their friendship to us, and neutrality in our present unhappy disputes with Great Britain.

The order of the day put off and adjournment made till to Morrow.

References

Allen, J. (2017). *An introduction to the crusades*. Toronto, ON: University of Toronto Press.

Alonso, V. (2007). War, peace, and international law in Ancient Greece. In K. A. Raaflaub (Ed.), *War and peace in the ancient world* (pp. 206–225). Oxford: Blackwell.

Ammons-Blanfort, D'Alessio, S., & Stolzenberg, L. (2023). Self-help and Black firearm crime. *Crime & Delinquency*, *69*(1), 178–207.

(1639/1969). *Articles of militarie discipline*. Edinburgh: Da Capo Press.

Aquinas. (1485/1947). *Summa theologica*. Tr. Fathers of the English Dominican Province. Cincinnati, OH: Benziger Brothers.

Asbridge, T. (2005). *The first crusade: A new history: The roots of conflict between Christianity and Islam*. Oxford: Oxford University Press.

Augustine. (1950). *City of God*. New York: Modern Library.

Augustine. (1958). *On Christian doctrine* (D. Robertson Jr, Trans.). New York: The Liberal Arts Press.

Augustine. (1961). *Confessions* (R. Pine-Coffin, Trans.). New York: Penguin Books.

Barthelemy, D., & White, S. (1996). The "Feudal Revolution". *Past and Present*, *152*, 196–223.

Bartlett, C. (1995). *English longbowmen: 1330–1515*. Oxford: Osprey Press.

Bassiouni, M. C. (2008). The new wars and the crisis of compliance with the law of armed conflict by non-state actors. *Journal of Criminal Law and Criminology*, *98*(3), 711–810.

Beaulac, S. (2004). The Westphallian model in defining international law: Challenging the myth. *Australian Journal of Legal History*, *8*, 181–213.

Bédoyére, G. de la. (2020). *Gladius: The world of the Roman soldier*. Chicago, IL: University of Chicago Press.

Bell, L. (2007). Conflcit and reconciliation in the Ancient Middle East: The clash of Egyptian and Hittite Chariots in Syria, and the world's first peace treaty between "Superpowers". In K. Raaflaub, (Ed.), *War and peace in the Ancient world providence*. RI: Wiley.

Bisson, T. (1994). The "Feudal Revolution". *Past and Present*, 142 6–42.

Bisson, T. (1997). The 'Feudal Revolution' replay. *Past and Present*, *155*, 205–225.

Black, D. (1976). *The behavior of law*. San Diego, CA: Academic Press.

Black, D. (1998). *The social structure of right and wrong* (Revised ed.). San Diego, CA: Academic Press.

Blau, P., & Meyer, M. (1987). *Bureaucracy in modern society* (3rd ed.). Chicago: McGraw Hill.

Bonét, H. (1949). *The tree of battles: An English version with introduction* (G. W. Coopland, Trans.). Cambridge, MA: Harvard University Press.

Bonger, W. (1916). *Criminality and economic conditions* (H. Horton, Trans.). New York: Agathon Press, Inc.

Bowman, J. (1999). Councils, memory and mills: The early development of the peace of God in Catalonia. *Early Medieval Europe*, *8*(1), 99–129.

Bracey, D. (2006). *Exploring law and culture*. Long Grove, IL: Waveland Press.

Bradford, A. S. (2001). *With arrow, sword, and spear: A history of warfare in the ancient world*. London: Praeger.

Brand, C. E. (1968). *Roman military law*. Austin: University of Texas Press.

Callister, G., & Whitbread, R. (2022). *Battle: Understanding conflict from hastings to helmand*. South Yorkshire: Pen and Sword Books.

Castiglione, B. (1528/1959). *The book of the courtier* (Tr and Ed F. Simpson). New York: Ungar Publishing.

Caxton, W. (1485/1926). *The book of the order of Chivalry. Early English text society*. Oxford: Oxford University Press.

Chambliss, W. J. (1964). A sociological analysis of the law of vagrancy. *Social Problems*, *12*(1), 67–77.

Chandler, J. (2022). The Continental Army and 'Military Europe': Professionalism and restraint in the American War of Independence. *War in History*, *29*(2), 323–340.

Charni, G. de. (n.d.). *De Chivalerie* (Dr. T. Hatton, Trans.). Unpublished manuscript.

Clausewutz, C. von. (1832/1993). *On war*. New York: Everyman's Library.

Code of Hammurabi, The. (n.d.). (C. Jones, Trans). Retrieved from https://www.gutenberg.org/files/17150/17150-h/17150-hhtm. Accessed on January 26, 2023.

Coleman, P. (1918). *The international law and custom of Ancient Greece and Rome*. London: Macmillan and Co Ltd.

Connell, R. (1995). *Masculinities*. Berkeley, CA: University of California Press.

Connell, R. (2002). *Gender*. Cambridge: Polity.

Cooley, C. (1901). *Human nature and the social order*. New York: Charles Scribner's Sons.

Cooper, N. (1981). Gustav Adolphus and military justice. *Military Law Review*, *92*, 129–137.

Cowdrey, H. (1970). The peace and the truce of God in the eleventh century. *Past & Present*, *46*, 42–67.

Cox, R. (2013). A law of war? English protection and destruction of ecclesiastical property during the fourteenth century. *English Historical Review*, *128*(535), 1381–1417.

Croxton, D. (1999). The peace of Westphalia of 1648 and the origins of sovereignty. *The International History Review*, *21*(3), 569569–569591.

Cruickshank, C. (1969). *Army Royal: Henry VIII's invasiob of France, 1513*. Oxford: Clarendon Press.

Curry, A. (2008). The military ordinances of Henry V: Texts and contexts. In C. Given-Wilsom, A. Kettle, & L. Scales (Eds.), *War, government and aristocracy in the British Isles, c. 1150–1500. Essays in honour of Michael Prestwick* (pp. 214–249). Suffolk: Boydell Press.

Curry, A. (2011). Disciplinary ordinances for English and Franco-Scottish armies in 1385: An international code? *Journal of Medieval History*, *37*, 269–294.

Duby, G. (1978). *Medieval marriage: Two models from twelfth-century France* (E. Forster, Trans.). Baltimore, MD: John Hopkins University Press.

Durant, W. (1950). *The age of faith. Vol IV. The story of civilization*. New York: Simon & Schuster.

Durkheim, E. (1893/1984). *The division of labor in society*. (W. Halls, Trans.). New York, NY: Free Press.

Durkheim, E. (1912/1915). *The elementary forms of the religious life* (J. Swain, Trans.). New York: The Free Press.

Erikson, K. (1996). *Wayward Puritans: A study in the sociology of deviance*. Boston: Allyn and Bacon.

Evans-Pritchard, E. (1969). *The Nuer: A description of the modes of livelihood and political institutions of a nilotic people*. New York: Oxford University Press.

Ferguson, R. (2013). Pinker's list: Exaggerating prehistoric war mortality. In D. P. Fry (Ed.), *War, peace, and human nature: The convergence of evolutionary and cultural views* (pp. 112–131). New York: Oxford University Press.

Froissart. (1968). *Chronicles* (G. Brereton Ed. And Trans.). New York: Penguin Books.

Garland, Y. (1975). *War in the ancient world*. New York: W. W. Norton.

Garland, Y. (1984). Hellenistic science: It's application in peace and war: War and Siege craft. *The Cambridge Ancient History*, *7*(P II), 353–362.

Gies, F. (1984). *The knight in history*. New York, NY: Perennial.

Gillespie, A. (2011a). *A history of the laws of war. Vol 1: The customs and laws of war with regards to combatants and captives*. New York: Hart Publishing.

Gillespie, A. (2011b). *A history of the laws of war. Vol II: The customs and laws of war with regards to civilians in tomes of conflict*. New York: Hart Publishing.

Goffman, E. (1959). *The presentation of self in everyday society*. New York: Doubleday Anchor.

González de León, F. (2004). Spanish military power and military revolution. In G. Mortimer (Ed.), *Early modern military history, 1450–1815* (pp. 25–42). New York, NY: Palgrave.

Gordon, G. (2013). The trial of Peter von Hagenbach: Reconciling history, historiography and international criminal law. In K. Heller & G. Simpson (Eds.), *The hidden history of war crimes trials*. New York: Oxford University Press.

Grose, F. (1786). *Antiquities respecting a history of the English army from the conquest to the present time* (Vol. 1). London: C. Clarke.

Grose, F. (1788). *Antiquities respecting a history of the English army from the conquest to the present time* (Vol. 2). London: C. Clarke.

Grotius, H. (1625/1971). The law of war and peace. In L. Friedman (Ed.). *The law of war: A documentary history* (Vol. 1, pp. 16–146). New York, NY: Random House.

Hagedorn, J. (1988). *People and folks: Gangs, crime and the underclass in a Rustbelt City*. Chicago: Lake View Press.

Hampton, V. D. (2011). Viking age arms and armor originating in the Frankish kingdoms. *The Hilltop Review*, *4*(2), 36–44.

Harris, M. (1968). *The rise of anthropological theory: A history of theories of culture*. New York: Harper Collins.

Hartigan, R. S. (1982). *The forgotten victim: A history of the civilian*. Tampa, FL: Precedent Publishing.

Head, T. (1999). The development of the peace of God in aquitaine (970–1005). *Speculum*, *74*(3), 656–686.

Heider, K. (1977). *Grand Valley Dani: Peaceful warriors* (3rd ed.). San Diego, CA: Harcourt Brace publishers.

Hirschi, T. (1969). *Causes of delinquency*. Berkeley, CA: University of California Press.

Hobbs, T. (1651/1985). *Leviathan*. (C. Macpherson, Ed.). New York: Penguin Classics.

Hoebel, E. (1954). *The law of primitive man*. Cambridge, MA: Harvard University Press.

Hoebel, E. (1978). *The Cheyenne: Indians of the great plains* (2nd ed.). San Diego, CA: Harcourt Brace publishers.

Holá, B., Nzitatira, H., & Weerdesteijn, M. (2022). Introduction: Atrocity crimes and atrocity studies. In B. Holá, H. Nzitatira, & M. Weerdesteijn (Eds.), *The Oxford handbook on atrocity crimes* (pp. 1–23). New York: Oxford University Press.

Hoyos, D. (2019). *Carthage's other wars: Carthaginian warfare outside the 'Punic Wars' against Rome*. South Yorkshire: Pen and Sword Press.

Hurl-Eamon, J. (2022). Enslaved by the uniform: Contemporary descriptions of eighteenth-century solidering. *War in History*. On-line First. doi:10.1177/09683445221105258

Jacobs, B., & Wright, r. (2006). *Street justice: Retaliation in the criminal underworld*. Cambridge: Cambridge University Press.

Jankowski, M. (1991). *Islands in the street: Gangs and American urban society*. Berkeley, CA: University of California Press.

Jochnick, C., & Normand, R. (1994). The legitimation of violence: A critical history of the laws of war. *Harvard International Law Jouranl*, *35*, 49–95.

Josephus. (2001). The wars of the Jews: Or, the history of the destruction of Jerusalem. Project Guttenberg. Retrieved from https://Gutenberg.org/ebooks/2850. Accessed on January 29, 2023.

Journals of the Continental Congress 1774–1779. (1775/1905, June 30). *Articles of war*. (Vol II, pp. 111–123). Washington, DC: Government Printing Office. Retrieved from https://avalon.law.yale.edu/18th_century/contcong_06-30-75.asp. Accessed on December 29, 2022.

Journals of the Continental Congress. (1776, September 20). *Articles of war*. Retrieved from https://avalon.law.yale.edu/18th_century/contcong_09-20-76.asp. Accessed on December 29, 2022.

Katz, J. (1988). *Seducations of crime*. New York, NY: Basic Books.

Kauzlarich, D., & Kramer, R. (1998). *Crimes of the American nuclear state: At home and abroad*. Boston: Northeastern University Press.

Kauzlarich, D., Mullins, C., & Matthews, R. (2003). A complicity continuum of state crime. *Contemporary Justice Review*, *6*(3), 241–254.

Keegan, J. (1976). *The face of battle: A study of Agincourt, waterloo, and the somme*. New York: Penguin Books.

Keeley, L. H. (1996). *War before civilization: The myth of the peaceful savage*. New York: Oxford University Press.

Keen, M. (1978). *Chivalry*. New Haven: Yale University Press.

Keen, M. (1995). Richard II's Ordinances of War of 1385. In R. Archer & S. Walker (Eds.), *Rulers and ruled in late medieval England: Essays presented to Gerald Harriss*. London: The Hambledon Press.

Keen, M. H. (1965). The laws of war in the late middle ages. In *Routledge library editions: Military and naval history* (Vol. 16). London: Routledge.

Keepie, L. (2008). The army and the navy. In A. Bowman, E. Champlin, & A. Lintott (Eds.), *The Cambridge ancient history* (Vol. 10, pp. 371–396). Cambridge: Cambridge University Press.

Kehoe, A. (1989). *The ghost dance ethnohistory and revitalization*. New York: Holt, Rinehart, and Winston.

LaFree, G. (1989). *Loosing legitmacy: Street crime and the decline of social institutions in America*. Boulder, CO: Westview.

Lanni, A. (2008). The laws of war in Ancient Greece. *Law and History Review*, *26*(3), 469–489.

LeBlanc, S. (2003). *Constant battles: Why we fight*. New York: St. Martin's Press.

Luban, D. (2013). Military necessity and the cultures of military law. *Leiden Journal of International Law*, *26*, 315–349.

Lutz, E., & Reiger, C. (2009). *Prosecuting heads of state*. Cambridge: Cambridge University Press.

Mackenzie, M. (2012). *Female Soldiers in Sierra Leone: Sex, security, and post-conflict development*. New York, NY: New York University Press.

Macmunn, G. (1920). *Gustavus Adolphus: The Northern Hurricane*. London: Hodde and Stoughten Ltd.

Martinez, A. (2017). Disciplinary ordinances for English armies and military change, 1385–1513. *History*, *102*(351), 361–385.

McCauley, C., & Moskalenko, S. (2008). Mechanisms of political radicalization: Pathways toward terrorism. *Terrorism and Political Violence*, *20*(3), 415–433.

McCauley, C., & Moskalenko, S. (2017). Understanding political radicalization: The two pyramids model. *American Psychologist*, *72*(3), 205–216.

McGarry, R., & Walklate, S. (2019). *A criminology of war?* Bristol: Bristol University Press.

McNeill, J. T., & Gamer, H. M. (Trans.). (1990). *Medieval handbooks of penance: A translation of the principal libri poenitentiales and selections from related documents*. New York, NY: Columbia University Press.

McVitty, E. A. (2014). False knights and true men: Contesting chivalric masculinity in the English treason trials, 1388–1415. *Journal of Medieval History*, *40*(4), 458–477.

Merton, R. (1938). Social structure and anomie. *American Sociological Review*, *3*(5), 672–682.

Messerschmidt, J. (2014). *Crime as structured action: Doing masculinities, race, class, sexuality, and crime* (2nd ed.). Lanham, MD: Rowman and Littlefield.

Messerschmidt, J. (2018). *Masculinities and crime: A quarter century of theory and research*. Lanham, MD: Rowman and Littlefield.

Messner, S., & Rosenfeld, R. (2007). *Crime and the American dream* (4th ed.). Boston, MA: Thomson Wadsworth.

Michell, H. (1940). *The economics of Ancient Greece*. New York: Cambridge University Press.

Miller, J. (2008). *Getting played: African Americn girls urban inequality and gendered violence*. New York, NY: New York University Press.

Minear, R. (1971). *Victors' justice: The Tokyo war crimes trial*. Tokyo: Charles E. Tuttle Co.

Morgan, G. (1997). *Images of organization* (2nd ed.). Thousand Oaks, CA: Sage.

Mortimer, G. (2004). War by contract, credit and contribution: The thirty years war. In G. Mortimer (Ed.), Early modern military history, 1450–1815 (pp. 101–117). New York, NY: Palgrave.

Mullins, C. (2006). *Holding your square: Masculinities, stretlife, and violence*. Cullompton-Devon: Willan Publishing.

Mullins, C. (2011). War crimes in 2008 Georgia-Russia conflict. *British Journal of Criminology*, *51*(6), 918–936.

Mullins, C. (2016). Sexual violence during war. In R. McGarry & S. P. Walklate (Eds.), *Palgrave handbook on criminology and war* (pp. 117–132). London: Palgrave.

Mullins, C., & Rothe, D. (2008). *Blood, power, and bedlam: Violations of International Criminal Law in Post-Colonial Africa*. New York: Peter Lang Press.

Mullins, C., Wright, R., & Jacobs, B. (2004). Gender, streetlife, and criminal retaliation. *Criminology*, *42*(4), 911–940.

Murphy, N. (2015). Henry VIII's invasion of France: The Gascon expedition of 1512. *English Historical Review CXXX*, *542*, 25–56.

Napier, C. (1837). *Remarks on military law and the punishment of flogging*. London: T and W Boone.

Neff, S. (2005). *War and the law of nations: A general history*. New York: Cambridge University Press.

Neville, C., (Ed.). (1990). A plea roll of Edward I's Army in Scotland, 1296. *Miscellany of the Scottish Historical Society* (Vol. *XI*, pp. 7–134). Edinburgh: Pillans & Wilson, Ltd.

Newhall, R. (1940). *Muster and review: A problem of English military administration 1420–1440*. Cambridge, MA: Harvard University Press.

Oehler, C. (1997). *The Great Sioux Uprising*. New York: Da Capo.

Ögren, K. (1996). Humanitarian law in the articles of war decreed in 1621 by King Gustavus II Adolphus of Sweden. *International Review of the Red Cross, 313*.

Otterbein, K. (2009). *The anthropology of war*. Long Grove, IL: Waveland.

Parker, G. (2020). Dynastic war: 1494–1660. In G. Parker (Ed.), *The Cambridge history of warfare* (2nd ed., pp. 147–166). Cambridge: Cambridge University Press.

Pausanias. (1898/2013). In J. Frazer (Ed.), *Pausanias's description of Greece*. Cambridge: Cambridge University Press.

Perrow, C. (1984). *Normal accidents: Living with high-risk technologies*. New York, NY: Basic Books.

Perrow, C. (1996). *Complex organizartions: A critical essay* (3rd ed.). New York, NY: McGraw-Hill.

Polybius. (1889). *Histories* (Tr E. Shuckburgh, Trans.). New York: MacMillan and Co. The Internet Archive. Retrieved from https://archive.org/details/historiespolybi00hultgoog/page/n7/mode/2up. Accessed on January 29, 2023.

Porter, E. (1946). The articles of war. *The Historian*, *8*(2), 77–102.

Power, M. (1991). *The Egalitarians—Human and Chimpanzee an anthropological view of social organization*. New York: Cambridge University Press.

Pritchett, W. K. (1971). *The Greek state at war. Part I*. Berkeley, CA: University of California Press.

Pritchett, W. K. (1974). *The Greek state at war. Part II*. Berkeley, CA: University of California Press.

Pritchett, W. K. (1991). *The Greek state at war. Part V*. Berkeley, CA: University of California Press.

Reckless, W. (1961a). *The crime problem*. New York, NY: Appleton Centruy.

Reckless, W. (1961b). A new theory of delinquency and crime. *Federal Probation*, *25*, 42–46.

Reuter, T., & Wickham, C. (1997). Debate: The 'Feudal Revolution'. *Past and Present*, *155*, 177–208.

Rodgers, C. (2004). The Medieval legacy in early modern military history, 1450–1815. In G. Mortimer (Ed.), *Early modern military history, 1450–1815* (pp. 6–24). New York, NY: Palgrave.

Roesdahl, E. (1987). *The vikings*. New York: Penguin.

Roe, T. & Watts, W. (1632). *The Swedish Discipline: Religious, civile, and military*. London: Nath: Butter and Nish.

Roth, R. (2009). *American homicide*. Cambridge, MA: Harvard University Press.

Rothe, D., & Mullins, C. (2006). *The international criminal court: Symbolic gestures and the generation of global social control*. Lanham, MD: Lexington Books.

Rousseau, J. (1762). *Du Contract Social, Ou, Principes du Droit Politique*. Geneva: Chez Marc Michel Rey.

Rueda, G., & Tanner, S. (2016). To prevent the existence of people dedicated to 'causing trouble': Dirty work, social control, and paramilitaries in Columbia. *British Journal of Criminology*, *56*, 87–104.

Rutar, T. (2022). The prehistory of violence and war: Moving beyond the Hobbes-Rousseau quagmire. *Journal of Peace Research*. Online first. doi:10.1177/00223433221090112

Saccio, P. (2000). *Shakespeare's English kings: History, chronicle, and drama* (2nd ed.). Oxford: Oxford University Press.

Sandholtz, W. (2007). *Prohibiting plunder: How norms change*. New York: Oxford University Press.

Saul, N. (1997). *Richard II*. New Haven, CT: Yale University Press.

Singha, R. (2016). The "rare infliction": The abolition of flogging in the Indian army, circa 1835–1920. *Law and History Review*, *34*(3), 783–818.

Steuben, F. (1779/1786/2019). *Regulations for the order and discipline of the troops of the United States*. Carlisle, MA: Applewood Books.

Stewart, W. (1985). *True blue: The loyalist legend*. Toronto, ON: Collins.

Strauss, B. (1983). Aegospotami reexamined. *American Journal of Philology*, *104*(1), 24–35.

Sykes, G., & Matza, D. (1957). Techniques of Neutraloization: A thery of delinquency. *American Sociological Review*, *22*(6), 664–670.

Thucydides. (2009). *The Peloponnesian war* (M. Hammond, Trans.). New York: Oxford University Press.

Totten, S. (2012). *Genocide by attrition: The Nuba Mountains of Sudan*. Piscataway, NJ: Transaction Publishers.

Treaty of Westphalia. (1648). Retrieved from https://www.jstor.org/stable/41932578. Last accessed January 27, 2023.

Troyes, C. (1970). *Romans de la Table Ronde*. Folio: Gallimard.

Underwood, P., Pfaff, S., & Hechter, M. (2018). Threat, deterrence, and penal severity: An analysis of flogging in the royal navy, 1740–1820. *Social Science History*, *42*(3), 411–439.

Vaughan, R. (2002). *Charles the Bold: the last Valois duke of Burgundy*. Suffolk: Boydell Press.

Vegetius, F. (2019). *De Re Militari* J. Harper and L. Adet, trans. Dubai: Harper-Mclaughlin-Adet.

Visigothic Code. (634/1910). (Scott, Trans.). Boston: The Boston Book Company.

Walklate, S., & McGarry, R. (2015). *Criminology and war: Transgressing the borders*. Oxfordshire: Routledge.

Watkin, W. (1942). The middle ages: The approach to the truce of God. *Rice Institute Pamphlet*, *XXIX*(4), 291–309.

Weber, M. (1919/2015). *Weber's rationalism and modern society* (D. Owen and T. Strong, Trans. and Ed.). Indianapolis: Hackett Books.

Wilson, P. (2004). New approaches under the old Regime. In G. Mortimer (Ed.), *Early modern military history, 1450–1815* (pp. 135–154). New York, NY: Palgrave.

Wilson, I. (2021). *The book of Geoffroi de Charny*. Suffolk: The Boydell Press.

Winlow, S. (2001). *Badfelllas: Crime, tradition and new masculinities*. London: Berg.

Winthrop, W. (1920). *Military law and precedents*. Washington, DC: G.P.O. Library of Congress. Retrieved from https://www.loc.gov/item/war20000086/. Accessed on December 2, 2022.

Witt, J. (2012). *Lincoln's code: The laws of war in American history*. New York, NY: Free Press.

Wood, E. (2006). Variation in sexual violence during war. *Politics & Society*, *34*(3), 307–341.

Index

Printed and bound by CPI Group (UK) Ltd, Croydon, CR0 4YY

13/09/2026

14961059-0001